ENVIRONMENT & POLICY

VOLUME 47

The titles published in this series are listed at the end of this volume.

INSTITUTIONAL DYNAMICS IN ENVIRONMENTAL G

Institutional Dynamics in Environmental Governance

Edited by

Bas Arts

Wageningen University, The Netherlands

and

Pieter Leroy

Nijmegen University, The Netherlands

Springer

A C.I.P. Catalogue record for this book is available from the Library of Congress.

ISBN-10 1-4020-5078-X (HB)
ISBN-13 978-1-4020-5078-7 (HB)
ISBN-10 1-4020-5079-8 (e-book)
ISBN-13 978-1-4020-5079-4 (e-book)

Published by Springer,
P.O. Box 17, 3300 AA Dordrecht, The Netherlands.

www.springer.com

Printed on acid-free paper

Dedication page

The book editors would like to thank the authors for investing intellect, creativity and time into this volume, the Springer editor Esther Verdries for a smooth cooperation, Lieke Michiels van Kessenich for formatting the manuscript, Edwin Beschler for language editing and an anonymous referee for the feedback and recommendation to Springer.

Contents

About the Authors

Dirk Bogaert is a lecturer at the Department of Social Welfare Studies, Ghent University and at the Arteveldehogeschool Ghent. He is also a senior researcher at the Maritime Institute of Ghent University.

Froukje Boonstra is a researcher in public administration at Alterra, Wageningen University and Research Centre.

Ann Crabbé is a researcher at the Faculty of Political and Social Sciences, University of Antwerp.

Sara de Boer is a researcher in public administration at Alterra, Wageningen University and Research Centre.

Jaap Gersie is a senior lecturer at the Department of Political Sciences of the Environment, Nijmegen University.

Henri Goverde is a professor in political science at Wageningen University and Research Centre, and associate professor in public administration at Nijmegen University.

Jacques Klaver is a senior lecturer at the Department of Political Sciences of the Environment, Nijmegen University.

Duncan Liefferink is a senior researcher at the Department of Political Sciences of the Environment, Nijmegen University.

Frans J.G. Padt is a researcher at the Department of Political Sciences of the Environment, Nijmegen University.

Mariëlle van der Zouwen is a lecturer at the Department of Forest and Nature Conservation Policy, Wageningen University and Research Centre.

Jan van Tatenhove is an associate professor at the Department of Social Sciences, Environmental Policy, Wageningen University and Research Centre.

Bruno Verbeeck is a researcher at the Faculty of Political and Social Sciences, University of Antwerp.

Mark Wiering is a lecturer and senior researcher at the Department of Political Sciences of the Environment, Nijmegen University.

Emiel Ypma is a project employee of Environmental Permits and Planning at Witteveen+Bos, branch office Maastricht.

About the Editors

Bas Arts was an associate professor at the Department of Political Sciences of the Environment, Nijmegen University. From 2006 onwards he is professor and chair of the Forest and Nature Conservation Policy Group at Wageningen University and Research Centre.

Pieter Leroy is professor and chair of the Department of Political Sciences of the Environment, Nijmegen University.

List of Tables

List of Figures

Chapter 1

Institutional Dynamics in Environmental Governance

Pieter Leroy and Bas Arts

This book is the third in a series that results from the research programme of the Department of Political Sciences of the Environment at Nijmegen University, the Netherlands. This research programme is entitled 'new arrangements in environmental policies'. The programme was initiated in the late 1990s, building upon a longstanding experience and expertise in environmental policy issues. It essentially deals with innovation and tradition in environmental policies, and aims at an interpretation thereof from an institutional dynamics' perspective.

When launching this programme, we were driven by a variety of empirical observations on the one hand and inspired by a series of theoretical considerations on the other. We enumerate some of the thought provoking empirical observations in the first section, while the second section sets out our theoretical sources of inspiration. By then we will also have identified the starting points and the main ambitions of our research programme, while indicating its gradual development hitherto. We conclude by sketching the outline of this volume, which is to be considered yet another step in the research programme's further development. The main question in all chapters of this volume is how to interpret the institutional dynamics in recent environmental governance. The ultimate chapter summarises some answers to this and related questions, and indicates our further research endeavours.

SOME EMPIRICAL OBSERVATIONS

As many other scholars in the field, we observe some considerable changes in the environmental policies since the 1990s, as compared to the initial stages of this policy domain in the 1970s and 1980s. From the early 1980s onwards we have been engaged in a series of both fundamental and policy oriented research projects on issues such as (national and European) waste

B. Arts and P. Leroy (eds.), Institutional Dynamics in Environmental Governance, 1–19.

policies, nature conservation, groundwater policies, environmental policies towards industries, region-specific environmental planning and the like. These projects, although limited and specific in some cases and more encompassing in others, revealed some overall changes in environmental policies from the late 1980s and early 1990s. One can list these changes, more or less arbitrarily it seems, as follows:

- The introduction and the increasing use of concepts such as 'sustainability', 'biodiversity', 'integrated assessment', 'environmental quality' and others, reflect a discursive turn in environmental policies. This discursive turn indicates a substantial change in the definition of the problems, in their naming and framing, and in the preferred ways to tackle them. In short, environmental problems have been increasingly linked to other fields of societal concern, such as social, economic and technological issues and, accordingly, their solution has been increasingly linked to other policy domains, such as agriculture, infrastructure, traffic, technology etc. Hence the responsibility for their solution was no longer with environmental policy departments and agencies solely. In brief, from the 1990s onwards environmental policy gradually became a *multi-sector* field, appealing for shared responsibilities among different policy domains, and raising issues about policy co-ordination and policy integration.
- These discursive changes and their implications were paralleled by the introduction and the relative success of a second set of concepts: 'stakeholders approach', 'shared responsibility', 'integrated management', 'co-production' and the like. These concepts explicitly pointed at (or appealed to) the renewal of roles and responsibilities of the agencies involved, and on new configurations and coalitions between them. In its initial stages, environmental policy was largely state dominated. Now it became a matter of shared responsibility. And this wasn't lip-service solely, but led into new social practices as well. We observed the increasing environmental concern - *con amore* or *à contrecoeur* – with industries and their efforts towards private standard setting on the one hand, the active involvement of formerly opposing environmental action groups in different policy processes on the other. In brief, environmental policies increasingly became a *multi-actor* field. This not only meant the (quantitative) widening of the circle of the actors involved. Moreover it led to qualitative changes in the roles and interrelations of the agencies involved, in their sharing of responsibilities, etc.
- Inspired and legitimised by these new substantial and strategic concepts, the interplay of a wider arena of agencies gave rise to the

emergence of new forms of interaction and new practices in policy making. Environmental policies not only were state dominated initially, they also mainly built upon regulatory strategies and were managed in accordance with the formerly predominant blue print planning principles. From the late 1980s onwards, however, we observed a variety of regional and local initiatives and projects with stakeholders engaging in different sorts of negotiations, we witnessed the emergence of new participatory approaches, and we observed state-industry as well as industry-NGO-negotiations, often resulting in voluntary agreements or private-public partnerships (Mol et al., 2000). We will not assess here whether or not these new styles and practices of policy making actually increased their legitimacy and their effectiveness (Leroy, 2002). We restrict to the observation that environmental policies display an increasing variety in their processing, organisation and management. Hence one could label environmental policies as *multi-process or multi-rule*, referring to this multitude of projects and processes, each of them having its own rules for accession, interaction and decision-making, either paralleling or even – as it seemed in some cases – replacing classical, constitutional patterns and rules of policy making.

- Finally, we point at the increasingly transboundary and transnational character of environmental policies. While the European Union gradually developed its own environmental policy, both local and transnational operating private companies and NGOs urged the nation-states concerned to co-ordinate their policies on, for instance, the Rhine and the North Sea. It is just one example to illustrate the interplay of top-down and bottom-up initiatives, of governmental and non-governmental actions that contributed to a rapid internationalisation of environmental policies. Internationalisation, however, in itself does not mean a decreasing role for the local level and an ever growing importance for the global level. Rather do we observe the *multi-level* character of environmental policies. The latter means that policies increasingly are designed, discussed and implemented at different levels of government simultaneously. As these levels employ different definitions of the problem, allow different agencies to participate, and operate along different rule systems, it is most likely that they come up with different approaches and with possibly conflicting strategies, but also create new opportunities for interest groups to intervene at different levels. Hence, once again, the need for policy co-ordination.

As mentioned, we observed these changes and analysed them in articles and reports on a variety of environmental issues and environmental policy subdomains in the Netherlands, Belgium, Germany, and at European and global level (Arts, 1998; Bouwer and Leroy, 1995; Bouwer, 1997; Leroy, 1994; Liefferink, 1996; Van Tatenhove, 1993). Many other scholars reported similar changes and shifts in environmental policies in other European countries (Jänicke and Weidner, 1997; Jordan, 1993; Paehlke and Torgerson, 1990). Although these changes have been listed and labelled differently by different authors, they consent that these changes relate to both policy content and policy strategy, to both policy ruling and policy organisation. Therefore our ambition was to develop a framework for the common understanding and interpretation of these changes, based upon a thorough empirical analysis, and yet starting from a clear theoretical positioning. That is what our research programme is all about, that is what this book is all about.

SOME THEORETICAL CONSIDERATIONS

As said, similar changes in environmental policy making were observed and reported in different European and other western countries in the early 1990s. They were analysed by different scholars in varying terms of interpretation by for instance Weale (1992), Sabatier and Jenkins-Smith (1993), Jänicke (1993), Jänicke and Weidner (1997), Lascoumes (1994) and many others who provided inspiring explanatory schemes and approaches. Although these approaches from abroad were well discussed and appreciated, Dutch environmental policy research in the 1980s and 1990s tended to regard the changes one observed as mainly strategic and instrumental in character. Over time of course Dutch scholars evolved in their preferred approaches, and we even observed a paradigm shift in Dutch environmental policy research (Leroy and Nelissen, 2002). Nevertheless, reviews of PhD theses and textbooks from the 1980s and early 1990s on the environmental policy domain reveal a certain bias towards a strategic interpretation of the renewal of environmental policy (Glasbergen, 2002; Leroy and Nelissen, 1999). These approaches were primarily, although largely implicitly, based upon a rational choice paradigm, respectively on rather synoptic views on (environmental) policy making. Only a minority of studies paid attention to the political, institutional or otherwise labelled 'context' (Frouws, 1993). Although it is speculative, one might relate this bias to the fact that many of these environmental policy studies were commissioned by governmental authorities, emphasising self-evidently the practical relevance thereof, and thus inducing a 'management' bias (Leroy, 1995). Anyway, Dutch environmental policy analyses from the 1980s primarily conceived changes and reforms in environmental policies as the strategic responses of agents, mainly public agencies, aiming at greater effectiveness and efficiency, at increased legitimacy etc. Moreover, most of these studies had a restricted scope, highlighting changes in the environmental policy domain whilst somewhat insulating it from its wider societal and political context.

As said, the predominant approaches to environmental politics and policies gradually evolved in the Netherlands and abroad (see below), and so did ours. With our research programme 'new arrangements in environmental policies', we aimed at capturing both policy substance and policy organisation aspects, both strategic and institutional aspects of the changes we observed. In the remainder of this section we will gradually elaborate our ambition, by positioning ourselves in the midst of different sources of inspiration. It should be clear, however, that we did not (and do not) aim at a grand theory. Rather do we aim at a practical 'meso level theory' or approach.

A Double Ambition

First, inspired by classical sociology on the one hand and by its recent reformulation by Giddens (1984, 1990), we essentially wanted our approach to restore the balance between the meaning and impact of rational behaviour by agencies involved on the one hand, and structural factors that drive (or block) policy innovation on the other. Our institutional dynamics' approach aims at a mid-position, doing justice to agencies and structures.

Secondly, inspired by contemporary environmental sociology (Beck, 1992; Buttel, 1997; Lash, Szerzinsky and Wynne, 1996; Redclift and Woodgate, 1997; Yearley, 1996; and many others), we wanted to link the events and trends on environmental issues to more encompassing societal and political trends that we thought of great importance. We regard the environmental issue as an example *par excellence* of the problems that highly modernised societies face, and that they have to respond to (Barry, 1999; Irwin, 2001). In our view, environmental problems thus largely represent more fundamental and more encompassing issues of late modern societies, and should be analysed and dealt with accordingly. Environmental policies, therefore, have to be regarded from a broader perspective than, for instance, classical public administration approaches tend to do.

Consequently, we opted for a research programme with a double ambition:

1. to analyse recent changes (and patterns of stability) in environmental policies as institutional dynamics,
2. and to relate these 'specific' changes in day to day environmental policies in a plausible way to current structural and encompassing societal and political trends.

This double ambition urged for the gradual development, the application and the sustained testing and elaboration of a theoretical position and an analytical framework. Concepts such as 'institutionalisation', 'political modernisation' and 'policy arrangements' became pivotal in our approach. We will explain these central concepts below, as we gradually developed, operationalised and tested them over the years. In retrospect our first book (Van Tatenhove, Arts and Leroy, 2000) roughly sketched our approach and applied it to the empirical evidence that we had gathered at that time. The second book (Arts and Leroy, 2003) reported the mainly theoretical debate we had with some colleagues on the validity, the applicability and the added value of our approach. In the meantime we further refined and nuanced our approach theoretically, and elaborated and applied it empirically in a series of articles, reports and PhD-dissertations. To restrict to the latter here, we refer to the dissertations by Boonstra (2004), Bogaert (2004) and Van der Zouwen (2006), who all contributed to this volume as well.

Sources of Inspiration and Main Concepts

The central assumptions and concepts of the approach are discussed at full length in the chapters 2 and 3 of this volume, while chapter 4 draws upon them to develop an evaluative perspective. Here we will only summarise their quintessence, whilst indicating their theoretical backgrounds and foundations. The latter originate from a series of authors and debates in current sociology, political sciences, public administration and international relations, either in general or with regard to environmental issues in particular. Without going into the details of every single issue and debate, we enumerate these sources of inspiration below, while elaborating the starting points of the research programme. As said, three concepts are pivotal: institution, modernisation and policy arrangements.

First, we refer to a basic concept of sociological tradition: *institution*. The concept has been defined, discussed and redefined a thousand times from classical sociology till our time, and the emergence of neo-institutionalism in the 1980s and 1990s has refuelled the debate recently

(Hall and Taylor, 1996; March and Olson, 1989; Scott, 2001). Without ignoring the different issues and the subtly varying stances therein, the concept is crucial to us since it refers primarily (a) to the phenomenon whereby over time day to day actors' behaviour solidifies into patterns and structures, whereas these patterns in turn structure day to day actors' behaviour. As a consequence and secondly, the concept refers (b) to the gradual sedimentation of meanings into rules of behaviour and organisational structures, that in turn reproduce and recreate these meanings. In other words, the concept of institution marks the crossroads of the actor-structure duality – largely addressed by Giddens, and discussed in detail in chapter 2 – on the one hand, and the substance-organisation duality on the other, recently addressed by a series of authors from either social constructivism or new institutionalism (Hajer, 1995; Hay and Wincott, 1998). Both dualities, or dialectics, have been well known since classical sociology, the first in a sometimes caricaturised Durkheim-Weber opposition, the second in a similarly virtual and often caricaturised Marx-Weber opposition.

The first duality, the so-called duality of structure, has been addressed extensively by Giddens (1984, 1990), in a reaction to the persistent dualism in social sciences. Some theories, he argues, pay a lot of attention to the intentions, reasons and motives of acting agencies, thereby underestimating the 'structured', better, the institutionalised or rule-directed character of these actions. Other theories, to the contrary, focus on institutions and their dominance, largely ignoring the impact of (un)-intended actions and of rule-altering behaviour, and the opportunities of institutional change. Essentially, Giddens points at the sustaining intentionalist-structuralist divide in social sciences. The second duality, the so-called substance-organisation duality, is classic to social sciences as well. It essentially goes back to two opposing schools of thought in (social) philosophy: an idealistic approach, that largely builds upon ideational mechanisms to explain social change, human progress (or the lack thereof), opposed to a materialistic approach, that ascribes social stability and change mainly to material circumstances and variables.

Not only classic, but also recent institutionalism reflect both dualities, as some authors regard institutions mainly as the solidified outcomes of common knowledge and beliefs (discursive or cognitive institutionalism) (Hajer, 1995), whereas others emphasise the integrative and regulatory roles of institutions, paying attention primarily to their autonomy and dominance (historic institutionalism) (Hay and Wincott, 1998). Other authors distinguish actor-oriented institutionalism from structure-oriented institutionalism (and all positions in between these extremes), and yet they claim a mid-position for themselves, aiming at reconciling differing positions and bridging one or both dualities (Hirsch, 1997; Scott, 2001).

Given these sometimes furious academic debates, we risk to oversimplify things, and yet it is attractive to think of these two dualities or divides as the extremes of two continua. In brief: from actor to structure, and from discourse to organisation (Figure 1.1). We then, with a lot of other scholars, deliberately position our conception of 'institutions' in the midst of these crossing continua.

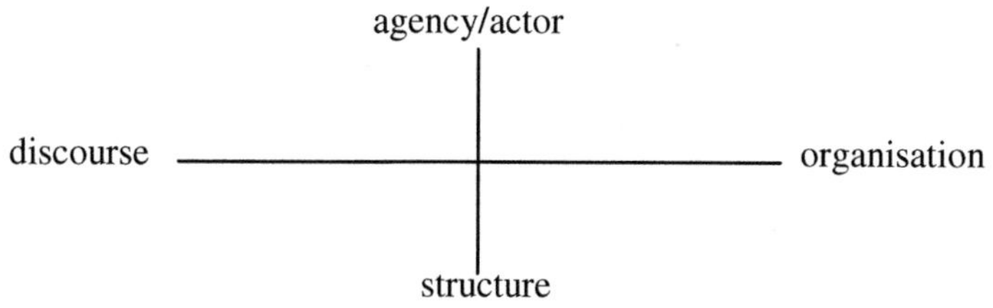

Figure 1.1. Crossing dualities in social sciences.

The advantage of such presentation is that it allows to position a series of paradigms and approaches, in the social sciences in general, and with regard to environmental policy analyses in particular. Let us restrict to the actor-structure duality first. Approaches laying emphasis on the agencies' behaviour and capacities largely build upon rational choice theories, assuming agencies to be rational, knowledgeable, well-informed etc., and behaving accordingly. From this perspective, environmental issues primarily appear as 'tragedies of the commons', 'prisoners dilemmas' and the like, in brief as market failures and due to the unintended outcomes of aggregated individual behaviour. Environmental policy then should mainly correct these market failures, but still build upon the rational choices a *homo economicus* is assumed to make (Weale, 1992). Approaches emphasising the 'structure' or the 'system', to the contrary, do regard environmental issues as the (inevitable) outcomes of (the combination of) a capitalist production system, a one-sided, solely instrumental process of (technological) modernisation, and the lack of capacity of the political system to control these. With both Weale (1992) and Barry (1999) we refer to authors originating from critical theory and/or from (neo-)Marxism, such as Habermas, Bahro and Gorz. Schaiberg's 'treadmill of production' offers a well known metaphor and analysis (Schnaiberg, 1980). These authors are sceptical, to say the least, on the capabilities of environmental policy measures which they regard as 'reformist', as these do not address the real driving forces, i.e. the 'systemic' causes of environmental degradation.

When bringing in the ideational-organisational or the discursive-material duality, the four quadrants that emerge are helpful to further characterise predominant approaches in recent environmental policy analysis, and to understand their relative positions. The upper right quadrant is quite well represented in Dutch environmental policy analyses from the 1980s, as we discussed above, with both policy instrumentation approaches (Bressers and Klok, 1987) and policy networks approaches (Glasbergen, 1995; Kickert et al., 1997). Both paid attention to strategies to overrule the negative outcomes of rational behaviour (or as it was labelled: environmental unfriendly behaviour), by altering it either by a smart instrumentation or through the creation of inter-organisational inter-dependencies. Ideational, discursive, cognitive and interpretative appro-aches with emphasis on agency have their place in the upper left quadrant, labelled by Weale (1992) as the 'discourse idiom'. As Dutch environmental policy analysis was largely dominated by public administration approaches that, to a large extent, neglected ideational aspects, approaches that fit into this quadrant were almost absent in the Netherlands. Over the last decade, however, it has been populated, in the Netherlands and at international level, with a series of (moderate or radical) social constructionist approaches that reaffirmed the role and relevance of discourses as constitutive elements in (environmental) policy making (De Jong, 1999; Dryzek, 1997; Termeer, 1993). As far as one conceives discourse coalitions or socio-cognitive configurations as more or less intentionally built 'devices' in order to realise a strategic discursive turn (in environmental policies), agencies are still pivotal. Sabatier and Jenkins-Smith (1993) do pay attention to discursive elements as well, but they rather belong to the bottom left quadrant, as they insist on longstanding coalitions and the relative stability of belief and knowledge systems as constituencies of environmental policies. Hajer (1995) in turn addresses the ideational-organisational duality, when assessing the relative success of 'ecological modernisation' and other innovative concepts and their impact upon the organisation of and strategy in environmental policies. In social sciences in general, the bottom-left quadrant should be populated by a Foucauldian school of thought, emphasising the structuring character of hegemonic discourses, e.g. of discursive fixation. In environmental policy analysis this paradigm is not well represented, although Sairinen's analysis of Finnish environmental policy combines traditional policy analysis with a 'governmentality' approach (Sairinen, 2000). Finally, the bottom-right quadrant, as indicated above, mainly accommodates authors inspired by critical theory, and again there is but a small sample of them in environmental policy analysis. One can point at publications from the

1970s and early 1980s by Bahro, Boockchin and Gorz, but in retrospect these are rather political statements than empirical analyses of environmental politics. In a way also (some interpretations of) Beck's analysis of our 'risk society' fits in well, as he describes environmental and other high consequence risks as intrinsically linked to processes of 'simple' modernisation.

In conclusion: as said we deliberately opt to position our conception of 'institutions' in the midst of these crossing continua, between intentionalist and structuralist approaches on the one hand, and between ideational and organisational ones on the other. That is not to say that we pretend to bridge all these different perspectives, and yet our conception is developed in dialogue with them, since we would like to build upon each of them. We do so, *per negativum*, to avoid one-sided approaches that do not do justice to the complexities of social reality; *per positivum*, to attempt to capture as much as possible of their theoretical and methodological richness.

Inspired by this richness and when applied to politics and policy processes, our concept of institutionalisation refers to the gradual stabilisation of definitions of problems and approaches, of strategies and solutions in and around specific policy domains. It also refers to the more or less fixed patterns of divisions of tasks and interactions that develop between the actors involved, to the stabilisation of more or less fixed rules of the game etc. From this perspective, we analysed and reconstructed the institutionalisation of Dutch environmental policies and some of its subdomains in our first book (Van Tatenhove and Leroy, 2000). In brief: we made clear that also the institutionalisation of environmental politics comprises cognitive, interactive, regulatory and normative dimensions. We referred to the gradual solidifying of institutional patterns in each of these dimensions, which in turn constrain day to day political behaviour, and create mechanisms of path dependency that agencies cannot easily overcome.

We look from a similar institutional perspective in this book, paying attention to the change and stability environmental politics displays, either in substantial and organisational matters, and induced by either agency or structure. It is the analysis, interpretation and characterisation of these patterns of stability and change that we envisage with the concept of 'policy arrangements', which will be discussed at full length in chapter 3 of this volume, and which we will return to below.

Before that, however, we turn to our second pivotal concept and source of inspiration: *modernisation*, either related to society and politics in general, or restricted to environmental politics particularly. As to the first, a series of scholars suggest that our western societies have reached a new, qualitatively different stage or form of modernity. We refer to Beck (1992), Giddens (1990), Lash et al. (1996) and many others. Here again, we are well aware of the subtle variety and divergences in their and other interpretations. Yet we believe they all point at processes of change that give a new direction to the long term modernisation of western societies. This new turn is said to be caused by technological, economic, societal, political and epistemological changes and, simultaneously, to have an impact on our economic, societal, political and scientific institutions. Scholars refer to processes such as globalisation (Castells, 1996-1998; Yearley, 1996), to the dematerialisation of our economies and the growth of non-material fluxes by ICT, others refer to high consequence risks, to the irreversibility of their environmental consequences (Spaargaren et al., 2000), and still others claim a growing and structural scientific uncertainty about complex issues, depriving science from its (presumed) former role as a legitimising institution (Irwin, 1995; Wynne, 1996).

It is striking that almost all authors in the modernity debate point at environmental issues as the manifestation *par excellence* of present-day modernity and the problems it provokes. Even before the 'risk society' thesis was widespread, scholars from environmental sociology and political sciences of the environment claimed environmental issues to have a catalytic role in societal, economic and political changes. Whether they labelled these changes as political modernisation (Jänicke, 1993) or as ecological modernisation (Mol, 1995), they regard recent societal responses to environmental issues as outstanding manifestations of a new modernity, including the building of new political and societal institutions that can organise the capacity (Jänicke and Weidner, 1997) and the legitimacy (Irwin, 2001) needed to adequately deal with these issues.

Chapter 2 will deal in more detail with this concept of modernisation and its challenges and consequences. We restrict our attention here to some political consequences that seem linked to this presumably all-pervading process of modernisation. Although quite different in scale, status and impact, all the processes referred to above (from globalisation to ecological modernisation) are said to provoke the erosion of the role of some long standing key institutions of our societies. The institutions affected comprise, as said, the formerly authoritative and legitimising role of science and technology (Irwin, 1995; Wynne, 1996), but it mainly affects the role of the nation-state.

We cannot and will not discuss the extensive debates on this latter issue, but just indicate some insights from political sciences that have been thought-provoking to us, and that in a way link our first concept, institutionalisation, to our second, (political) modernisation. Political scientists indeed have labelled a series of recent changes in western politics as *shifts in governance* (Van Kersbergen and Van Waarden, 2001). In general 'governance' refers to the fact that steering no longer is the privilege of governmental agencies, but is *de facto* (and in many cases also *de jure*) the common responsibility of a variety of agencies, representing governmental bodies, market agencies and civil society organisations. Although the phenomenon of multi-actor governance is not a new one –(as the tradition of neo-corporatist decision-making in some European countries makes clear), one witnesses either their transfer to new policy domains – one of which is the environmental – and the emergence of new forms thereof. Therefore, governance is a multi-dimensional concept as well, referring to (new) steering concepts and beliefs, to new policy practices, to rulings on processing, organisation, interaction, etc. Empirically the new roles and interaction patterns between governmental bodies, market representatives and civil society organisations as referred to above, the variety of negotiations, covenants and agreements between public and private actors, and other 'new phenomena' referred to in the opening section of this chapter, suggest their rapid proliferation in the environmental field. In other words: the empirical observations we made there, apparently represent a more encompassing change, observed and analysed by political scientists outside the environmental field as well. Some of these scholars suggest the new patterns of governance would or could provide more steering capacity than their 'government' predecessors. We think, however, it remains to be assessed in practice and from empirical evidence whether and to what extent these forms of multi-actor governance do indeed represent changes in legitimacy and responsibility, and do increase our society's problem solving capacity.

Simultaneously, scholars from political sciences refer to multi-level governance. Originating from European studies (Marks and Hooghe, 1996), the interpretation of the concept has been widening since. It now stands for the very fact that (multi-actor) policy making evolves at different levels of policy making simultaneously, that these levels might interfere, differ and conflict, and that agencies might find opportunities to play their role at different levels. The concepts of institutionalisation, modernisation and multi-level governance come together when scholars refer to the fact that, for instance, local environmental groups get in touch with experts and policy makers at European level, passing by their national governmental level and decision making procedures, thereby de facto creating new political spaces (or: political institutions in the making). Again, the examples of governance practices from politics in general come close to the empirical observations from the opening section of this chapter. Again, we thus deal here with changes that go beyond the boundaries of environ-ronmental politics solely. Still we will restrict to analysis and assessment of their character in empirical research in the environmental field.

Earlier on we have stressed our double ambition: (1) to look at environmental policy processes from an institutional perspective, balancing between agency and structure, and doing justice to substantial as well as to organisational aspects of policy processes; and (2) to take into account long term processes that characterise contemporary society, first captured under the umbrella concept of 'modernisation'. Recalling these ambitions bring us to our third pivotal concept: *policy arrangements*. As we did in our first and second books, we define a policy arrangement as the temporary stabilisation of the content and organisation of a particular policy domain at a certain policy level or over several policy levels – in case of multi-level governance. This definition implies two assumptions. (1) Based upon our institutionalisation concept we suggest that day to day policy processes and the interactions between the agencies involved gradually develop into more or less stable patterns, which we label policy arrangements, while these institutionalised patterns or policy arrangements comprehend both sub-stantial and organisational matters – and their interplay (2) Based upon the idea of modernisation and its composing processes as constituent for late modern societies, we suggest policy arrangements not only to be the result of strategic behaviour, but also to reflect long term contextual societal and political trends and processes.

Policy arrangements, thus, is an institutional concept. As such, the concept does not aim at explaining day to day policy processes, but aims at the analysis of institutional patterns of change and stability in the mid term. Our main goals then are, first, to describe and characterise arrangements – in many cases in a comparative perspective – and second to interpret and understand their relative stability or change, and the mechanisms behind these dynamics. In order to capture the assumptions mentioned above, we distinguish four dimensions of policy arrangements, each of which are equal sources of change and stability:

- the *actors* involved in the policy domain, and their *coalitions* (including their oppositions);
- the division of *resources* between these actors, leading to differences in *power* and *influence*;
- the *rules of the game* within the arrangement, either in terms of formal procedures or as informal rules and 'routines' of interaction; and

- the policy *discourses*, entailing the norms and values, the definitions of problems and approaches to solutions of the actors involved.

Although the former three dimensions primarily refer to organisational aspects and the latter one to the substantial aspects of a policy arrangement, their combination aims at capturing the ideational-organisational duality. At the same time we aim at bridging the agency-structure duality. Chapter 3 comprises a full elaboration of these four dimensions of the concept, their interrelations, their equal status in terms of explanation and *explanandum*, and the added value of looking at a given policy arrangement from each of the dimensions. Chapter 3 thus sets out the methodology of our approach.

INSTITUTIONAL DYNAMICS: TOWARDS ENVIRONMENTAL GOVERNANCE?

It might be clear from the above by which authors, scholars and debates we have been inspired, and yet these theoretical foundations are not taken for granted. Even though they might provide us with the conceptual ammunition that we look for while deploying our own research perspective, they provoke a series of theoretical, methodological and empirical questions that deserve closer reading and in-depth debate. The first part of this volume (chapters 2 to 4) mainly faces these theoretical and methodological aspects.

As announced, the next chapter discusses what '(political) modernisation' does mean, while avoiding any normative or prescriptive connotation, as we want to. The chapter looks at the implications for policy making in general and in the environmental field in particular (chapter 2). Chapter 3 covers rather operational and methodological questions: How can we use and operationalise the concept of 'policy arrangements' for empirical research, while doing justice to the actor-structure and substance-organisation dialectics? Chapter 4 then questions whether and how we can assess and evaluate the output and outcome of these new environmental policies, while overcoming classical policy evaluations' methodologies and shortcomings?

Although theoretical and methodological in character, each of these three chapters draws some empirical evidence and illustrations from one case: the (rather poor) position of Dutch organic farming. The project that we carried out on this very issue is looked upon from three different angles in these three consecutive chapters: from a 'political modernisation' perspective (chapter 2), as an example to be analysed from the four perspectives offered by the 'policy arrangements' concept (chapter 3), and as a topic for policy evaluation (chapter 4).

The following chapters of this volume (chapter 5 to 12) are mainly empirical in character, although and self-evidently, they all build upon the arrangements approach developed so far. Although dedicated to varying subdomains, they all cover some general empirical questions arising from the theoretical foundations mentioned above: is there any empirical evidence for substantial and organisational changes in policy making in general? Do we observe an actual shift 'from government to governance' in environmental policy making in particular? To what extent do we observe changes that, although spectacular in specific cases, tend to be ephemeral as well? Is there any empirical evidence for suggestions on changes towards multi-actor and multi-level policy making? Under what circumstances are these changes likely to institutionalise, or to fade away rapidly? And: do these changes increase society's capacity to deal with the complex environmental problems we face?

To deal with these and more specific questions, chapters 5 to 12 draw empirical evidence from research that has been set up along the lines of our approach and analysis, either at our department or within a short distance. It covers environmental domains such as water management, nature conservation policy, cultural heritage, region-specific environmental policies, and policies vis-à-vis or within industrial sectors. The chapters mainly cover empirical evidence from the Netherlands and Flanders, in some cases in a comparative perspective, but in other cases also at European level and even beyond.

Chapters 5 and 6 do have a similar, comparative approach of the Netherlands and Flanders, covering water policies and nature conservation policies respectively. Both chapters investigate how similar discourses, 'integrated water management' and 'nature development in ecological networks' respectively, do develop in quite different institutional contexts. The chapters are not restricted to differences in implementation processes, but look at the legitimacy and impact of innovative discourses, and on the different ways pre-existing institutions are affected by and react to these changes, partly induced by European initiatives.

Chapter 7 takes the comparative perspective one step further, as it compares nature conservation policies in traditional 'nature areas' in Spain, the UK and the Netherlands. It makes clear that multi-actor policies in some cases seem to take hold and persist for long periods of time, whereas in other cases traditional patterns of governmental decision-making still prevail. Multi-level governance, similarly, emerges in some cases, whereas other national policy practices successfully resist transnational interference.

Chapter 8, on cultural heritage policies, to the contrary, establishes a growing influence of international discourses on national policies and rulings in this relatively new field. Empirical research in the US (Arizona), Norway and the Netherlands points at the mechanisms of transnational interference and institutionalisation: formal regulations, but also exchanges of practices between professionals and experts from governments and NGOs in the field.

Dutch region-specific environmental policies, as it developed throughout the 1990s, is at stake in chapters 9 and 10. Chapter 9 looks at three regional projects thereof, establishing the how's and why's of the changes the renewal induced by these very projects will institutionalise over time. 'Congruency' with already existing institutional arrangements seems to be the crucial factor. Chapter 10 also pays attention to the way these region-specific policies reflect 'political modernisation', e.g. principles and patterns of multi-actor and multi-level policies. Maybe even more, though, these policies have been coloured by 'new public management' principles. The latter, in some cases, do contradict the former, resulting in rather hybrid institutional arrangements.

Chapters 11 and 12 deal with the emergence of new policies towards and within industrial sectors. The former chapter does so while comparing initiatives, efforts and results of corporate environmental management in the Netherlands and the Czech Republic. The very comparison of developments in these two quite different economic and political contexts does reveal the main driving forces of these strategies and their likely institutional impact in each of these countries. Chapter 12 illustrates the interplay between traditional government practices towards industries on the one hand and the changes induced by a so-called target group approach in Flemish environmental policies on the other. Despite the lip service paid to the latter, the former seems to get the bulk of political and administrative support, and therefore seems to survive any attempt to change the existing government-industry relations.

Chapter 13, finally, presents an overall assessment. First, we compare and integrate the empirical evidence gathered in the previous chapters: Do the policy arrangements that have been analysed throughout the volume point at institutional dynamics indeed, or do they rather indicate lasting stability? Can we draw some empirical conclusions on 'political modernisation' from these cases? A second cluster of conclusions to be addressed is more theoretical and methodological in character: does the policy arrangements' approach allow us to identify the driving forces of change and stability? Which of the suggested driving forces seems decisive? To what extent can we assess their level of steering capacity? All this leads us to a critical assessment of the research done so far, and opens perspectives for the work still to be done.

REFERENCES

Arts, B. (1998), *The political influence of global NGOs*, PhD Dissertation Nijmegen University, International Books, Nijmegen/Utrecht.

Arts, B. and P. Leroy (eds.) (2003), *Verandering van politiek, vernieuwing van milieubeleid: klassieke en post-moderne arrangementen,* Nijmegen University Press, Nijmegen.

Barry, J. (1999), *Environment and social theory*, Routledge, London/New York.

Beck, U. (1992), *Risk society – towards a new modernity,* Sage, London.

Bogaert, D. (2004), *Natuurbeleid in Vlaanderen, natuurontwikkeling en draagvlak als vernieuwingen?*, Dissertatie, Radboud Universiteit Nijmegen/Instituut voor Natuurbehoud, Brussel.

Boonstra, F. (2004), *Laveren tussen regio's en regels: verankering van beleidsarrangementen rond plattelandsontwikkeling in Noordwest Friesland, de Graafschap en Zuidwest Salland,* Koninklijke Van Gorcum, Assen.

Bouwer, K. and P. Leroy (eds.) (1995), *Milieu en ruimte: analyse en beleid*, Boom, Meppel.

Bouwer, K. (1997), *Van milieubeleid naar omgevingsbeleid?*, Katholieke Universiteit Nijmegen, Nijmegen.

Bressers, J.Th.A. and P.J. Klok (1987), Grondslagen voor een instrumententheorie, *Beleidswetenschap*, nr. 1, pp. 77-97.

Buttel, F.H. (1997), Social institutions and environmental change, in: M. Redclift and G. Woodgate (eds.), *The international handbook of environmental sociology*, Edward Elgar, London, pp. 40-54.

Castells, M. (1996-1998), *The information age: economy, society and culture*, Volume II, the power of identity, Blackwell Publishers, Malden/Oxford.

De Jong, D.M. (1999), *Tussen natuurontwikkeling en Landschaftsschutz – sociaal-cognitieve configuraties in het grensoverschrijdende natuurbeleid*, PhD Dissertation, Nijmegen University, Eburon, Delft.

Dryzek, J. (1997), *The politics of the earth, environmental discourses*, Oxford University Press, Oxford.

Frouws, J. (1993), *Mest en macht: een politiek-sociologische studie naar belangenbehartiging en beleidsvorming inzake de mestproblematiek in Nederland vanaf 1970,* Landbouwuniversiteit Wageningen, Wageningen.

Giddens, A. (1984), *The constitution of society,* Polity Press, Cambridge.

Giddens, A. (1990), *The consequences of modernity*, Polity Press, Cambridge.

Glasbergen, P. (1995), *Managing environmental disputes – network management as an alternative*, Kluwer, Dordrecht.

Glasbergen, P. (2002), Beleidswetenschappelijk milieuonderzoek, in: J.J. Boersema, T. Pulles, J. van der Straaten and J. Bertels (eds.), *De oogst van milieu*, Boom, Amsterdam, pp. 250-269.

Hajer, M.A. (1995), *The politics of environmental discourse: ecological modernization and the policy process,* Oxford University Press, Oxford.

Hall, P.A. and R.C.R. Taylor (1996), Political science and the three new institutionalisms, *Political Studies*, Vol. 44, no. 4, pp. 936-957.

Hay C. and D. Wincott (1998), Structure, agency and historical institutionalism, *Political Studies*, Vol. 46, no. 5, pp. 951-957.

Hirsch, P.M. (1997), Ending the family quarrel: towards a reconciliation of 'old' and 'new' institutionalism, *American Behavioural Scientist*, Vol. 40, pp. 406-418.

Irwin, A. (1995), *Citizen science: a study of people, expertise and sustainable development*, Routledge, London.

Irwin, A. (2001), *Sociology and the environment*, Polity Press, Cambridge.

Jänicke, M. (1993), Über ökologische und politische Modernisierungen, *Zeitschrift für Umweltpolitik und Umweltrecht*, no. 2, pp. 159-175.

Jänicke, M. and H. Weidner (eds.) (1997), *National environmental policies: a comparative study of capacity building*, Springer, Berlin.

Jordan, A. (1993), Integrated pollution control and the evolving style and structure of environmental regulation in the UK, *Environmental Politics*, Vol. 2, no. 3, pp. 405-427.

Kickert, W.J.M., E.H. Klijn and J.F.M. Koppenjan (eds.) (1997), *Managing complex networks: strategies for the public sector*, Sage, London.

Lascoumes, P. (1994), *L'éco-pouvoir: environnements et politiques*, La Découverte, Paris.

Lash, S., B. Szerzinsky and B. Wynne (eds.) (1996), *Risk, environment and modernity*, Sage, London.

Leroy, P. (1994), De ontwikkeling van het milieubeleid en de milieubeleidstheorie, in: P. Glasbergen (eds.), *Milieubeleid: een beleidswetenschappelijke inleiding*, VUGA, Den Haag, pp. 35-58.

Leroy, P. (1995), *Environmental science as a vocation*, Katholieke Universiteit Nijmegen, Nijmegen.

Leroy P. and N.J.M. Nelissen (1999), *Social and political sciences of the environment – three decades of research in the Netherlands*, International Books, Utrecht.

Leroy, P. (2002), Environmental politics, participation and political inequality, in: L. Draetta and F. Lai (eds.), Naturalia, sciences sociales et environnement: entre cadres théoriques et approches empiriques, *EUROPAEA,* Vol. VIII, no. 1-2, pp. 153-167.

Leroy, P. and N.J.M. Nelissen (2002), The paradigm shift in environmental policy research, in: P.P.J. Driessen and P. Glasbergen (eds.), *Greening society – the paradigm shift in Dutch environmental politics*, Kluwer, Dordrecht.

Liefferink, D. (1996), *Environment and the nation state*, Manchester University Press, Manchester.

March, J.G. and J.P. Olsen (1989), *Rediscovering institutions – the organizational basis of politics*, Free Press, New York.

Marks, G. and L. Hooghe (1996), European integration from the 1980s: state-centric versus multi-level governance, *Journal of Common Market Studies*, Vol. 34, no. 3, pp. 341-378.

Mol, A.P.J. (1995), *The refinement of production: ecological modernisation theory and the chemical industry*, Van Arkel, Utrecht.

Mol, A.P.J., V. Lauber and D. Liefferink (eds.) (2000), *The voluntary approach to environmental policy: joint environmental approach to environmental policy-making in Europe*, Oxford University Press, Oxford.

Paehlke, R. and D. Torgerson (1990), *Managing leviathan: environmental politics and the administrative state*, Belhaven Press, London.

Redclift, M. and G. Woodgate (eds.) (1997), *The international handbook of environmental sociology*, Edward Elgar, Northampton.

Sabatier, P.A. and H.C. Jenkins-Smith (eds.) (1993), *Policy change and learning: an advocacy coalition approach*, Westview Press, Boulder.

Sairinen, R. (2000), *Regulatory reform of Finnish environmental policy*, PhD Dissertation Helsinki University of Technology, Helsinki.

Schnaiberg, A. (1980), *The environment*, Oxford University Press, New York/Oxford.

Scott, W.R. (2001), *Institutions and organisations*, Sage, Thousand Oaks.

Spaargaren, G., A.P.J. Mol and F.H. Buttel (2000), *Environment and global modernity*, Sage, London.

Termeer, C.J.A.M. (1993), *Dynamiek en inertie rondom het mestbeleid: een studie naar veranderingsprocessen in het varkenshouderijnetwerk*, VUGA, 's Gravenhage.

Van der Zouwen, M. (2006), *Nature policy between trends and traditions – dynamics of nature policy arrangements in the Yorkshire Dales, Doñana and the Veluwe*, PhD Dissertation Nijmegen University, Eburon, Delft.

Van Kersbergen, C. and F. van Waarden (2001), *Shifts in governance: problems of legitimacy and accountability,* NWO, Den Haag.

Van Tatenhove, J.P.M. (1993), *Milieubeleid onder dak? Beleidsvoeringprocessen in het Nederlandse milieubeleid in de periode 1970-1990, nader uitgewerkt voor de Gelderse Vallei*, Pudoc, Wageningen.

Van Tatenhove, J.P.M., B. Arts and P. Leroy, (eds.) (2000), *Political modernisation and the environment: the renewal of environmental policy arrangements*, Kluwer Academic Publishers, Dordrecht.

Van Tatenhove, J.P.M. and P. Leroy (2000), The institutionalisation of environmental politics, in: J.P.M. van Tatenhove, B. Arts and P. Leroy, (eds.) (2000), *Political modernisation and the environment: the renewal of environmental policy arrangements*, Kluwer Academic Publishers, Dordrecht, pp. 17-33.

Weale, A. (1992), *The new politics of pollution*, Manchester University Press, Manchester.

Wynne, B. (1996) May the sheep safely graze?, in: S. Lash, B. Szerzinsky and B. Wynne (eds.), *Risk, environment and modernity*, Sage, London, pp. 44-83.

Yearley, S. (1996), *Sociology, environmentalism, globalization*, Sage, London.

Chapter 2

Political Modernisation

Bas Arts and Jan van Tatenhove

INTRODUCTION

The concept of 'political modernisation' is one of the key notions in the policy arrangements approach. It tries to capture those structural transformations in political domains in contemporary societies, which have or may have consequences for day-to-day policy practices. In turn, developments within certain policy practices may contribute to – or contradict – these structural transformations. Europeanisation offers an obvious example: while one can regard Europeanisation as a structural transformation process, one witnesses the mobilisation of EU rules and funds by policy actors at the local level, in order to achieve certain policy goals, thereby indirectly contributing to the Europeanisation of domestic policy practices. It is this two-way process – or duality – between structural transformations on the one hand and policy practices on the other which we deal with in this chapter. The central questions are: How can we understand the concept of political modernisation? How do processes of political modernisation affect policy practices and vice versa? How can we understand and explain processes, events and outcomes within policy arrangements? And how should we study the interplay of structural processes of political modernisation and day-to-day policy-making in empirical research?

The concept of 'political modernisation' has been interpreted quite differently. Some use it normatively and 'locally', as a programme to reform given political and democratic institutions. Others link the concept directly to the governance debate, transcending this normative and local focus. Again others consider 'political modernisation' as a purely analytical concept to understand structural transformations in relation to day-to-day political practices (and vice versa). In this chapter we elaborate upon the second and third perspectives.

Characteristic for an analytical perspective on political modernisation is, firstly, to link policy analysis to sociological and political

B. Arts and P. Leroy (eds.), Institutional Dynamics in Environmental Governance, 21–43.

science theories on modernity and modernisation. We especially relate to the debate on second modernity and reflexive modernisation. This literature offers fruitful insights into the structural transformations of current societies, implying various consequences for politics, policy-making and governance. Also the reverse relationship, from policy practices to structural transformations, is theorised about in this literature. In this sense political modernisation is *not* a normative programme, but an analytical tool to understand change and stability of policy in a rapidly changing world. Secondly, (political) modernisation is *not* a simple, diachronic and evolutionary process, for example from 'tradition' to 'early modernity' and to 'late modernity' (A → B → C). Although we acknowledge a certain path of development in time and space, this path is in our view *complex*, *synchronic* and (largely) *unplanned*. This includes the juxtaposition of traditional and modern structures and their merging into hybrid ones, as well as multi-facetted loops and feedbacks, such as the 'modernisation of tradition' and the 'traditionalisation of modernity' running parallel. Also, structures differ in time and space, so that we prefer to speak in the plural, of tradition*s* and modernit*ies*.

The format of this chapter is as follows. The next section starts with the discussion about the 'duality of structure' literature to grasp the mutual relationships between political modernisation and policy agents embedded in policy arrangements at the theoretical level. With that, we distance ourselves from simple mechanical causal models, in which for example structure is assumed to determine processes and outcomes of interaction. Instead, duality implies a subtle, two-way, multi-consequential model, in which structural processes in and structural properties of social systems constrain and enable meaningful action, while agents (re)produce and transform these processes and properties through their meaningful conduct at the same time. Yet they do so *indirectly* (through long social chains, hence together with 'unknown others'), mostly *unintended* (e.g. local agents do not generally intend to strengthen a process such as Europeanisation) and only in the *longer* run (since systems and structures generally do not change that easily). Subsequently, we deal with the concept of political modernisation. Its background, definition(s) and theoretical grounding will be clarified. After discussing modernisation and modernity we deal with the changing relations between state, civil society and market, and with patterns and structures of governance in the first and second phase of political modernisation. In the following sections, we pay attention to methodological matters. We will introduce two analytical perspectives, labelled institutional and strategic analysis respectively, to deal with political modernisation and the duality of structure in empirical research. The institutional analysis refers to analysing certain practices from a structural perspective, while 'putting the conduct of agencies between brackets' (Giddens). This implies a focus on structural transformations - understood as political modernisation – as well as on the structural properties properties of policy arrangements – rules, discourses and resources structures. In contrast, strategic analysis starts the analysis with the actions, ideas, power, etc., of agencies, while putting between brackets the structures in the context of which these actors have to operate. We will illustrate the application of these analytical distinguishable approaches by applying them to the case of Dutch organic farming. This case has no other meaning than to illustrate our theoretical claims and our methodological tools. This case reappears in the next chapters, While this chapter analyses the case mainly from an institutional perspective, the next chapter will unfold a strategic analysis thereof (Liefferink, this volume), while the subsequent chapter will take it as an example of our policy evaluation efforts (Arts and Goverde, this volume). With that, we can display the coherence between consequent perspectives and ways of application and operationalisation of the policy arrangement approach.

DUALITY OF STRUCTURE

Theoretical Debate

The famous sentence of Marx' *Eighteenth Brumaire of Louis Bonaparte* – "human beings make their own history, but not in circumstance of their own choosing" – is an aphorism that appears more cogent in the preface to most works in social theory than it does in the conclusions (Cohen, 1989). The struggle with the structure–agency problem is, hence, not new for social scientists. According to McAnulla (2002) the structure–agency question is the most important theoretical issue within the human sciences, while political scientists have argued that structure–agency questions should be recognized as central to the way we study politics.

In this section we discuss different ways of dealing with the structure–agency problem, starting with Giddens' structuration theory. In general, agency refers to individual or group abilities (intentional or otherwise) to affect their environment, whereas structure refers to context: the material and ideational conditions which define the range of actions available to actors. During the 1970s and 1980s, Giddens (1979, 1981, 1984) developed his structuration theory, as a reaction to the dualism in the social sciences between theories which are 'strong on action, weak on institutions' on the one hand and theories which are 'strong on institutions, weak on action' on the other. Whereas the first kind of theories have given a great deal of attention to action, intentions, reasons and motives, underestimating the rule-directed character and unintended consequences of action, the latter have placed the unacknowledged conditions and unintended consequences of action in the forefront, emphasising problems of institutional organisation and change. The divide between structuralist and intentionalist theories is still a central cleavage in the social and political sciences. On the one hand, we have structuralism, functionalism and social-economic approaches, whereas on the other end of the spectrum we find rational choice, network and group approaches, but also a variety of interpretative approaches. According to Giddens (1981, pp. 36-37)

> "(...) the dualism of subject and object (...) must cede place to recognition of a *duality* that is implicated in all social reproduction, *the duality of structure*. By the 'duality of structure' I refer to the essentially recursive character of social life: the structural properties of social systems are both medium and outcome of the practices that constitute those systems".

Structures guide and constrain human agency and the behaviour of actors in social practices (medium), while human agencies produce structures at the same time (outcome). However, Giddens does not consider structure and agency as two independent sets of phenomena. Structure simultaneously 'enters' into the constitution of social practices and 'exists' in the generating moments of this constitution (Giddens, 1979, p. 5). With these claims, Giddens' structuration theory seems to provide a useful basis for the reconciliation of action and structure. It offers insights in the patterning of social relations in collectivities, reproduced across time and space and in various locales.

However, during the 1990s structuration theory has been subject to considerable criticism (see for an overview the four volumes edited by Bryant and Jary, 1997; also relevant are: Archer, 1996; Clegg, 1989; Cohen, 1989; Dotty, 1997; Wendt, 1999). The main *theoretical* criticism holds that structuration theory stays at the voluntarist and subjectivist side of the duality of structure, because it dissolves the notion of structure in a theory of human action (as Giddens claims that structures only exist in human conduct and memory). With that position, structures as such seem to become 'virtual', whereas structures of signification, legitimisation and domination are, according to these critics, *real*, otherwise they can neither produce constraints nor be reproduced. In addition, McAnulla (2002, pp. 279-280) adds two *methodological* points: (1) by insisting that structure and agency are mutually constitutive and are in fact one and the same thing, it becomes very difficult to examine the nature of the interrelationship, or the dialectics, between structure and agency; and (2) there is a huge problem in using structuration theory in empirical research. Therefore, some believe that an 'analytical dualism' of agency and structure is to be preferred above the 'duality of structure', because otherwise one is unable to fruitfully analyse agents on the one hand and structures on the other.

Although the 'duality' and the 'virtuality' of structures are *theoretically* very relevant notions, in order to prevent a crude objectivation and reification of structures, we agree with the critics that these concepts are very difficult to handle at the *methodological* level. While Giddens accepts the bracketing of either structure or agency in order to analyse one of the two at the methodological level, he nonetheless adopts an agency-centred analysis for the most part. Critics of structuration theory, such as critical-realists, believe that structure exists independent of human agency, because structures produce 'real' effects. In our methodological approach we partly give in to these critics by developing a model in which agency and structure are of a *different* order and logic. In so doing, we draw some lessons from other 'dialectical approaches', as McAnulla calls them, such as the strategic-relational approach (Jessop, 1990) and the morphogenetic approach (Archer, 1996).

The key concept in the *strategic-relational approach* is strategy. Unlike Giddens, Hay and Jessop make a clear distinction between structure and agency. Structure is the starting point of analysis and action only takes place within a pre-existing structured context, which is strategically selective. "Actors are reflexive and formulate strategy on the basis of partial knowledge of the structures. It is possible for actors to formulate strategies which overcome the problems created for them by strategically selective contexts" (McAnulla, 2002, pp. 280-281). The strategic-relational approach stresses the ability of agents to alter structural circumstances through an active process of strategic learning: agents are reflexive, capable of reformulating their own identities and interests (although within limits), and able to engage in strategic calculations about their current situation.

In her *morphogenetic approach* Archer (1996) makes a clear analytical distinction between structure and agency (she prefers the notion of 'dualism' instead of 'duality'). Both exercise unique properties and powers and, as such, are irreducible to one another. According to Archer "structures as emergent entities are not only irreducible to people, they pre-exist them, and people are not puppets of structures because they have their own emergent properties which mean they either reproduce or transform social structures rather than create them" (Archer, 1996, in: McAnulla,

2002, p. 286). To grasp the structure–agency problem, Archer developed two cycles of change over time. One relates to the relationship between structure and agency, the other relates to the relationship between culture and agency. She does so to accentuate the ideational aspects of social life and to avoid conflating the material (structure) with the ideational (culture).

The cycles of change can be summarized as follows. In social and cultural interactions agents are strongly influenced by the context in which action takes places (structural and cultural conditioning). These structural and cultural conditions are the result of past actions and affect the interactions and the interest people have. However, during social interaction, agents also have at least some degree of independent power to affect events. As a result of these actions, the structural conditions might change. This process of structural or cultural elaboration (or reproduction) is a result which no group or individual wanted, but nonetheless emerges as the outcome of conflict or compromise. The changed structural (and cultural) context marks the beginning of a new circle of change. Given this picture, structure is hardly ever newly created; rather it is modified or transformed as a result of actions. Archer calls this process of change *morphogenesis.*

The Duality of Structure and the Policy Arrangement Approach

Central to our approach is the institutionalisation of policy arrangements as the result of the interplay of processes of political modernisation and policy innovation. In new institutionalism (Lowndes, 2002; Sweet, 2001; Van Tatenhove and Mak, 2005), institutions are seen as sets of 'rules' that guide and constrain the behaviour of individual actors. In general, institutionalisation is the process of production and reproduction of policy arrangements, by which rules of the game are formed and defended. On the one hand, policy arrangements are produced by human agencies in interaction, resulting in accepted rules, coalitions and discourses ('structuration'). On the other hand, once formed, policy arrangements and the rules which go along with them constrain the interactions of the agents involved ('stabilisation').

What these dialectical approaches make so interesting for our study of the institutionalisation of policy arrangements is, firstly, that there is a *fruitful* analytical distinction to be made between structure and agency and, secondly, that the ways structure affects agency and agency affects structure are of a *different* order and logic. While the structural properties of policy arrangements constrain and enable interactions in policy arrangements (Van Tatenhove et al., 2000), interactions in policy arrangements do *not*, in turn, (directly) change the structural process of political modernisation. One of the problems with the policy arrangement approach up till now has been a lack of understanding of how the structural process of political modernisation changes as a result of interactions in policy arrangements. In other words, a new understanding of the duality of structure is needed. Inspired by the dialectical models, we can give a more sophisticated interpretation of the duality of structure for the policy arrangement approach.

Political modernisation refers to structural transformation processes within the political domain of society (see next section). In that sense, political modernisation is an ongoing process of 'structural conditioning'. Structural processes, such as globalisation, Europeanisation, the rise of information technology, etc., but also the structural properties of policy arrangements (rules, resources, discourses; see for their operationalisation: Liefferink, this volume), are the context or conditions in which agencies' actions take place. These structural processes and properties constrain and enable agencies. To advance their interests and while trying to affect policy outcomes, actors act upon the structural properties and opportunities of policy arrangements. In other words, they mobilise resources, make use of rules, frame discourses and build coalitions. As a result of these interactions, the structural properties of policy arrangements might be modified (although not necessarily so). However, the change that may, as a result, occur in the structural conditions of policy arrangements *as whole*, i.e. processes of political modernisation, is *not* the intended consequence of the dynamics within a *single* arrangement, but is the unforeseen and unintended consequence of a great variety of actions in several policy arrangements. In this sense, structure is *not* newly created; rather it is indirectly modified or transformed as a result of social interaction in a *diversity* of policy arrangements.

POLITICAL MODERNISATION

Different Views

In daily politics as well as in scientific literature different conceptualisations of political modernisation do exist (Table 2.1).

First of all, there exists a normative usage in political discourse, such as the 'modernisation of democracy', or the 'modernisation of local politics', which expresses the normative demand to reform certain existing political institutions in order to improve their functioning (Boogers, 2000).

Table 2.1. Different conceptualisations of political modernisation

Political modernisation	Day-to-day politics (normative)	Public administration (analytical and normative)	Political sociology (analytical)
Definition	Institutional reform	Shifts in governance	New relationships between state, market and civil society

A second conceptualisation is directly related to the governance debate and to public administration (as a science). Here political modernisation is a synonym for 'shifts in governance' or 'a shift from government to governance' (Jänicke, 1993; Van Kersbergen and Van Waarden, 2001). Thirdly, political modernisation is used as an analytical tool to understand the effects of structural processes on day-to-day policy making by focusing on new relationships between state, civil society and market (Van Tatenhove, 1999). In this section, we elaborate upon the analytical perspective on political modernisation, combining elements of the second and third interpretations of political modernisation.

The concept of political modernisation first of all expresses the shifting locus and focus of politics. Politics and policy are no longer framed within the nation-state model alone, but within a diversity of society-centred forms of governance. In this new era of politics, the locus of politics has shifted from classical-modernist institutions to new sites, new actors and new themes. These shifts are reflected in the new policy vocabulary, emphasising governance, complexity, access, trust, deliberation, networks and flows, considerably changing the traditional political science vocabulary of representative democracy, political parties, interest mediation, social movements, international politics, political power, political participation and the citizenry (Arts and Van Tatenhove, 2005; Bovens et al., 1995; Gibbins and Reimer, 1999; Hajer, 2000; Hajer and Wagenaar, 2003; Urry, 2004). Secondly, as stated earlier, political modernisation should not be considered a normative or political programme, but as an analytical tool, based on political-sociological and political science theories. Consequently, special attention will be paid to: (1) politics in 'the second stage of modernity' (Beck, 1992, 1994, 2000; Urry, 2004); (2) the shifting relationships between state, market and civil society, nationally as well as internationally; and (3) shifting relations in structures of governance (Kooiman, 1993; Pierre, 2000). Thirdly, the concept of political modernisation is meant to link policy analysis to political analysis. Too often, policy analysts remain caught within the domains of their discipline, either ignoring overall political change (and persisting in their synoptic-rational models) or proclaiming (too) radical policy change at sector levels (heralding a post-modern era), without seriously addressing the mediating and tempering political-institutional context (Arts and Van Tatenhove, 2005).

A Substantive Definition

Given the above considerations, we define 'political modernisation' as the shifting relationships between the state, market and civil society in political domains of societies – *within* countries and *beyond* – as a manifestation of the 'second stage of modernity', implying new conceptions and structures of governance. Inspired by Held (1995), we define 'the political domain of society' as the setting in which different groups (from state, civil society and market) produce and distribute resources (power and domination), rules (institutions) and meaning (discourses) in order to shape public life. Below we will clarify and elaborate upon the central elements of this definition, such as modernisation, the relationship between state, market and civil society and governance.

Modernity and Modernisation

In general, modernity refers to modes of social life organization, which emerged in Western countries from the seventeenth century onwards, the influence of which subsequently became more or less worldwide. It is a cluster of cultural and structural processes, of typical institutional forms, which came into being on the crossroads of capitalism, industrialism and the nation state (Giddens, 1990). To understand political modernisation as a relevant process for environmental policy, we make a distinction between the first and second stages of political modernisation (Beck, 2000). These stages have partly *diachronically* developed (historically, the first stage preceded the second one), partly *synchronically* (today we witness all kinds of hybrid structures of 1st and 2nd modernity). In general, the first modernity has been 'nation-state centred', whereas the second stage has developed beyond the 'nation-state model'. In this second stage of modernity,

> "the indissoluble link of society and nation-state is fundamentally broken with the emergence of a logic of *flows* including (…) the flows of risks (…). In such a situation modernity is radicalized, subjecting itself to reflexive processes. Second or reflexive modernization disenchants and dissolves its own taken-for-granted foundations" (Urry, 2004).

More specifically, the *first phase of modernity* is closely linked to the project of (early) modernity itself. The dominant discourse is the 'manageable society'. This is reflected in the centrality of the nation-state and the regulatory state. Also, the emergence of international organisations and the conception of international order has been shaped within the Westphalian model, which entrenched the principle of territorial sovereignty (Held, 1995). Moreover, the state was considered to be the supreme regulatory body within its boundaries, both within capitalist and centrally planned societies. At the same time, society was believed to be highly 'manageable' by state regulation. In the early days of environmental policy, this faith in 'manageability' was reflected in the development of sectoral legislation, the setting of environmental standards and planning, and the development of environmental impact assessment.

The *second phase of modernity* is closely linked to what some call *post*-modernity, and others *late or reflexive* modernity (Albrow, 1996; Beck, 1992, 1994, 1999, 2000; Beck and Beck-Gernsheim, 2002; Beck et al., 1994; Gibbins and Reimer, 1999). According to Beck, contemporary society has entered the second stage of modernity. The first thesis of Beck is that we live in a global risk society, as a consequence of the modernisation process. The so-called 'new risks', such as the ecological ones, have been man-made, mainly unintended and unforeseen, beyond class (we are all subject to potential harm, rich and poor), beyond country level (as many of these risks are globalised) and cannot be sufficiently dealt with by the modern institutions of state, market, civil society and science (as these stood at the roots of this risk production process). This leads to Beck's second thesis: that the risk society forces us to 'reflexive modernisation'. Confronted with these new risks, we 'simply' have to reflect on and re-invent modernity, although our immediate 'reflexes' will lead us into more problem-solving by the classical institutions. Yet 'reflection' also leads to new political practices outside the formal institutions of the nation state, which Beck labels 'sub-politics'. Examples from the environmental field are standard-setting for sustainable development by market and civil society parties, e.g. in the forestry area, or the generation of nuclear-free electricity by citizens-owned companies (Arts and Van Tatenhove, 2002).

The transition from first to second modernity is characterised by the rise of the network society (Castells, 1996-1998) and the risk society (Beck, 1992), and with that, by new ordering principles, such as flows, networks and risks. Technological innovations, globalisation and individuallisation accompany these structural changes and affect the interrelations between state, civil society and market on the one hand and emerging structures and patterns of governance on the other.

Interrelations of State, Civil Society and Market

The relationships between state, market and civil society are shifting due to 'horizontal' as well as 'vertical' processes. The former refer to a blurring of the distinctions between these subsystems at national levels, the latter to a relocation of politics below and beyond the nation state. Below, we will deal with these two types of processes more in-depth.

Historically, the early modernity project was accompanied by the liberal-democratic order (Dubbink, 1999). This order was characterised by so-called *differentiation*, the formal and organisational split between state, market and civil society. Each of these subsystems should have their own rationales, norms and logic of action: respectively public interests, political representation and bureaucracy (state), private interests, interest groups and competition (market) and civic interests, social movements and solidarity (civil society). According to the liberal-democratic ideology, these spheres should be as separate as possible. The state should not interfere in economic affairs nor should the market have a duty in terms of public responsibilities. This division of labour would lead to the best for all, to maximum welfare. Of course, reality in post-War Europe was different. The state did interfere in the market in many cases, while economic interests groups exercised political influence (e.g. in etatist and neo-corporatist arrangements). Recently, however, this process of *de-differentiation* has intensified. The state has been overloaded and has, as a consequence, transferred public duties to both society and the market (Pierre, 2000). The market has been challenged to take public responsibility, e.g. to promote sustainable development and social corporate responsibility (Bendell, 2000). And society has been re-politicised (Beck's 'sub-politics'). In other words, there is not so much left of the old (ideal-type) separation of tasks. At the level of policy making, this is expressed in new experiments of 'reflexive policy making', in which parties of all three spheres try to design new policy practices, based on new rules beyond the traditional divides (Pestman and Van Tatenhove, 1998).

Besides these *de-differentiation* processes, or 'horizontal shifts', the nation-state model also lost its exclusiveness under the influence of 'vertical shifts', like globalisation and individualisation. Individualisation should not be read as the emergence of the free, rational 'me-first' individual, as a consequence of growing wealth, neo-liberalisation, etc., but as the emergence of institutionalised individualism (Beck and

Beck Gernsheim, 2002). That is: the new individualism is a structural expression of a highly differentiated society as well as of new patterns of social integration. To give an example: today, political subjects prefer to (loosely) organise themselves in the form of ad hoc transnational advocacy networks rather than in classical, national political parties (Keck and Sikkink, 1998). Also, the individual has become globalised. Ever more, one feels himself being less embedded in a certain nation or considers himself less the citizen of a certain state (although 'nationalism' is definitely not to be considered a phenomenon of the past). Through production and consumption flows, the media, ICT, tourism, social networks, global activism, etc., the individual is directly linked to the rest of the world.

It should be realised, though, that individualisation and globalisation are 'grand' processes and manifest themselves differently in various spheres of society. Table 2.2 summarises a number of relevant, order-specific globalisation and individualisation processes, the consequence of which is that the relationships between these spheres have become blurred (Beck, 1994; Bovens et al., 1995; Castells, 1996-1998; Duyvendak, 1997; Held, 1995; Inglehart, 1997; Strange, 1996). However, it is an empirical question which transformation processes are more or less relevant for a certain policy issue and policy arrangement and, hence, are relevant for a certain policy analysis. Almost all empirical chapters in this volume (chapters 5 to 12) deal with these empirical questions. We will summarise their empirical findings and the theoretical implications thereof in the last chapter.

Table 2.2. Order-specific manifestations of globalisation and individualisation

	Globalisation	Individualisation
State	Relocation of politics; diffusion of authority	Gap between politics and citizenry; sub-politics
Market	Economic internationalisation; new opportunities and risks	Re-organisation of the firm; 'new' consumerism
Civil society	European and cosmopolitan citizenship	New forms of integration and segregation

Governance

Processes of political modernisation reflect different structures and patterns of governance. In other words, it is claimed that the *de-differentiation*, globalisation and individualisation of the state, market and civil society imply new conceptions and structures of governance. This buzzword of the late 1990s and early 2000s in political sciences, public administration and management sciences alike generally refers to a 'paradigm shift' or 'turn' in the way we govern societies and organizations today (Hajer and Wagenaar, 2003; Held and McGrew, 2002; Héritier, 2001, 2002; Hooghe and Marks, 2001; Jordan, 2001; Pierre, 2000; Van Kersbergen and Van Waarden, 2001). To put it bluntly, the old paradigm of top-down, state-led, command & control ways of steering, according to the governance literature, no longer suffice (Bovens et al., 1995; Dubbink, 1999; Hajer, 2000). Instead, we find new forms of governance and policy instruments: network-like arrangements of public and private actors, self-regulation by business organizations, public-private and civic-private partnerships, emission trading systems, certification programs, etc. (Bendel, 2000; Kickert et al., 1997; Kolk, 2000). Some refer to this as a 'shift from government to governance' or as 'governance without government' (Van Kersbergen and Van Waarden, 2001). As a result, we witness the entrance of 'new' private and societal actors in public policy-making, also conceptualized as *multi-actor* governance or network governance (Kohler-Koch and Eising, 1999). In addition, these new forms of governing and steering are to be found at and in-between different *levels* of public policy-making, which is generally referred to as *multi-level* governance (Hooghe and Marks, 2001). In general, governance refers to a society-centred way of governing or steering, accentuating coordination and self-governance, manifested in different types of policy arrangements, which are an expression of an increasing encroachment of state, civil society and market (Van Tatenhove, 2003; Van Tatenhove and Mak, 2005).

The presumed shift from government to governance is a reaction to the steering and governance problems associated with early modernity. Firstly, the classical-modernist nation state could not bring security and prosperity for all, either in the developed or underdeveloped world. Neither could it guarantee that it would do so in the future, given its declining capacities and powers in the light of growing globalisation and Europeanisation tendencies. More and more, monolithic state governance has been replaced by forms of network governance, new public management, good governance, informal governance and systems of joint multi-level governance, in which regions, nations and international organizations jointly and through complex procedures of participation and decision-making co-determine political outcomes (Held and McGrew, 2002; Hooghe and Marks, 2001; Kohler-Koch and Eising, 1999). Secondly, the regulatory state has lost credibility, due to the crisis of the Western, Keynesian welfare state, the failure of state intervention in many developing countries, as well as the collapse of the socialist state model in Eastern Europe in the late 1980s (Pierre, 2000). Also, privatisation and de-regulation programmes have strengthened these processes. Thirdly, top-down policy-making turned out to be less effective, efficient and legitimate as it had claimed. Therefore, governance has not only become multi-layered, but also pluralized (Kooiman, 1993; Rhodes, 2000; Weiss and Gordenker, 1996). This means that the participation and influence of players from the market and civil society, e.g. epistemic communities, NGOs or business, has increased at all levels of policy-making (Haas, 1992; Princen and Finger, 1994). Also, self-governance practices, without direct state involvement, have become much more common phenomena. Finally, society turned out to be less manageable than believed, given its growing complexity. The effects of policy-making are in many cases unknown, unintended or unforeseen. As a consequence, governance optimism of the early phase of modern politics has been replaced by governance relativism, or even worse, by governance pessimism.

Death of the State?

From the above analysis, which builds on the notions of governance, second modernity and a blurring of state-market-society boundaries, one might easily conclude that we support a 'retreat-of-the-state', a 'death-of-the-state' or a 'hollowing-out-of-the-state' thesis (Albrow, 1996; Strange, 1996). Although it is definitely the case that the state has partly retreated from certain domains, like economic or environmental policy, this claim, however, can not be held true in general (Van Kersbergen and Van Waarden, 2001). As Hirst (2000) makes clear, the state remains rather dominant in those fields where it has traditionally been considered 'the sovereign', such as the monopolisation of collective violence, internal and external security, taxation and currency, law and order and social consensus building. Having said that, we may observe some shifts beyond the nation state model in these areas as well: UN peace keeping forces intervening in sovereign states, the introduction and EU-regulation of the Euro, and citizen initiatives to maintain law and order in their neighbourhoods. Even more so, the power of the state has *increased* in some instances, the (inter)national regulation of the Internet being one example (Knill and Lehmkuhl, 2002). Therefore, we would not proclaim a general 'death of the state'. Yet its position, role, power and authority are definitely transformed in the light of political modernisation processes, as analysed in the above.

INSTITUTIONAL ANALYSIS

So far, we dealt with a meta-theory, 'duality of structure', as well as with a theory, 'political modernisation'. Now the question is how to operationalise these. In other words, how to make use of these concepts in empirical research? In the above, we made a methodological distinction between institutional and strategic analysis, the former focusing on structure, the latter on agency in empirical research. Now we will elaborate on these two methodologies more in depth, starting with the institutional focus.

An institutional analysis is meant to analyse policy practices from a structural perspective, putting the conduct of agencies between brackets. This implies a focus on processes of political modernisation and on the way these affect the structural properties of policy arrangements. These structural properties are analytically distinguished into the four so-called dimensions of an arrangement: agencies, discourses, resources, rules and discourses. They will be explained at full length in the next chapter (Liefferink, this volume). From an institutional perspective, it should be assessed how these structural properties and processes constrain or enable policy actors in achieving certain outcomes and, hence, whether structures favour a change of policy processes and outcomes or not. But first of all, we should determine what the relevant structural processes and properties consist of with regard to a certain policy domain. As stated, this is an empirical question. Theoretically, one may assume that globalisation and individualisation are relevant, but in what form, shape and depth depends on the issue under investigation. We distinguish the following steps in an institutional analysis:

1. a selection and elaboration of relevant political modernisation processes (e.g. economic globalisation, Europeanisation of rule-making, relocation of political authority to sub-national levels, new governance discourses, new relationships between state and market, etc.) for policy arrangement A, which is our object of study;
2. an analysis of the structural properties of policy arrangement A (rules of the game, policy discourses, division of power), in relation to the selected structural transformation processes;
3. an analysis of how these structural processes and properties relate to each other as well as manifest themselves in policy arrangement A;
4. an analysis of how these structural processes and properties constrain or enable agents to act in a certain way and to achieve certain policy outcomes.

It should be noted – given our premise of the duality of structure – that the last step in this analytical scheme should be done with caution. It is always tempting to entirely explain the conduct of agencies as a consequence of certain structures. However, this would imply a rather crude determinism. Therefore structural explanations should be always confronted with peoples' intentions and motives to act in a certain way and not otherwise. For as far as these match our structural hypotheses (e.g. 'these are the rules', 'it is best to follow the majority view', 'you cannot decide against the industry's interests', etc.), the latter can be rather safely adopted. If not, agency-oriented explanations should enrich our institutional analysis.

Organic Farming

As indicated, we would like to illustrate our methodological considerations with an empirical case, organic farming. Recently, we conducted a research project on this topic for the Dutch Environmental Assessment Agency, focusing on long-term perspectives for this sector in the Netherlands (Arts et al., 2001). Below, we present a secondary analysis of this research, without going into empirical details, but restricting to the perspectives elaborated in this chapter.

Although the number of organic farms, their land area as well as their turn-over, have more or less doubled in the Netherlands in the period 1997-2003, the Dutch organic farming sector is still small compared to other countries in Europe (Biologica, 2004). For example, about 2,2% of total agricultural area is used for organic farming in the Netherlands, while comparable figures in Austria and Switzerland are 13% and 10% respectively. Moreover, recent figures show a decline of growth figures. The number of organic farms, for example, is even decreasing in the Netherlands today (Biologica, 2005). These developments can be explained, we assume, both by structural trends as well as by actors' interventions.

In our case study on organic farming, five potentially relevant structural trends were distinguished: the retreat of the state, internationalisation, 'sciencification', ecological modernisation and post-materialism (Arts et al., 2001). These processes, though differently, may have put pressure on the Dutch organic policy arrangement. For example, the (partial) retreat of the state, as an expression of new governance practices in this policy field, may create both new opportunities and restrictions for organic farmers; internationalisation, particularly the Europeanisation of agriculture, may bring about new 'outside' rules and resources, as well as more competition from foreign organic sectors; the 'sciencification' of the farming and food sector may lead to an increasing role of scientific knowledge actors and discourses within the sector; ecological modernisation may lead to a greening of mainstream agriculture, which may be a threat to organic farming; post-materialism may induce an increase of demand for organic products.

Of course, one can question the empirical validity of these trends and their actual impact, but by employing different hypotheses and scenarios, one can generate different expectations and validate these empirically. For example, a (partial) retreat of the state would have to become manifest in the policy arrangement itself as well as in its recent history. This would imply a change of actor constellation, power relations, rules of the game and (governance) discourse. To some extent, we find these changes in the Dutch organic sector, especially the call for a more market-oriented policy and the entry of new market players, such as large retailers. Hence, we see new relationships between state and market emerging. At the same time, the Ministry of Agriculture still plays an important role. Similar questions can be asked and empirically validated with regard to the other trends, which were identified in the above. All these seem to have been more or less relevant for the sector. For example, Europeanisation has resulted in new rules for organic farming (e.g. on *Eko* labelling), scientification to some additional research (although the mainstream research institutions remain dominant in this field), and ecological modernisation also seems a trend in mainstream agriculture, with more emphasis on environmental management, green labelling (*Milieukeur*) and animal rights. This has led to some additional competition pressure for organic farming, e.g. between the two labels. One trend, which was hypothesised, seems however not very relevant for Dutch organic farming: post-materialism. So far the average Dutch consumer is not willing 'to go organic', although consumption figures have increased the last couple of years (Biologica, 2004, 2005).

To some extent, given the above analysis, processes and outcomes within the Dutch organic farming arrangement can be explained by structural trends, such as liberalisation, privatisation and (some) ecological modernisation. Especially the partial retreat of the state and a lack of post-materialisation (which becomes manifest in relatively low consumption figures of organic products) are considered the main causes of the rather low success rate by the sector, according to some key stakeholders. Yet this is only half the story. To understand the way social interactions develop as well as certain policy outcomes are produced, explanations at the agent level are indispensable as well. With that, we enter the sphere of strategic analysis.

STRATEGIC ANALYSIS

Starting points of a strategic analysis are the actions, ideas, and influence of actors in day-to-day interactions in policy arrangements. Now the structures, within which these actors have to operate, are put between brackets. The focus of analysis is on how agencies make use of rules, resources and discourses in order to get things done. At the same time, by doing so, agencies reproduce or modify structural properties of the policy arrangements in which they operate, and by that, overall structures might be even changed as well. However, for a proper analysis in terms of the duality of structure, two levels should be distinguished: firstly, the structural properties of policy arrangements and, secondly, the structural process of political modernisation. The former may be *directly* related to the social interaction and preferred outcomes of actors. For example, the adoption of new participation rules for NGOs modifies the rules of the game. Political modernisation as a general process, however, is only *indirectly* related to intentional human conduct. More often than not, it is the *unintended* outcome of social interactions and outcomes in many policy arrangements across time and space. For example a possible unintended outcome of the reduction of tariffs by governments in several countries around the world is a further liberalisation of world trade in agricultural products. We distinguish the following four steps in a strategic analysis:

1. an analysis of social interactions and policy outcomes in policy arrangement A;
2. an analysis of the change or stabilisation of the structural properties (rules, resources, discourses) of policy arrangement A, as a consequence of these social interactions and policy outcomes;
3. a reiteration of the analytical steps 1 and 2 for (related) policy arrangements B... Z;
4. an analysis of structural reproduction or transformation processes (political modernisation), as a consequence of change and/or continuity in policy arrangements A... Z.

What these four steps in our view make very clear is that there is no direct causal link – theoretically nor methodologically – between the actions of individual policy agents and 'grand' political modernisation processes. For example, a student who conducts research on a local nature conservation project in a specific town might find out that concerned individuals *à titre personnel* rather than local authorities and formal representatives of NGOs are involved in this local project. From these observations, he however cannot conclude that the participation of these individuals immediately contributes to the individualisation of politics in Western societies. It may be definitely a *manifestation* of this individualisation process, but that is an institutional observation (see previous section). Instead, he should relate this phenomenon to the structural properties of the (local) nature conservation arrangement itself (interaction rules, local governance discourse, and division of resources). The researcher has to assess in what way the interactions between actors involved have resulted in a modification of rules and resources of the policy arrangement. Then, in a next step, a comparison might be made with other (related) policy arrangements across time and space. If similar developments are detectable, one can more safely assume that developments in nature conservation contribute to political individualisation processes. However, in bounded research practices – in terms of time, resources and focused research questions – one may wonder whether such an elaborated strategic analysis is achievable and justified. Therefore, it is very legitimate to limit oneself to the first two steps only.

Organic Farming

When assessing the Dutch policy arrangement of organic farming from a strategic analysis perspective, the first thing that stands out is the diversity of actors in the arrangement. We see governmental and non-governmental as well as organic and non-organic players. However, most striking is not the diversity of actors, but the inclusion of mainstream agricultural organisations and large retailers in the policy arrangement, actors which were considered the 'enemy' by organic organisations not so very long ago. But this inclusion should not be equated with integration, as the mainstream and organic fields hitherto remain rather different worlds. The result is a fragmented policy arrangement, in which interactions are not intense, and in which co-operation and trust between actors are low. Power relations are asymmetrical, with governmental and mainstream organisations residing in the centre, and non-governmental and organic organisations in the periphery. As a result, actors are confronted with very contrasting policy objectives, as some players are advocating, whereas others are frustrating the further development of organic farming.

Although the arrangement is fragmented, some changes have nonetheless taken place, such as a change of interaction rules, which have made at least some interaction between 'mainstreamers' and 'organics' possible. Yet a sharp distinction between their discourses is very characteristic for the arrangement. The core of the organic discourse is the objective to realise growth by converting mainstream agriculture into organic farming as much as possible, whereas the mainstreamers consider organic agriculture as just another option to generate some additional income for farmers who are in economic trouble at best. Some think of integrating both agricultural philosophies, contributing to the sustainability and transition discourses, but these are still in the minority. Besides, several organic organisations still prefer small-scale production and selling sites, which contradicts the business philosophy of mainstream agriculture and of the big retailers.

As a consequence of this fragmentation, we believe that the Dutch organic sector is 'muddling through', without realising impressive growth results. Hence, continuity prevails, so that one cannot see much structural modification within and beyond this policy arrangement, as a result of social interactions and policy outcomes. An exception is the fact that mainstream organisations and retailers have been tolerated as relevant stakeholders in the arrangement, although not very enthusiastically by all, which indicates changes in the rules of the game. Yet their contrasting discourses and asymmetrical power relations have remained stable so far and account for continuity in terms of a fragmented and rather unsuccessful policy arrangement. Together with the (non)manifestation of some structural trends in the arrangement (e.g. retreat of the state, lack of post-materialism, Europeanisation; see previous section), these factors help to understand the current state-of-the art of the Dutch organic farming policy arrangement.

CONCLUSION

In this chapter we dealt with the understanding and explanation of social processes and political outcomes in policy arrangements. In order to prevent (too much) voluntarism or determinism, the thesis of the 'duality of structure' was introduced. This thesis, firstly, implies consideration of agency and structure as indissolvable at the theoretical level, secondly, consideration of them as logically different at the methodological level. The latter implies the need to complement an institutional analysis with a strategic one.

The strategic analysis is largely a prelude to insights to be developed in the next chapter, where the concept of policy arrangements will be elaborated upon in full detail. The institutional analysis is further elaborated upon in this chapter. To that end, the concept of political modernisation was introduced and analysed from a political-sociological perspective. With that, political modernisation is in our view linked to the second stage of modernity, to shifting relations between state, market and civil society, as well as to new discourses and practices of governance. The case of Dutch organic farming subsequently made clear how political modernisation processes can account for certain policy processes and outcomes. Yet a full understanding of these processes and outcomes points at the need to include agency-oriented explanations as well, and thus indicates the importance of the 'duality of structure' thesis.

REFERENCES

Albrow, M. (1996), *The global age: state and society beyond modernity*, Polity Press, Oxford.

Archer, M.S. (1996), *Realist social theory: the morphogenetic approach*, Cambridge University Press, Cambridge.

Arts, B., M. Bruns, P. Leroy, D. Liefferink and J.P.M. van Tatenhove (2001), *Biologisch groeien?! Een multi-actor analyse van het beleidsarrangement biologische landbouw (2000-2020)*, Katholieke Universiteit Nijmegen, Nijmegen.

Arts, B. and J.P.M. van Tatenhove (2002), Institutional innovation and the environment: 'frontstage' and 'backstage' politics, *Gaia: Ecological Perspectives in Science, Humanities, and Economics*, no. 1, pp. 64-65.

Arts, B. and J.P.M. van Tatenhove (2005), Policy and power – A conceptual framework between the 'old' and 'new' policy idioms, *Policy Sciences*, Vol. 37, no. 3/4, pp. 339-356.

Beck, U. (1992), *Risk society – towards a new modernity*, Sage, London.

Beck, U. (1994), The reinvention of politics: towards a theory of reflexive modernization, in: U. Beck, A. Giddens and S. Lash (eds.), *Reflexive modernization: politics, tradition and aesthetics in the modern social order*, Polity Press, Cambridge, pp. 1-55.

Beck, U., A. Giddens and S. Lash (1994), *Reflexive modernization: politics, tradition and aesthetics in the modern social order*, Polity Press, Cambridge.

Beck, U. (1999), *World Risk Society*, Polity Press, Cambridge.

Beck, U. (2000), The cosmopolitan perspective: sociology of the second age of modernity, *British Journal of Sociology*, Vol. 51, no. 1, pp. 79-106.

Beck U. and E. Beck-Gernsheim (2002), *Individualization – institutionalized individualism and its social and political consequences*, Sage, London.

Bendel, J. (eds.) (2000), *Terms of endearment: business, NGOs and sustainable development*, Greenleafe Publications, Sheffield.

Biologica (2004), *Eko-Monitor: Cijfers en trends, Jaarrapport 2003,* bron: ww.biologica.nl.

Biologica (2005), *Eko-Monitor: Cijfers en trends, Jaarrapport 2004,* bron: ww.biologica.nl.

Boogers, M. (2000), Over moderniseren van lokaal bestuur, in: N.J.M. Nelissen, H. Goverde and N. van Gestel (2000), *Bestuurlijk vermogen: analyse en beoordeling van nieuwe vormen van besturen*, Coutinho, Bussum, pp. 325-354.

Bovens, M., W. Derksen, W. Witteveen, F. Becker and P. Kalma (1995), *De verplaatsing van de politiek, een agenda voor democratische vernieuwing*, Wiarda Beckman Stichting, Amsterdam.

Bryant, G.A. and D. Jary (eds.) (1997), *Anthony Giddens, critical assessments,* Volumes I to IV, Routledge, London.

Castells, M. (1996-1998), *The information age: economy, society and culture*, Volume II, the power of identity,Blackwell Publishers, Malden/Oxford.

Clegg, S.R. (1989), *Frameworks of Power*, Sage, London.
Cohen, I.J. (1989), *Structuration theory: Anthony Giddens and the constitution of social life*, MacMillan Education Ltd, London.
Dotty, R.L. (1997), Aporia: a critical exploration of the agent-structure problematique in international relations theory, *European Journal of International Affairs*, Vol. 3, no. 3, pp. 365-392.
Dubbink, W. (1999), *Duurzaamheid als patstelling: over de onvriendelijke betrekkingen tussen openbaar bestuur, markt en 'civil society'*, Eburon, Delft.
Duyvendak, J.W. (1997), *Waar blijft de politiek? Essays over paarse politiek, maatschappelijk middenveld en sociale cohesie*, Boom, Amsterdam.
Gibbins, J.R. and B. Reimer (1999), *The politics of postmodernity: an introduction to contemporary politics and culture*, Sage, London, pp. 134-166.
Giddens, A. (1979), *Central problems in social theory*, Macmillan, London.
Giddens, A. (1981), *A contemporary critique of historical materialism, Vol. 1 Power, property and the state*, Macmillan, London.
Giddens, A. (1984), *The constitution of society*, Polity Press, Cambridge.
Giddens, A. (1990), *The consequences of modernity*, Polity Press, Cambridge.
Haas, P.M. (1992), Introduction: epistemic communities and international policy coordination, *International Organization*, Vol. 46, no. 1, pp. 1-35.
Hajer, M.A. (2000), *Politiek als vormgeving*, Vossius AUP, Amsterdam.
Hajer, M.A. and H. Wagenaar (eds.) (2003), *Deliberative policy analysis: understanding governance in the network society, theories of institutional design*, Cambridge University Press, Cambridge.
Held, D. (1995), *Democracy and the global order: from the modern state to cosmopolitan governance*, Polity Press, Cambridge.
Held, D. and A. McGrew (eds.) (2002), *Governing globalization: power, authority and global governance*, Polity Press, Cambridge.
Héritier, A. (2001), *New modes of governance in Europe: policy-making without legislating?*, Max Planck Project Group, Preprint 01/14, Bonn.
Héritier, A. (eds.) (2002), *Common goods: reinventing European and international governance*, Rowman & Littlefield Publishers, Lanham.
Hirst, P. (2000), Democracy and governance, in: J. Pierre (eds.) (2000), *Debating governance: authority, steering and democracy*, Oxford University Press, Oxford, pp. 13-36.
Hooghe, L. and G. Marks (2001), *Multi-level governance and European integration,* Rowman & Littlefield Publishers, Lanham.
Inglehart, R. (1997), *Modernization and postmodernization – cultural, economic and political change in 43 societies*, Princeton University Press, Princeton.
Jänicke, M. (1993), Über ökologische und politische Modernisierungen, *Zeitschrift für Umweltpolitik und Umweltrecht*, no. 2, pp. 159-175.
Jessop, B. (1990), *State theory: putting the capitalist state in its place*, Polity Press, Cambridge.
Jordan, A. (2001), The European Union: an evolving system of multi-level governance, or government?, *Policy & Politics*, Vol. 29, no. 2, pp. 193-208.
Keck, M.E. and K.A. Sikkink (1998), *Activists beyond borders: advocacy networks in international politics*, Cornell University Press, Ithaca.
Kickert, W.J.M., E.H. Klijn and J.F.M. Koppenjan (eds.) (1997), *Managing complex networks: strategies for the public sector*, Sage, London.
Knill, C. and D. Lehmkuhl (2002), Private actors and the state: Internationalization and changing patterns of governance, *Governance – An International Journal of Policy and Administration*, Vol. 15, no. 1, pp. 41-64.

Kohler-Koch, B. and R. Eising (eds.) (1999), *The transformation of governance in the European Union*, Routledge/ECPR Studies in European Political Science, London and New York.

Kolk, A. (2000), *Economics of environmental management*, Pearson Education Ltd, Edinburg.

Kooiman, J. (eds.) (1993), *Modern governance: new government-society interactions*, Sage, London.

Lowndes, V. (2002), Institutionalism, in: D. Marsh and G. Stoker (eds.), *Theory and methods in political science* (2nd edition), Palgrave MacMillan, New York, pp. 90-108.

McAnulla, S. (2002), Structure and agency, in: D. Marsh and G. Stoker (eds.), *Theory and methods in political science* (2nd edition), Palgrave MacMillan, New York, pp. 271-291.

Pestman, P. and J.P.M. van Tatenhove (1998), Reflexieve beleidsvoering voor milieu, ruimtelijke ordening en infrastructuur? – Nieuwe initiatieven nader beschouwd, *Beleidswetenschap,* Vol. 12, nr. 3, pp. 254-272.

Pierre, J. (eds.) (2000), *Debating governance: authority, steering and democracy*, Oxford University Press, Oxford.

Princen, T. and M. Finger (eds.) (1994), *Environmental NGOs in world politics: linking the global and the local*, Routledge, London.

Rhodes, R.A.W. (2000), Governance and public administration, in: J. Pierre, *Debating governance: authority, steering and democracy*, Oxford University Press, Oxford, pp. 54-90.

Strange, S. (1996), *The retreat of the state: the diffusion of power in the world economy*, Cambridge University Press, Cambridge.

Sweet, A.S., W. Sandholtz and N. Fligstein (eds.) (2001), *The institutionalization of Europe*, Oxford University Press, Oxford.

Urry, J. (2004), Introduction, in: U. Beck and J. Willms, *Conversations with Ulrich Beck*, Polity Press, Cambridge, pp. 1-10.

Van Kersbergen, C. and F. van Waarden (2001), *Shifts in governance: problems of legitimacy and accountability*, NWO, Den Haag.

Van Tatenhove, J.P.M. (1999), Political modernisation and the institutionalisation of environmental policy, in: M. Wissenburg, G. Orhan and U. Collier (eds.), *European discourses on environmental policy*, Ashgate, Aldershot, pp. 59-78.

Van Tatenhove, J.P.M., B. Arts and P. Leroy, (eds.) (2000), *Political modernisation and the environment: the renewal of environmental policy arrangements*, Kluwer Academic Publishers, Dordrecht.

Van Tatenhove, J.P.M. (2003), *Multi-level governance and the 'institutional void': the interplay between frontstage and backstage politics*, paper presented at workshop 21, ECPR Joint Sessions of workshops, 28 March – 2 April 2003.

Van Tatenhove, J.P.M. and J. Mak (2005), *Shifting relations in governance in the EU: winners and losers of informal governance*, paper for workshop in European governance, Amsterdam, January 2005.

Weiss, T. and L. Gordenker, (eds.) (1996), *NGOs, the UN and global governance*, Boulder, London.

Wendt, A.E. (1999), *Social theory of international politics*, Cambridge University Press, Cambridge.

Chapter 3

The Dynamics of Policy Arrangements: Turning Round the Tetrahedron

Duncan Liefferink

INTRODUCTION

The overall objective of the policy arrangements approach is to analytically link changes in day to day policy practices to broader, structural changes in contemporary society. The theoretical conceptualisation of this link and the character of the structural transformations in contemporary society were worked out in the previous chapter. The present chapter brings us down to the level of policy practices.

The central question of the chapter is how to analyse and understand change and stability within policy arrangements. This question involves, among other things, the definition of the policy issue at stake, the identification of actors taking part in policy making and implementation, and the written and unwritten rules governing their behaviour. Several 'meso level' theories are available to this end, such as discourse analysis (Hajer, 1995), various policy network approaches (Glasbergen, 1989; Marsh and Rhodes, 1992) or the advocacy coalition approach (Sabatier and Jenkins-Smith, 1993). Building upon these the policy arrangements approach offers four dimensions to describe and analyse day-to-day policy processes: actors and coalitions, resources and power, rules of the game, and discourses. We will define these four dimensions hereafter. The former three deal with the organisation of policy arrangements, the latter one with their substance. Our approach, more than most other meso-level policy theories which tend to focus on only one or two of those dimensions, provides an excellent basis for an *encompassing* and *dynamic* analysis of policy processes. The primary goal of this chapter is to demonstrate and further develop this feature of the policy arrangements approach.

The first section below goes into this approach and stresses that all four dimensions of the policy arrangement are indissolubly interrelated, i.e. that a change in one dimension seldom stands alone and tends to have an impact on one or more of the other dimensions. This is visualised with the

B. Arts and P. Leroy (eds.), Institutional Dynamics in Environmental Governance, 45–68.

help of a tetrahedron, in which each corner represents one dimension. The analysis of a policy arrangement usually makes sense only if all dimensions are interconnected. This, in turn, makes it possible to describe how changes in one dimension affect other dimensions, i.e. to capture the full *dynamics* of change within a given policy arrangement.

The four-dimensional analysis of policy arrangements also allows for four different *analytical* perspectives on one and the same policy arrangement, dependent on the research question. Each perspective will highlight different aspects of the arrangement and requires its own methodology. One can for instance start the analysis from (a change in) actors/coalitions, or one can scrutinise the arrangement-wide consequences of altered rules of the game. The next section systematically describes these four possible analytical perspectives and specifies which types of research questions they are able to handle. Both theoretical and more practical, policy-oriented questions are taken into account. In addition, methodological consequences are explored. The exercise is illustrated with a case we already know from the previous chapter: the development of organic farming in the Netherlands. The previous chapter (Arts and Van Tatenhove, this volume) stressed the structural changes affecting – or not – the contemporary and future situation of organic farming, restricting itself to what is called an institutional analysis. This chapter will develop a more strategic analysis, starting from the aforementioned dimensions of a policy arrangement. The same policy game is thus watched from four different angles.

In the final section the four-dimensional view on policy arrangements will be used for developing a basic *typology* of policy arrangements, building upon the well-established trichotomy of etatism, liberal-pluralism and neo-corporatism. Since in those types of arrangements the role of the state remains central, it is proposed to add 'sub-politics' as a fourth type. This type is, as indicated in the previous chapter as well, loosely based on the notion introduced by Beck (1994), and refers to arrangements that are dominated by private actors and that develop outside formal political institutions. Apart from that, three additional features of policy arrangements are addressed: their degree of formality, the basic political character of the issues addressed by them, and their relationship with cognate arrangements. These features can be used to further specify the basic typology referred to above.

THE CONCEPT OF POLICY ARRANGEMENTS

A policy arrangement has been defined as "the temporary stabilisation of the content and organisation of a particular policy domain" (Van Tatenhove et al., 2000, p. 54). Daily interactions between policy actors are assumed to gradually develop into more or less stable patterns. These patterns may include the substantive delineation of the problem at stake and of possible solutions, but also the processes of give-and-take between the actors and the formal and informal rules according to which these processes take place. As stated in the introductory chapter of this volume, these processes are usually referred to as institutionalisation. The structures thus formed in turn shape subsequent behaviour. Such structures are not fixed, however. Like language, structures are 'used' by people who are able to change their behaviour. Speakers of a given language may gradually adopt new grammatical or syntactical rules, or invent new expressions. They are not able, though, to change the entire language at once. The same applies to the very concept of 'policy arrangements', which are defined as temporary stabilisations in ongoing processes of institutionalisation. As discussed in the previous chapter, the concept thereby attempts to capture the 'duality of structure'(Giddens, 1984).

The structure of a policy arrangement can be analysed along the following four dimensions, the former three referring to the organisational, the latter one to the substantial aspects of policy:

- the *actors* and their *coalitions* involved in the policy domain;
- the division of *resources* between these actors, leading to differences in *power* and influence, where power refers to the mobilisation and deployment of the available resources, and influence to who determines policy outcomes and how;
- the *rules of the game* currently in operation, in terms of formal procedures of decision making and implementation as well as informal rules and 'routines' of interaction; and
- the current policy *discourses*, where discourses entail the views and narratives of the actors involved (norms, values, definitions of problems and approaches to solutions).

As stated in the introductory chapter, the policy arrangement approach as a whole builds upon a series of sources of inspiration, e.g. on a variety of theories and approaches from sociology, politics etc. This applies to the four dimensions and their further elaboration as well, where we draw upon different approaches in policy analysis. Complementary to the approaches and scholars mentioned in the introductory chapter, we will therefore list some further sources of inspiration hereafter. These four dimensions draw heavily upon, in particular, network theory of the 1990s (Marsh and Rhodes, 1992), enriched with elements from discourse analysis (Dryzek, 1997; Hajer, 1995; Van Tatenhove et al., 2000). In contrast with these approaches, however, the crucial point we want to make is that the four dimensions do not just sum up to define a policy arrangement. They are inextricably interwoven. This interrelatedness is essential for understanding a policy arrangement at a given point in time. In addition, it allows us to analyse the dynamics of a policy arrangement over time. The interrelatedness of the four dimensions can be symbolised by a tetrahedron, in which each of the corners represents one dimension (Figure 3.1).

The symbol of the tetrahedron visualises that any change in one of the dimensions may induce change in other dimensions. The appearance of new actors or a change in the composition of coalitions, for instance, may add new elements to the prevalent discourse or lead to another distribution of resources. Similarly, the introduction of extra resources (e.g. subsidies, knowledge, skills) or their withdrawal may attract new actors, exclude others or instigate new coalitions. A change in formal procedures, such as rules of participation or voting, may have similar effects. Finally, new ideas may enter the tetrahedron through the dimension of discourse. Examples are concepts like 'public-private partnership' or 'sustainable development'. Such concepts may mobilise new types of expertise or legitimacy, in other words new resources, or form the nucleus of new coalitions. As a consequence of the indissoluble interrelatedness of the four dimensions, repercussions across dimensions are likely to occur – even though they do not necessarily have to do so in each and every case. Therefore, the analysis of a policy arrangement should in principle address the entire tetrahedron.

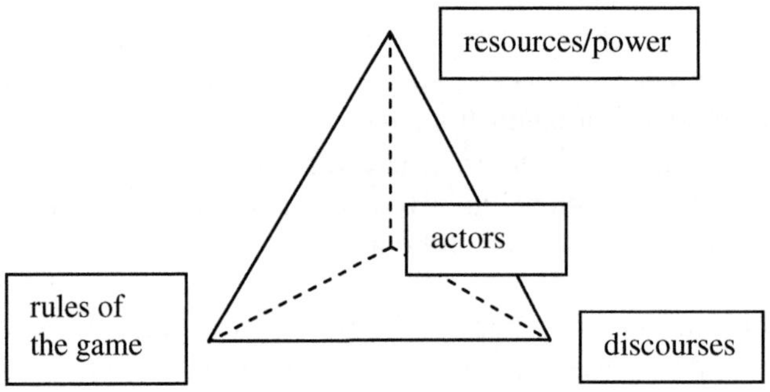

Figure 3.1. The tetrahedron, symbolising the interconnectedness of the four dimensions of a policy arrangement.

The argument of the interconnectedness of the four dimensions does of course not imply that policy arrangements are always harmonious, stable and internally consistent. Incongruence among the dimensions of an arrangement or 'institutional voids', e.g. the absence of shared rules (Hajer, 2003), may in fact result in shorter or longer periods of instability and shock wise changes (Boonstra, this volume). Alternatively, as we will see later on in this chapter, it may lead to a policy arrangement which hardly moves at all. The issue of 'congruence' of arrangements as an indicator of their performance will be discussed in the next chapter (Arts and Goverde, this volume).

Policy arrangements, moreover, do not operate in a vacuum. They are part of society. This means, on the one hand, that changes in individual policy arrangements may add up to more structural trends, for instance an inclination to involve stakeholders such as business and non-governmental organisations (NGOs) in policy making or the increased use of voluntary agreements in environmental policy. On the other hand, changes in the broader social, cultural, political or economic context or in fact the physical environment may have an impact on, for instance, power relations between actors involved in specific policy processes. Thus, structural change in individual policy arrangements often originates in broader processes of (social, political etc) change. In the present paper, we will not go into these possible drivers of change, as these are discussed in the previous chapter (Arts and Van Tatenhove, this volume). Instead, we will focus on the analysis of the dynamics at the 'micro-level', i.e. the question how the four dimensions within one policy arrangement interrelate and make the tetrahedron 'revolve'.

ANALYSING POLICY ARRANGEMENTS: A MATTER OF PERSPECTIVE

The main message of the previous section was that the analysis of a policy arrangement only makes sense if it is comprehensive. That is, if it encompasses all four dimensions of policy arrangements distinguished above – actors/coalitions, resources/power, rules of the game, and discourses – as well as their interrelations. In practice, the analysis may in fact start at any corner of the tetrahedron, as long as all corners and the connections between them are eventually covered. This is not to say, however, that the choice of a starting point is unimportant. On the contrary, different starting points imply the use of different conceptual and methodological tools. In a more practical sense, this is useful also in terms of delimiting the research task. But perhaps most importantly, different starting points shed different light on the policy arrangement at stake. Which phenomena one prefers to highlight depends on the research question underlying the analysis.

In the present section, we will elaborate our multi-perspective approach to the analysis of policy arrangements with the help of the same case as used in the previous chapter, the development of organic farming in the Netherlands. In the present chapter, however, we will scrutinise the internal dynamics of the arrangement rather than its structural ramifications. We will systematically subject the case to different types of research questions. Where relevant, we will distinguish between scholarly, theoretically informed research questions and more applied, policy-oriented research questions. In addition, we will address some methodological implications. It will turn out that the dimension where we start provides the key to 'unlocking' the other dimensions. Thus, by departing from all four corners of the tetrahedron subsequently, we will watch the same policy game from four different angles. The empirical material for this exercise will be taken mainly from Arts et al. (2001) and Hofer (2000).

Actors/Coalitions

For research questions focusing on the positions and roles of actors in a given policy arrangement, it is most suitable to enter the tetrahedron from the actor/coalitions corner. Questions of this type can on the one hand be theoretically inspired, for instance by macro-theories on changes in the relationship between state, market and civil society. To mention just a few examples: Does, as is often assumed, the nation-state retreat in favour of international and sub-national levels in the face of globalisation and European integration? And if so, how are policies made and implemented in this system of multi-level governance? Does late-modern society lead to the emergence of new coalitions and various kinds of sub-politics, initiated by private actors such as firms, social movements and even individuals, outside formal political institutions (Beck, 1994)? On the other hand, research into the positions and roles of specific actors can be more practice-oriented. It can help to assess the options available to actors such as government departments, firms or NGOs to improve their stakes in the policy process. For this reason, in fact, a large part of privately funded, strategic policy research implies an actor perspective.

In addition to this, an actor perspective is the most tangible way to get to an overview of the policy arrangement around a given issue. It also comes closest to how policy actors themselves view their own situation. In day-to-day practice, people deal with other people. It is only through them that our other analytical categories, i.e. resources/power, rules and discourses, materialise. They often do so in the form of 'allies' and 'enemies'. Not surprisingly, therefore, many policy studies start by determining *who* is involved in the policy area under consideration. They then go on to analyse the power relations between these actors and the institutional context in which they operate. This is, for example, the case in the Dutch policy network approach, as represented by Glasbergen (1989), and it is how we will proceed in the present section.

Analysing a policy arrangement from an actor perspective starts by identifying the relevant actors and their influence in the policy process. This can be done through the study of policy documents, but also 'in the field'. In doing so, it is useful to distinguish between central and more peripheral actors and to cluster actors that fulfil similar roles in the arrangement.

In the organic farming case, we asked a limited number of experienced, well-informed practitioners to position all relevant players in the field in a figure consisting of three concentric circles, indicating influence, and four spheres or segments, indicating the different roles performed by the actors (see Figure 3.2; of course the number and character of clusters can be different for other cases). The outcomes were validated with other practitioners. Some minor adjustments were then made, but generally speaking there turned out to be a remarkably high consensus on the positions of the various actors. The original version of Figure 3.2 (Arts et al., 2001) contains several dozens of actors. As the figure only serves as an illustration in the present context and in order not to make things unnecessarily complicated, these have been left out here. A figure like this, when properly filled in, provides a good basis for looking at the relative position of and at the power relations between the actors involved. When turning to the dimension of power and resources, in other words, our initial analytical starting point in the actor dimension implies a focus on the relative power of actors *vis-à-vis* each other, i.e. 'relational power'.

With regard to organic farming in the Netherlands, it is striking that the core of the figure is almost entirely dominated by actors normally associated with traditional agriculture. In the Netherlands, more than in almost any other country, this association with traditional agriculture implies a focus on resource intensity and high productivity. This goes in particular for the 'state' and 'expert system' segments. In the 'market' segment, some organic trade firms and associations appear, but in terms of size and resources they are in fact tiny in comparison with the regular agricultural and food chains operating in the same segment. Only in the 'interests' segment, a truly 'organic' association dominates, i.e. Biologica, the principal umbrella organisation for organic interests. Although this might be taken as an indication of Biologica's exceptionally influential position, this is probably not the case.

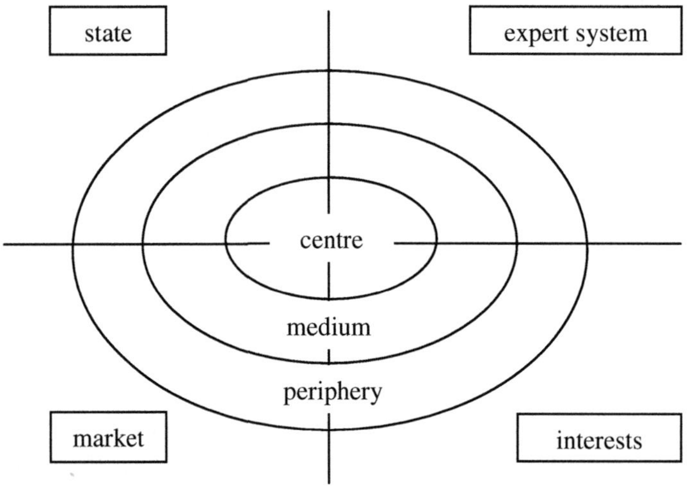

Figure 3.2. Example of a 'map' of actors and their relative positions in a policy arrangement.
Source: Arts et al., 2000 (adapted).

It rather suggests that Biologica is in fact fairly isolated in articulating the interests of organic farming in the Netherlands. Other 'organic' players, on the one hand, have far more marginal positions in the arrangement than Biologica. Traditional agricultural interest groups, on the other hand, are not eager to promote 'organic' interest. At the same time, they hardly need to invest much of their resources in defending their own 'traditional' interests, as these are sufficiently taken care of by the majority of core actors anyway. This picture reflects, in short, that organic farming does not in fact present a serious challenge to traditional agriculture in the Netherlands.

Having identified the most important actors and power relations in the arrangement, we can add another dimension to the analysis by grouping actors according to the views they have about the policy domain at stake. Such exercise is reminiscent of the work by Sabatier and Jenkins-Smith (1993) on advocacy coalitions. It should be noted, however, that advocacy coalitions are based on shared beliefs (i.e. an attribute of *actors*) which cannot be fully equated with discourses (i.e. 'storylines' or 'narratives' prevailing in a given *policy arrangement*). In our case, two discourses on the future development of organic farming in the Netherlands can be distinguished. A radical one is based on the idea of sustained *competition* between traditional and organic farming. According to this view, organic farming should maintain its own expert system and its own marketing channels, and – as a long term perspective – eventually push traditional products from the market. Not surprisingly, this discourse is not supported by the traditional agricultural community. But perhaps more surprisingly, it is not supported by 'mainstream' organic groups either. They rather cherish a more pragmatic view, by which the existing gap between traditional and organic farming gradually comes to be closed. In this perspective of *assimilation*, organic farming makes increasing use of the traditional agricultural research infrastructure and traditional marketing channels, e.g. regular supermarkets instead of small, specialised shops. This should eventually lead to a reform of traditional agriculture 'from inside'. In a moderate form (i.e. without the explicit long term perspective), this view finds support among many traditional actors too, including the organisations of traditional farmers. Pressed by environmental problems and a steady stream of animal diseases associated with traditional agriculture, they have gradually come to recognise the need of developing more environmentally friendly forms of farming. In this context, organic farming is seen as an option for the future at least worth considering. Commercial considerations may play a role here as well. Organic products now constitute a small but potentially growing niche market. Regular trade and retail are in principle ready to step in, as did supermarkets for instance in Austria and Denmark (Hofer, 2000).

As far as the rules of the games are concerned, finally, an 'actor-based' analysis implies a focus on the rules governing the interaction between the actors involved. In the organic 'game' in the Netherlands, those rules are almost fully controlled by the state. Since the 1991 EU Regulation on organic farming (2092/91), for instance, the leading organic food label EKO is controlled by the state (see below). Most major (and traditional) research institutes in the agricultural field, moreover, have recently been privatised, but still maintain close links with the state. In the present situation, finally, the conversion of individual farmers from (highly intensive) regular to organic agriculture is heavily dependent upon state subsidies. The relatively low conversion rate in the Netherlands may in fact be partially explained by the modest level of those subsidies.

The above actor-based analysis of the policy arrangement around organic farming in the Netherlands makes clear that resources as well as rules are strongly focused around the state and, consequently, around traditional agriculture. As we have seen, the world of traditional farming is not radically against organic farming, but it is not particularly active in promoting it either. Organic food is essentially seen as a small and harmless niche market, or – more positively – as one possible way out of the protracted crisis of traditional agriculture. At the same time, however, organic farmers lack resources to have a strong position of their own. This may explain, among other things, a good deal of pragmatism and the prevalence of a discourse of assimilation among major organic groups, notably Biologica.

Resources/Power

The analysis of resource dependencies and power relations is central to several theoretical approaches in political science. One can think of traditional (neo-)marxism or more recent approaches such as studies of multi-level governance. In the latter case, research questions focus on (shifts of) resources and power between, for instance, the nation state, sub-national levels and the EU. Within these approaches, to be sure, one can choose to concentrate on the resources and power of one particular (type of) actor, e.g. NGOs or the national environment ministry. Questions of shifting resources and power are addressed even more directly in practice-oriented research evaluating the impact of policy interventions. Such interventions often amount to the introduction of certain resources into or the withdrawal of resources from the policy arrangement, for example by way of subsidies, taxes or the production and dissemination of particular expertise. Evaluation can be done either *ex ante*, i.e. in advance in order to estimate the impact of a planned policy intervention, or *ex post*, i.e. afterwards to measure the impact actually realised, perhaps as a basis for revising or fine-tuning the policy. On a further elaboration of the policy evaluation potential of the policy arrangement approach, see Arts and Goverde (this volume).

The empirical analysis to be undertaken in this perspective comes close to what is propagated by the British school of policy network analysis (Marsh and Rhodes, 1992; Rhodes, 1986). The core idea of this approach is that actors around a given policy issue are to different degrees dependent upon each other for resources, e.g. money, information, or political legitimacy. In this way, by linking the dimensions of resources/power and actors, we are again (as in the previous section) identifying power relations between actors, i.e. 'relational power'. By mapping these resource dependencies, moreover, it will become clear that certain actors are, as it were, driven into each other's arms because they share control over important resources. Thus, we can identify different 'resource coalitions'. It should be noted that in one policy arrangement, money may be the central stake, while in another arrangement, the exchange of, for instance, knowledge and expertise may be crucial. In the policy game, moreover, resources can be seen as 'weapons', i.e. actors attempt to determine outcomes with the help of resources, but at the same time as 'prizes', i.e. during the process actors attempt to improve their situation by changing the distribution of resources to their advantage (Rhodes, 1986, p. 19-20). In this context, rules play an ambiguous role. On the one hand, they can be used strategically, i.e. as legal resources, in the policy game. On the other hand, they are not, as for instance money or personnel, exclusively controlled by certain actors. Instead, they are part of the actors' mutual knowledge (Giddens, 1984, p. 17-18). Nevertheless, they can be changed by actors who have the power to do so. The ambiguous nature of rules in this context is further stressed by the fact that such 'regulatory power' is often based again upon formal or informal rules. The same actually goes for discourses. Discourses can be used as 'weapons' for gaining, for instance, political legitimacy, but without being under any actor's exclusive control, some actors may be able to change the content of the narratives prevailing in the arrangement, or even to introduce wholly new ones. Such 'discursive power' is often based upon political legitimacy.

Turning to our case of organic farming in the Netherlands, the position and role of the organic umbrella organisation Biologica can very well be understood from the perspective of resource dependencies. In the first place, Biologica itself is a sort of resource coalition. It brings together a number of smaller organisations representing different strands in organic agriculture (e.g. biodynamic, 'regular' organic, etc.). While discursive differences persist within Biologica, the organisation's main aim is to pool resources (money, personnel, and legitimacy) so as to increase the political impact of the organic sector. However, as we have seen, Biologica's position vis-à-vis traditional agriculture and traditional farmers organisations is weak. Therefore, Biologica is particularly active in forging strategic alliances with a large variety of other actors, ranging from environmental and consumer organisations and the Dutch green party *Green Left*, to banks and supermarkets. The main resource paid into these alliances by Biologica, the single 'authorised' voice of the Dutch organic sector, is clearly political legitimacy.

At a more practical level, a resource based approach may help us to analyse the impact of specific policy interventions, e.g. the impact of state subsidies for conversion from regular to organic farming. The level of these subsidies in the Netherlands is comparatively low. According to Biologica, it is in fact far too low to compensate for the loss of income during the conversion period. The low conversion rates and the low overall percentage of organic farming (2,2% of all agricultural land in the Netherlands in 2003; Biologica, 2004) suggest that they have a point here. However, the development of the Dutch home market for organic food has been even slower (in 2003: 1,6% of total food consumption in the Netherlands; Biologica, 2004). More than in other countries, both consumers and retailers have been very reluctant to 'go organic'. Who could break this stalemate? The state is basically unwilling to intervene in the market for organic food, only partly as a result of the changing role of the state, one of the structural transformations discussed in the previous chapter. This non-intervention is further legitimated with reference to a production and market oriented discourse which has also long dominated Dutch agricultural policy at large (Ministerie van LNV, 2000). This basically liberal discourse has been further strengthened with the present central/right wing government. According to it, the role of the state should not be more than giving an initial push in the beginning of the production chain (i.e. the conversion subsidies), after which the market is supposed to do its work. The organic sector itself, however, lacks the resources for convincing either the general public or the supermarkets, or both, of the merits of organic products.

Rules

As a third entrance into a policy arrangement there is the dimension of rules. Rules are the mutually agreed formal procedures and informal routines of interaction within institutions. Formulated this way, rules have a particularly strong connection with the actor dimension of the arrangement. When rules are connected with the dimension of resources and power, we are back again at the notion of 'regulatory power', introduced above. Turning to the dimension of discourses, finally, we may try to identify the discourses *underlying* the rules of interaction prevailing in the network. As will be further elaborated below, these discourses mainly deal with general ideas about governance, i.e. about the relationships between and the share of responsibility of state, market and civil society.

Entering the tetrahedron via the rules dimension is a suitable strategy for studying the influence of institutional change on particular policy areas. Hence it offers an opportunity of linking the institutional analysis, emphasised in the previous chapter, and the strategic one that we deal with here. One could think of the influence of evolving European Union rules on national institutions, often referred to as Europeanisation. But one does not have to focus on change to study the impact of institutions. Comparative research allows for institutional analysis at a more general level, addressing not only change in particular institutional constellations, but also by singling out the impact of their more stable, enduring features, e.g. electoral systems, or the division of competences between national and sub-national levels in federal systems. This is typically done by studying one policy issue or policy field in different countries. This perspective may remind one of neo-institutional analysis (March and Olsen, 1989). Furthermore, starting from the rules dimension is of course helpful for evaluating (*ex ante* or *ex post*) the effect of the introduction of new rules or procedures on other dimensions of the policy arrangement.

A nice example in the field of organic farming is the differential impact of rules on the labelling of organic food products in the Netherlands and Denmark (Hofer, 2000). The Dutch EKO label was developed in the 1980s as a private initiative, while the state deliberately held aloof. Although the name of the EKO label became relatively well-known among the public, its market share remained below 1%. The Danish label, the 'red Ø', was introduced in 1989. It was owned and controlled by the state. Organic farmers were reluctant at first, but changed their minds when they saw that the 'red Ø' was implemented forcefully and that, moreover, the strong state involvement could be used as an argument for the quality and credibility of the label *vis-à-vis* consumers and retailers. In 1996 the market share of organic food in Denmark amounted to 5%. In the course of the 1990s, however, EU Regulation 2092/91 on organic farming had to be implemented. Among other things, it required state control of organic food labels. For Denmark nothing really changed, but in the Netherlands the formerly private EKO label was put under state supervision. Contrary to the experience with the Danish state-owned 'red Ø', however, this did not improve the effectiveness of the Dutch label? This was due, firstly, to the fact that the state still hardly associated itself with the label. It limited itself to its technical control task, but did not put any effort in strengthening the label's position on the market. This was of course perfectly in line with the 'reticent state' philosophy referred to above, according to which the market should function by itself. At the same time, it reflected a considerable degree of distrust between the state and the organic sector. In the eyes of Dutch organic farmers, strong state involvement would in fact hardly increase the credibility of the label. This situation, secondly, was aggravated by the extension to food products, also in the mid-1990s, of the state-owned *Milieukeur* label, which had existed for some years but initially covered non-food products only. The standards of this label were less strict than those of the EKO label. Although the performance of the agri-environmental *Milieukeur* on the market had turned out quite poor, the competition between the two labels increased confusion among consumers and thus posed an at least indirect threat to the EKO label.

The example illustrates that the impact of different or changing rules cannot be studied in isolation. We saw that the question of state control as such did not tell anything about the functioning of the Dutch and Danish organic food labels. Why things worked out so differently in the two countries could only be understood against the background of the other dimensions of the respective policy arrangements, in particular the distribution of public resources and the prevalent discourse on the role of the state.

Discourses

The final dimension of the tetrahedron to be discussed here is discourses. It is important to note from the outset that discourses are relevant at two different levels. The first level refers to general ideas about the organisation of society, particularly the relationship between state, market and civil society, i.e. about the preferred mode of governance. Such ideas clearly exceed specific policy issues or sectors. Through the views of the actors involved, however, they may have an impact on specific policy arrangements. As pointed out above, for instance, they may have important implications for the rules of interaction in the arrangement. The second level concerns ideas about the concrete policy problem at stake, e.g. about the character of the problem, its causes and possible solutions. Discourses at this level imply substantive strategic positions of actors in the arrangement. Groups of actors around one particular discourse, or discourse coalitions, may be discerned at both levels, i.e. not only at the second, issue-specific level, but also at the governance level. Moreover, as we will see below, considerable incongruences between the two levels may exist. If and how such incongruences can be reduced depends not least on the distribution of discursive power in the arrangement (Arts and Goverde, this volume).

From a theoretical point of view, entering the tetrahedron through the dimension of discourses may clearly be interesting to study the empirical effects of political modernisation, i.e. changing ideas about governance (Arts and Van Tatenhove, this volume; Hajer, 1995). More practically, the role of changing problem perceptions, induced among others by new scientific insights and often echoed by public information campaigns, may be scrutinised.

As we have seen, at the level of the policy arrangement around organic farming as such, a discourse of assimilation, rather than sustained competition, between organic and regular farming prevails in the Netherlands. However, due to the high cost of conversion, the number of organic farmers lags behind. Moreover, retailers and consumers persist in their wait-and-see behaviour, and research institutes continue to focus on traditional, intensive farming methods. The organic sector itself is not sufficiently powerful to get things moving, while regular farmers and farmers' organisations are only beginning to develop a more friendly attitude towards organic agriculture. Under the present circumstances, in other words, accelerating the process of assimilation would hardly be conceivable without close collaboration with the state. At this point, however, the discourse of assimilation collides with a second discourse, referred to earlier, that is dominant at the governance level. It implies that the state should limit itself to facilitating the development of the market and refrain from strong and focused interventions. Regardless of the political and ideological arguments involved here, this is important in view of the state's central position in the policy arrangement around organic farming. As discussed above, the state controls a number of central resources in the field. These notably include financial ones but also expertise. For many new initiatives in the field, therefore, the state is a necessary partner. Thus, the incongruence between the assimilation discourse on the one hand and the liberal, 'reticent state' discourse on the other plays an important role in explaining the slow development of the sector in comparison with most surrounding countries (Biologica, 2004, p. 7).

In more theoretical terms, our analysis shows that substantive discourses at the issue specific level on the one hand and governance discourses at the more general level on the other, are potentially incompatible. If this is the case, actors within the arrangement may be driven by conflicting ideas. This may, as it were, suffocate new developments and paralyse the policy arrangement. The organic farming case also suggests that such immobility may last for a considerable period.

Summing Up

In this section we have attempted to show how a policy arrangement can be analysed taking each of the four respective corners of the tetrahedron as starting point. By highlighting different features of the arrangement's dimensions, each perspective emphasised different aspects of the arrangement as a whole.

Analytically, the section can be summarised with the help of an annotated version of the tetrahedron (Figure 3.3). At first this annotated version seems complicated, yet it simply reflects the arguments brought forward so far. Looking at the rules dimension from the vantage point of actors, for instance, one focuses on the rules of interaction between the actors in the arrangement. Starting from actors and looking at resources, the focus is on power relations between actors, or on relational power. Far from being meant as a blueprint for empirical research, the figure draws attention to the analytical possibilities implied in the policy arrangements approach.

The case of organic farming was used to give some flesh and blood to the four analytical angles. This is an unusual exercise, to be sure, as normally one would prefer to restrict to one perspective, dependent on the research questions at stake. And even then, a full empirical analysis would require at least several pages. Our case, therefore, has been no more than an illustration to give the reader an idea of the empirical implications of our argument, which remains essentially analytical.

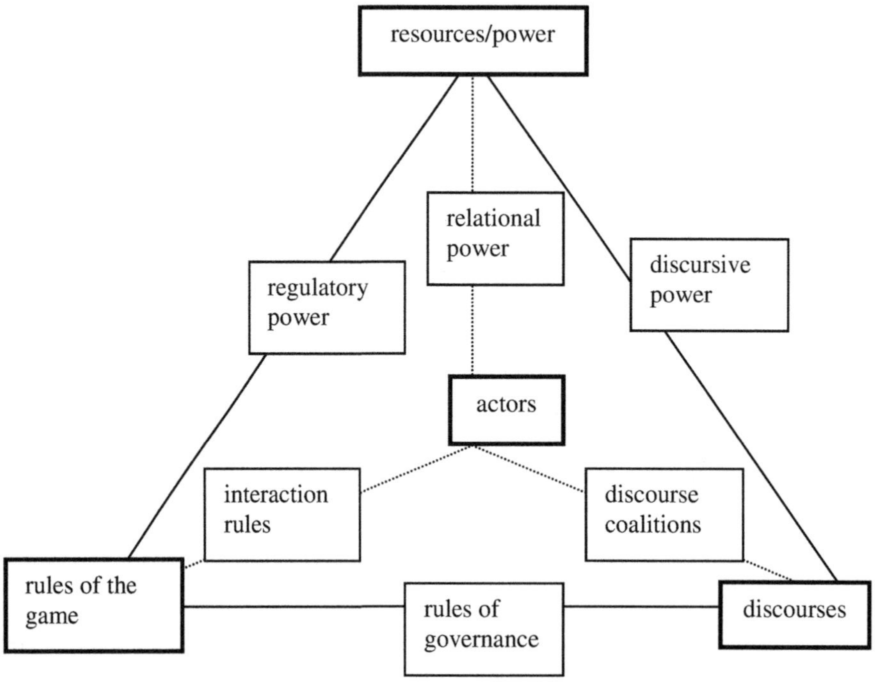

Figure 3.3. The tetrahedron: analytical perspectives.

A TYPOLOGY OF POLICY ARRANGEMENTS

The interconnectedness of the four dimensions of the tetrahedron not only makes it possible to analyse the process dynamics of policy arrangements. It also provides a good starting point for a comprehensive typology of such arrangements. To this end, we can make use of the fact that characteristics of one dimension of the tetrahedron have implications for other dimensions. That way, we can define ideal type combinations of features covering all dimensions of the arrangement.

A General Typology

In order to find such combinations, we can of course, as in the previous section, start at any corner of the tetrahedron and then work our way towards the others. For constructing a generally applicable typology, however, we prefer a more deductive approach, building upon the well-established trichotomy of etatism, liberal-pluralism, and neo-corporatism (Harvey, 1996; Padt, this volume; Van Waarden, 1995). Although one has to remain aware of the possible flaws of these traditional categories, using them as point of departure saves a lot of unnecessary work and makes our own exercise much easier to grasp. That is the pragmatic argument. From a theoretical perspective one can argue that these three categories do refer to distinguishable institutional features, and thereby urge one to pay attention to possible institutional transformations. We start our typology from the discourses dimension, in particular from the part that deals with prevailing ideas about the relationship between state, market and civil society or, in short: about governance. This makes sense as clear and far-reaching implications of the relationship between state, market and civil society can be observed throughout the organisation of a given policy arrangement, for instance in the number and type of actors involved, the distribution of major resources, or the rules governing the arrangement. It is an additional asset of choosing this particular vantage point that connections can be easily made between our typology and *shifts* in the ideas about the roles of state, market and civil society, i.e. about political modernisation and the structural transformations that this concept refers to (Arts and Van Tatenhove, this volume).

Etatism refers to the situation where state actors dominate the policy arrangement. Crucial resources are controlled by the state. Other actors are placed in a dependent position and have limited access to decision making. Etatist arrangements are likely to be buttressed by strict rules, conferring on the state the necessary authoritative instruments. In line with this, the prevailing substantive discourse in the arrangement is determined, or even imposed, by the state. Examples are not necessarily confined to policy arrangements in dictatorial regimes, e.g. Francoist Spain or worse. Examples also exist in more democratic countries, e.g. public health systems in several European countries. As said in the previous chapter, also environmental policy in its initial stages was predominantly state dominated.

Liberal-pluralism denotes a market-oriented model. No single actor dominates; resources are spread over a wide array of public and private parties. The latter may include business, but also actors from civil society such as NGOs. Newcomers can easily enter the arrangement. Liberal-pluralism presupposes basic democratic rules, accommodating open competition between the parties involved. Competition also extends to the dimension of substantive discourses, with different actors or actor coalitions promoting conflicting views of the policy problem at stake. Federal policy making in the US, where states, firms and interest groups compete for influence, provides typical examples of liberal-pluralism.

Neo-corporatism, finally, describes a situation where major resources are shared between state, market and civil society. Policies are made and implemented jointly, based on a commonly agreed substantive discourse. This is usually done in highly institutionalised settings, providing rules for negotiation and the search for consensus. Market players and civil society take part through a limited number of monopolistic representative associations (branch organisations, labour unions, NGOs, etc.). For other actors, gaining access to the arrangement is very difficult. Neo-corporatism is particularly common in Austria, the Netherlands, Belgium and the Nordic countries, especially with regard to socio-economic issues. But if taken in a slightly wider sense of the word, arrangements characterised by shared responsibility between public and private actors also occur elsewhere (Verbeeck and Leroy, this volume).

The traditional triad of etatism, liberal-pluralism and neo-corporatism, however, has one major shortcoming: its entire logic is directed towards *public* policies, even if, in the case of neo-corporatism, these are made by the state and private actors together. This does not sit well with more recent ideas about initiatives taken essentially or even exclusively by civil society outside the traditional institutional settings. One may think of grassroots actions by citizens or various initiatives by firms and/or NGOs. Hajer (2003) speaks of policies created in an 'institutional void', challenging the established rules and potentially re-shaping them. As in the previous chapter, we would like to subsume such initiatives under the term 'sub-politics', borrowed from Beck (1994). Sub-political arrangements are characterised by a membership which is usually limited to stakeholders in the problem concerned. Since the role of the state is minimal, major resources are controlled by private actors. Usually, sub-political arrangements challenge existing substantive discourses by presenting new, alternative ones. Within the arrangement, however, interaction is based upon the idea of a 'bottom-up' joining of forces, or in short: upon solidarity.

Table 3.1. Basic typology of policy arrangements

Characteristic / Ideal type	Access (number of actors in inner circle)	Control over major resources	Prevailing rule of interaction	General character of substantive discourses
Etatism	low	state	instrumentality	imposed
Liberal-pluralism	high	spread	competition	conflicting
Neo-corporatism	limited	shared	negotiation	agreed
Sub-politics	specific	non-state actors	solidarity	challenging

Table 3.1 summarises what we have now. It goes without saying that etatism, liberal-pluralism, neo-corporatism and sub-politics provide ideal types. In practice, arrangements will merely tend to one of the four models and seldom, if ever, represent 'pure' types.

The last column of the table, moreover, is limited to the general character of the substantive discourses circulating in the arrangement. This is because the organisational implications of different views on governance (the relationship between state, market and civil society) provide the basic logic for the table, whereas the issue-specific details of discourses are not helpful for constructing a general typology.

Finally, it should be noted that starting from the general discourse on the relationship between state, market and civil society, as we did for this typology, only works if these ideas are indeed reflected in the policy arrangement that is being considered. It assumes, in other words, that no or little incongruence exists between these ideas on the one hand and the actual organisation of the arrangement on the one hand. If such incongruence does turn up, it obviously calls for further analysis, as for instance in the case of organic farming in the Netherlands. Generally speaking, this arrangement can be characterised as liberal-pluralist. Although the state is in control of a number of important resources, it can hardly be maintained that it determines the arrangement as a whole. Neo-corporatist 'closed shops' between the state and privileged private actors do not occur either. A liberal discourse prevails and a relatively open set of private parties (organic vs. regular farmers, trade and retail, etc.) are left to compete for subsidies and market shares. At the same time, however, this *general* discourse on the mode of governance is not in line with the organisational implications of the *substantive* discourse of assimilation held by a number of players in the field, notably the organic farmers and their representatives. Given the rather marginal position of organic farming in the Netherlands, a policy of assimilation would require a much more collaborative, neo-corporatist, relationship between the state and the other parties involved. The organic sector has so far not been able to push through its views, however. As argued above, this has resulted in a good deal of immobility.

Further Specification of the Typology

The typology based on etatism, liberal-pluralism, neo-corporatism and sub-politics, presented in Table 3.1 covers a number of important characteristics of policy arrangements, but by no means all potentially relevant ones. Not addressed are for instance: the degree of formality of policy arrangements, the basic political character of the issues addressed by them, or their relationship with cognate arrangements. These characteristics may be important in explaining stability and change of policy arrangements, as the subsequent chapters of this book will show. However, it should be emphasised that the list is by no means exhaustive: in specific cases other aspects may prove more relevant. Hence, it is not our aim here to integrate all these aspects into our typology – and thus make it overly complex and impossible to work with. We rather propose to deal with them as additional aspects, which may be picked up and used whenever relevant to characterise in more detail a particular policy arrangement.

The degree of formality is to some extent implicated in the basic typology. Generally speaking, for instance, rules in etatist arrangements are likely to be more formal than in liberal-pluralist arrangement. In the latter case, relatively informal and implicit norms may govern actors' behaviour. Within one ideal type, however, considerable variation in the degree of formality may exist. It is very well conceivable that some liberal-pluralist arrangements are in fact strongly formalised. In the case of Dutch organic farming, in fact, the reticence of the state is quite well embedded in formal rules and procedures. Also neo-corporatist arrangements may either be based on formal rules of access, participation and resource exchange, or on more informal routines with a similar effect of ensuring that all represented interests are taken into account while at the same time excluding 'outsiders'. Scandinavian neo-corporatism, for instance, tends to be rather formalised, whereas the Austrian variant shows an intriguing mix of formal and informal elements (Lauber, 1996; Lehmbruch and Schmitter, 1982). Only sub-political arrangements may, almost by definition, be expected to be highly informal. The degree of formality is dealt with empirically in several chapters in this book (De Boer, this volume; Van der Zouwen, this volume; Verbeeck and Leroy, this volume).

As regards the political character of the issues addressed by policy arrangements, one may distinguish two basic categories: (1) issues calling primarily for the formulation and implementation of regulation, and (2) issues primarily calling for the re-distribution of certain resources. Those basic types of issues may arguably lead to different types of arrangements. According to Scharpf (1997), regulatory arrangements can be associated with relatively co-operative 'problem-solving' behaviour, whereas actors' behaviour in re-distributive arrangements tends to competitive 'bargaining'. Of course, again, the categories mix up in reality. Regulation, for example, usually has certain re-distributive effects, whereas primarily re-distributive policies can hardly do without some form of regulation. Generally speaking, however, it should be possible to define the principal character of the issue at stake. As to the first category, one may think of issues in the field of health, safety and environmental standards. The second category obviously includes social welfare policy, as well as the case discussed in this chapter, which is essentially about how to divide the (modest) Dutch organic apple-pie. This aspect clearly does not run parallel with our basic typology: both types of issues may be addressed by all four types of arrangements.

In today's policy intensive society, arrangements usually relate in one way or another to other arrangements. For our typology, it is useful to make a a basic distinction between policy arrangements which are hierarchically linked and those which are non-hierarchically linked. The former refers to arrangements that are embedded or nested, i.e. a broader arrangement provides framework conditions for the functioning of a more specific one (Koenig-Archibugi, 2002; Young, 1999). The form of these framework conditions may vary. The broader arrangement may for instance primarily determine problem perception, or membership, or interaction rules, or in fact combinations of these. The Dutch organic farming arrangements, for instance, is nested within the broader arrangement dealing with Dutch agricultural policy. This hierarchical relationship was noticed before and explains why various actors from the area of regular farming play such important roles in the organic farming arrangement. But arrangements may also belong to the second basic type and be interlinked in a non-hierarchical fashion. Koenig-Archibugi (2002) – who analyses global governance, but whose typology is equally applicable to arrangements at the national level – distinguishes 'clustered', 'overlapping' and 'competing' arrangements. In the cases of clustered and competing arrangements, there are two or more arrangements active in the same policy area. 'Overlapping' arrangements exist in adjacent, materially related policy areas, e.g. agricultural policy and groundwater protection, or housing and public transport policy, i.e. what is referred to in policy network analysis as 'horizontal interdependence' (Rhodes, 1986). In all non-hierarchical cases, arrangements are interlinked and various kinds of mutual impact are conceivable, but none of them is superior to the other(s) (for examples: Boonstra and Padt respectively, this volume). For the sake of consistency, finally, one might wish to distinguish 'independent' policy arrangements as a third basic type, but arrangements which are truly independent will be hard to find empirically (Wiering and Crabbé, this volume). To the contrary: the increasing (and partly non-hierarchical) interdependency of policy arrangements originating from different levels of administration has given rise to a widening of the concept of multi-level governance (Van der Zouwen, this volume).

We have now discussed three additional characteristics of policy arrangements, which may be used to further specify the basic typology of etatism, liberal-pluralism, neo-corporatism and sub-politics. This exercise allows us to characterise the policy arrangement around Dutch organic farming as a basically liberal-pluralist, fairly formalised, re-distributive arrangement, nested within the broader agricultural policy arrangement in the Netherlands.

The typology thus developed highlights a number of important constitutive features of policy arrangements, but it may in fact be extended by further aspects, dependent on the precise goal of the analysis. Apart from the single- or multi-level character of policy arrangements, already referred to, the characterisation of policy arrangements encompassing also the international level deserves attention. In view of the fundamentally different (more central) role of state versus non-state actors at the international level, our basic typology of etatism, liberal-pluralism, neo-corporatism and sub-politics does not apply here. In the present chapter, however, we will not address this question, not only for reasons of space, but also because a useful typology of international policy arrangements was already developed by Arts in the predecessor of this volume (Arts, 2000, p. 136-138).

CONCLUSION

The main purpose of this chapter was to develop an encompassing and dynamic view on policy arrangements. To this end, the four dimensions along which policy arrangements are structured were visualised with the help of a tetrahedron. It was argued, first, that the four corners of the tetrahedron are strongly interrelated: a change in one of the dimensions is likely to lead to changes also in one or more of the other dimensions. In order to capture dynamic processes of policy change within a given arrangement, therefore, the tetrahedron should be 'turned around', i.e. analysed from all sides. Second, it was demonstrated that the question where to start such a comprehensive analysis is not indifferent. Dependent on the research question at hand, one may start at one particular corner of of the tetrahedron – for instance actors, or discourses – and then proceed to the others. Each starting point implies its own analytical and methodological perspective. Finally, the four dimensions of the tetrahedron were used to develop a basic typology of policy arrangements.

It is essential to stress once again that neither the analytical approach nor the typology presented in this chapter are to be taken as straightjackets. Each problem requires its own solution. In this sense, the tetrahedron as well as the typology should be considered as practical tools in a fairly elementary toolbox. Just like hammers and screwdrivers, they may be applied in different ways, according to the user's requirements and skills. In many cases, moreover, they will have to be complemented by other, more refined and sophisticated tools. The purpose of this chapter, then, was not to formulate shock-proof instructions, but rather to give an idea of the versatility and broad applicability of the policy arrangement approach and to invite researchers to use their own creativity in further applying it.

REFERENCES

Arts, B. (2000), Global environmental policies: between 'interstatist' and 'transnational' arrangements, in: J.P.M. van Tatenhove, B. Arts and P. Leroy (eds.), *Political modernisation and the environment: the renewal of environmental policy arrangements*, Kluwer Academic Publishers, Dordrecht, pp. 117-44.

Arts, B., M. Bruns, P. Leroy, D. Liefferink and J.P.M. van Tatenhove (2001), *Biologisch groeien?! Een multi-actor analyse van het beleidsarrangement biologische landbouw (2000-2020)*, Katholieke Universiteit Nijmegen, Nijmegen.

Beck, U. (1994), The reinvention of politics: towards a theory of reflexive modernization, in: U. Beck, A. Giddens and S. Lash (eds.), *Reflexive modernization: politics, tradition and aesthetics in the modern social order*, Polity Press, Cambridge, pp. 1-55.

Biologica (2004), *Eko-Monitor: Cijfers en trends, Jaarrapport 2003*, bron: www.biologica.nl.

Dryzek, J. (1997), *The politics of the earth: environmental discourses*, Oxford University Press, Oxford.

Giddens, A. (1984), *The constitution of society,* Polity Press, Cambridge.

Glasbergen, P. (1989), *Beleidsnetwerken rond milieuproblemen*, VUGA Uitgeverij, Den Haag.

Hajer, M.A. (1995), *The politics of environmental discourse: ecological modernization and the policy process,* Oxford University Press, Oxford.

Hajer, M.A. (2003), Policy without polity? Policy analysis and the institutional void, *Policy Sciences,* Vol. 36, no. 2, pp. 175-195.

Harvey, D. (1996), *Justice, nature and the geography of difference*, Blackwell Publishers, Malden/Oxford.

Hofer, K. (2000), Labelling of organic food products, in: A.P.J. Mol, V. Lauber and D. Liefferink (eds.), *The voluntary approach of environmental policy: joint environmental policy-making in Europe*, Oxford University Press, Oxford, pp. 156-91.

Koenig-Archibugi, M. (2002), Mapping global governance, in: D. Held and A. McGrew (eds.), *Governing globalization: power, authority, global governance,* Polity Press, Cambridge, pp. 46-69.

Lauber, V. (1996), *Contemporary Austrian politics*, Westview, Boulder (Col.).

Lehmbruch, G. and P.C. Schmitter (1982), *Patterns of neo-corporatist policy-making*, Sage, London.

March, J.G. and J.P. Olsen (1989), *Rediscovering institutions - the organizational basis of politics*, Free Press, New York.

Marsh, D. and R.A.W. Rhodes (eds.) (1992), *Policy networks in British government,* Clarendon Press, Oxford.

Ministerie van LNV (2000), *Een biologische markt te winnen: beleidsnota biologische landbouw*, s-Gravenhage.

Rhodes, R.A.W. (1986), *The national world of local government,* Allen and Unwin, London.

Sabatier, P.A. and H.C. Jenkins-Smith (eds.) (1993), *Policy change and learning: an advocacy coalition approach*, Westview Press, Boulder.
Scharpf, F.W. (1997), *Games real actors play: actor-centred institutionalism in policy research,* Westview Press, Boulder.
Van Tatenhove, J.P.M., B. Arts and P. Leroy, (eds.) (2000), *Political modernisation and the environment: the renewal of environmental policy arrangements*, Kluwer Academic Publishers, Dordrecht.
Van Waarden, F. (1995), Persistence of national policy styles: a study of their institutional foundations, in: B. Unger and F. van Waarden (eds.), *Convergence or diversity: internationalization and economic policy response,* Avebury, Aldershot, pp. 333-72.
Young, O.R. (1999), *Governance in world affairs,* Cornell University Press, Ithaca.

Chapter 4

The Governance Capacity of (new) Policy Arrangements: A Reflexive Approach

Bas Arts and Henri Goverde

INTRODUCTION

The policy arrangements approach (PAA), as elucidated in the previous chapters, is mainly an analytical tool. It helps to describe, understand and explain policy practices from a specific perspective, but it does *not* offer instruments to evaluate and prescribe policy making. It is, of course, legitimate for any policy researcher to stick to analytical ambitions only. However, when one is involved in policy oriented research, the lack of evaluative and prescriptive tools in PAA is a disadvantage. Therefore this chapter is dedicated to designing such tools. Then, we inevitably enter into the 'normative sphere' of policy analysis.

To design an instrument for evaluation and intervention compatible with the PAA, insights from the policy evaluation literature in general as well as from the 'Governance Capacity Approach' (GCA) in particular will be borrowed (Nelissen et al., 2000). The GCA is meant to assess the governance capacity of 'new modes of governance' by evaluating their legal, political and economic qualities. A distinction is made between *indicative* and *performative* capacity, the former referring to the *potential* governance capacity of policy arrangements, the latter to their *real* performance. In order to assess governance capacity, we will make use of the so-called *JEP-triangle*, which is a key element of the GCA. It integrates different logics of and criteria for the evaluation and design of policy interventions. Besides, we will use the concept of *congruence* in order to cover the institutional aspects of policy evaluation and design (Boonstra, 2004; Grin et al., 2004). As an instrument for an institutional assessment of governance capacity is lacking in the original GCA, we will add this concept of congruence to our framework.

For several reasons, we think that both approaches – PAA and GCA– are compatible, even though the first is mainly analytical, the second mainly normative in nature. For example, both are rooted in the recent

B. Arts and P. Leroy (eds.), Institutional Dynamics in Environmental Governance, 69–92.

'new modes of governance' literature and share a critical view on rational, instrumental policy analysis. At the same time, neither stretches this criticism to the extent that it enters the spheres of radical social-constructivism or post-modernism. In fact, a middle ground between these paradigms is sought for in what we call a *reflexive* approach to policy evaluation and design. Although reflexivity can have different meanings, reflexive approaches are generally critical towards first modernity, instrumental rationality and objectivist science, which all assume the existence of a well-ordered and manageable nature and society. Such 'control and steering optimism' should in our view be questioned. At the same time, reflexive approaches maintain and cherish the idea of (collective) agency – scientists, policy makers, state departments, social movements, etc. – being capable and knowledgeable to reflect upon, respond towards and make a meaningful difference in a complex world.

To prevent sticking to abstract notions only, we will also in this chapter come back to (a secondary analysis of) the development of Dutch organic farming. Whereas chapter 2 analyses processes of political modernisation in the Dutch agricultural domain and their impact on organic farming, and chapter 3 analyses the policy arrangement on organic farming, we will assess and evaluate the governance capacity of this latter arrangement in its context of more encompassing transformations. Again the analysis of the case is by no means exhaustive, but just illustrative for the argument.

The format of this chapter is as follows. Firstly, we go into policy evaluation methodology. Different approaches and models will be reviewed. Next, the background, nature and suitability of the governance capacity approach (GCA) is addressed, including the introduction of criteria for good governance and of the so-called JEP-triangle. Thirdly, both approaches – PAA and GCA – are integrated into 'tools' for a reflexive evaluation and design respectively. Here the concept of congruence comes in. Then these tools are applied to the case of Dutch organic farming. Finally, some conclusions will be drawn on the applicability of our model as well as on the governance capacity of the Dutch policy arrangement on organic farming.

POLICY EVALUATION

According to Abma (2001), the economic, rational-instrumental approach is dominant in current policy evaluation methodology (Dunn, 1994; Swanborn, 1999). This has not always been the case, as the history of public administration shows a shifting dominance of juridical, political and economic approaches towards policy evaluation, putting emphasis on administrative ethics, political democracy and economic cost-effectiveness respectively (Denhardt, 2004; Nelissen et al., 2004; Schafritz and Hyde, 1997). However, due to the New Public Management movement of the 1980s and 1990s, which propagated a re-organisation of government in accordance with methods of business management, accountability norms and performance indicators have gained momentum and dominance (Nelissen et al., 1999; Osborne and Gaebler, 1992).

Measurement Model

Overall, in case of a rational-instrumental *ex post* evaluation, the 'goal variable' of a certain policy will be identified first. Next, it will be assessed whether this goal is achieved as an intended consequence of the policy intervention concerned – and not due to third variables or coincidence – and in a mode as efficient as possible (Swanborn, 1999). In contrast, *ex ante* evaluations in this tradition focus on the alternatives for a designed plan or policy by questioning which alternatives will effectively realise the political goal, while using available but scarce resources as efficiently as possible. Due to these types of *ex post* and *ex ante* evaluations, the criteria of 'effectiveness' and 'efficiency' have received the highest status in this literature.

Although we do not reject such models *in principle*, we argue that rational-instrumental evaluations are inherently one-sided and too limited (for a nuanced critique on rationalism: Giddens, 1984). These evaluations often suggest that rational, predictable and hence 'manageable' individuals, organisations and societies do exist and can be easily recognised, assumptions which in our view need to be questioned, as these might easily lead to an overstretched steering optimism. In addition, this methodology for evaluation is characterized by a so-called methodological individualism. As a consequence, the impact of structures, institutions as well as of structural processes on policy processes is undervalued. Finally, rational-instrumental approaches – still very popular today – seem to neglect current debates on reflexive and post-modern politics, which have put uncertainties in knowledge production, complexities in governance practices and learning processes in policy evaluation on the agenda, amongst others.

To overcome these shortcomings of instrumentalism and rationalism, other evaluation methods and techniques have been developed or re-valued. Abma (2001) distinguishes three models, which she labels 'measurement' (instrumental model), 'judgement' (multiple-criteria evaluation) and 'negotiation' (social-constructivist approach).

Judgement Model

The first measurement model was already briefly explained in the above. Multi-criteria evaluation extends this rationalist-instrumental measurement model by taking other logics and criteria into account (Snellen, 1987). Instead of being an 'objectivist measurer' of policy effects, the evaluator now becomes a 'judge' who assesses the quality of policy making on the basis of a range of normative and institutional criteria (not only effectiveness, but also legality, democracy, equity, institutional capacity, etc.). Van de Graaf and Hoppe (1992) claim that political judgement is a 'reflecting and representing form of evaluation', in which political subjects are able to account for their acts at four distinct levels of analysis: technical verification, situational validation, systemic support, and social choice. According to Fischer (1995), on which Van de Graaf and Hoppe base their view, these different types of political judgement produce a 'multi-level logic of policy evaluation', which go beyond rationalism and methodological individualism.

Negotiation Model

Although Fischer's model implies a policy evaluation on a much deeper, even fundamental, social level than the classical-instrumental one, the evaluator is still the outsider who claims authority by expertise. The third, social-constructivist model, however, rejects this approach. Following Abma (2001), performance measurement and value judgements are no longer adequate in situations of ambiguity, uncertainty and complexity, which are so characteristic for our late-modern society. The problem is that these types of evaluation seem to reduce and fix interests and values according to the demands of an objectivist-empirical method, undervaluing dynamics in policy processes and shifts in policy preferences. Also, the evaluator claims authoritative expertise, subordinating the one of stakeholders. Therefore, in the third, social-constructivist model, the evaluator acts mainly as a process facilitator who interacts with stakeholders to reconstruct their views on the policy matter concerned and stimulates deliberation, negotiation and mutual learning processes on the basis of these different views. Neither pre-set evaluation criteria nor final judgements of the evaluator are part of this methodology.

Reflexive Model

Below, we will mainly build on Abma's second 'judgement' model of policy evaluation. The main reason to do so is that this model matches the Policy Arrangement Approach (PAA) and Governance Capacity Approach (GCA) best. After all, both models go beyond rational, instrumental policy analysis and evaluation. The PAA does so by positioning itself on a continuum somewhere between rational and constructivist models of policy analysis (Arts et al., 2001). The GCA does so by criticizing New Public Management (NPM) (Nelissen et al., 2000), which overemphasises economic rationality and utility in policy making, evaluation and design. The GCA argues that other logics are relevant as well (particularly political and juridical logics). Although less explicitly, the PAA also subscribes to this criticism on rational and instrumentalist policy evaluation. Particularly the assumptions of the rational choice model – voluntarism, clear individual preferences, full information on behavioural options, maximising utility, methodological individualism (Swanborn, 1992) – are not shared (Van Tatenhove et al., 2000). Instead, the Giddensian notion of the 'reflexive and structured agency' is adopted, which assumes the knowledgeability and capability of agents, yet also posits the assumptions of *bounded* rationality, *routine* behaviour, *institutional* embeddedness, *unknown* preferences and *unintended* consequences (Giddens, 1984).

Although we will mainly build on Abma's second model, some of the critiques of social-constructivist approaches are nonetheless taken into account (Van der Meer and Edelenbos, 2002). In our view, it would be a loss to exclude the dynamics of dialogue and interaction with stakeholders in policy evaluation, aspects which are highly valued by social-constructivism. Yet we would not like to go as far as some critical thinkers do, namely 'de-valuating' the policy scientist into a subjectivist story teller or an interactive process facilitator at best. We think that evaluators can and may make their own judgement, as long as this is done in a transparent and self-critical mode. At the same time, we think that a dialogue with stakeholders and interactive evaluation techniques should be part of our approach. Arguments for dialogue and interaction are: to accommodate for differences and uncertainties in policy views respectively, to mobilise additional resources, to build legitimacy, to construct trust and to realise inclusiveness and (deliberative) democracy in policy making (Abma and In 't Veld, 2001; Hajer and Wagenaar, 2003; Pestman and Van Tatenhove, 1998).

To involve stakeholders is one thing, the question *how* is another. We think it is *not* very useful just to collect different views and interests and report this variety to the formal decision makers (all the more so since such an approach would contradict our idea of an evaluator as a judge). Besides collecting variation, a selection and integration process should also take place. For example Edelenbos and Van Eeten (2001) make a distinction between three phases of dialogue, which correspond with three roles of the policy evaluator. The first phase is called 'variation' during which the evaluator facilitates the uncovering of views and interests (e.g. through a Socratesian dialogue). The second phase is called 'selection'. Now the evaluator is condensing, structuring and integrating the different views and interests into more common frames (e.g. through ranking, clustering and factor analysis techniques). This process is done by the evaluator himself (the 'judge role'), although the result can again be debated with the stakeholders involved. The third phase is called 'retention' and refers to the handing over of the dialogue outcomes to the formal decision makers. Again, this role is primarily one of the policy evaluator himself. Hence, interactive policy making is not just sitting together or 'anything goes', but a structured and reflexive process of feeding commonly shared and potentially useful ideas into policy making.

As indicated before, we would like to label our approach 'reflexive evaluation'. Given the above considerations, reflexive evaluation should start with the premise that actors – either policy makers, scientists or civilians – are able to deliberately reflect on social practices and can decide whether they intend to maintain or change these (this first assumption comes close to the rational-instrumental model). In other words, agents can and may make a difference in a complex society. However, the second premise is that of 'structured agency', the assumption that these agents are embedded in rather stable social institutions. This second assumption is in line with institutional theorising. As a consequence, much conduct is 'rule-directed', this means based on routines and conventions, so that preferences for (radical) change do not emerge that easily; and if these emerge, attempts for social change are easily constrained by the 'given' institutional structure. That is why continuity generally seems more preferred to or the more logical outcome than (radical) change, so that too much steering optimism is unjustified. The third premise is that most policy making takes place in a dynamic context encompassing uncertainty and value dissent, so that reflection, instead of 'rational determinism' as well as interaction with stakeholders, instead of 'distant objectivism', need to be the starting points.

GOVERNANCE CAPACITY APPROACH (GCA)

Context

The context in which the GCA was designed related to the emergence of new modes of governance in the 1980s and 1990s. In and around government, all sorts of changes occurred during these decades. New issues in different policy fields appeared on the political agenda. Phenomena like globalisation, Europeanisation, individualisation as well as the public demand for decrease in organised crime, for safe-guarding social security, for better health service, for more attention to climate change, for asylum issues, all have had impact on governmental tasks and behaviour. Furthermore, new ideas revealed how the government should govern. Steering society today demands a government that in a professional manner can adapt itself to different management styles, depending on the contingencies. These new inputs have enhanced adaptations of styles of governing as well as of governmental institutions. Renewal of governmental institutions includes a huge diversity of phenomena, such as deregulation, decentralisation, 'doing more with less', liberalisation, interactive policy-making, contract management and client-oriented management. These types of new governance tools occur at all levels of government: national, regional, communal, inter-municipal, cross-border. Of course, older constructions of governing often constrained the new types of governance and continued to function simultaneously. Thus, a relevant question for research in public administration is how to judge the governance capacity of the new modes of governance vis-à-vis the older forms of government?

Definition

'Governance capacity' is broadly defined as the extent to which new forms of governance are able to successfully diminish or solve societal and administrative problems (Nelissen et al., 2000). Of course, success is a relative concept: criteria for evaluation should be developed in relation to different perceptions of problems by the stakeholders (as was outlined in the previous section). Two types of governance capacity can be distinguished:

a) *indicative* governance capacity: the potentials of the (new) modes of governance to contribute to the solution of societal or administrative problems, which are legitimately recognised by the stakeholders;

b) *performative* governance capacity: the performance of the (new) modes of governance in those practises that are meant to solve these societal or administrative problems.

In line with this distinction, it is useful to distinguish an *institutional* perspective on governance capacity on the one hand and a *strategic* perspective on the other. The institutional perspective on governance capacity reflects an indication of how (new) modes of governance will (probably) influence the institutional arrangements of policy making – i.e. relationships between public and private actors, rules of the game, division of resources – in such a way that a certain capacity to produce 'policy successes' is to be expected in the forseeable future. However, the extent to which this indicative governance capacity will be reflected in the practises of a policy arrangement depends on the actions of the stakeholders in that specific problem field. Consequently, the success of (new forms of) governance mainly depends on how stakeholders define, perceive and strategise for this success in relation to their own logics of action (based on their positions, values, interests, goals and attitudes). That is why the so-called performative governance capacity will be considered mostly from a *strategic* perspective.

The distinction between the institutional and the strategic perspective should not create the idea that governance capacity is either determined by institutions or by agencies. On the contrary, governance capacity is the result of efforts of public and private stakeholders, being embedded in institutions with formal and informal rules of the game, dependent upon the availability of resources and the presence of (different) discourses. Chapter 3 set out these phenomena (Liefferink, this volume). In other words, the governance capacity of an organisation, a network of actors or a sector depends on the quality of the functioning of a specific policy arrangement.

Criteria for 'Good Governance'

The abstract definition of governance capacity and the theoretical understanding of its relation to the concepts of policy arrangement and 'duality of structure' (Arts and Van Tatenhove, this volume) is only a first step in evaluating processes of governance in operational terms. Nelissen et al. (2000) have provided a second step in adopting criteria for 'good governance' that are fruitful to indicate and to assess governance capacity in a particular context (policy sector, policy arrangement, or policy act). For that purpose, these authors have introduced the JEP-triangle. The aim of this figure is to create a frame of reference for the evaluation of performative governance capacity in practises engaged with new forms of governance or policy arrangements. As this model integrates different logics and criteria for policy evaluation, it matches Abma's second, multi-criteria judgement model quite well (see previous section). Below, we will go into these different logics and criteria as well as into their relationships and (inherent) contradictions.

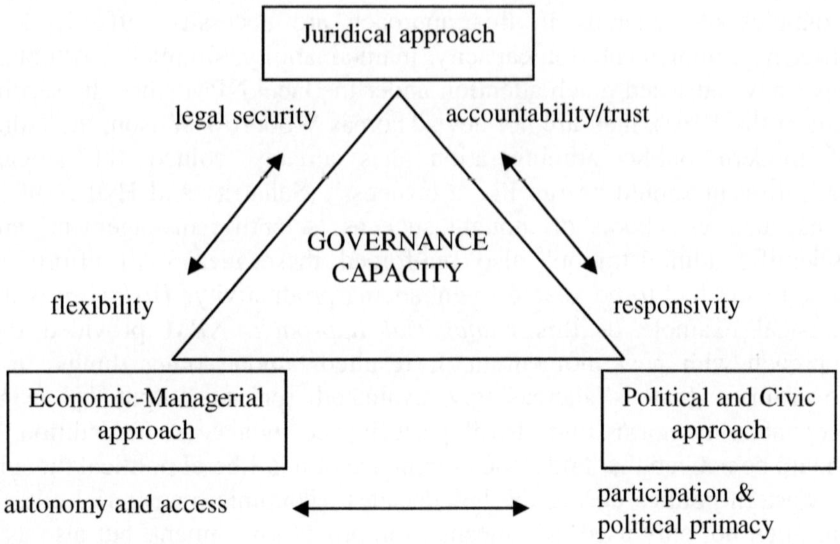

Figure 4.1. JEP-triangle.
Source: Adapted from Nelissen et al., 2000, p. 28.

Juridical Approach The juridical approach is related to the fact that government is grounded in a constitution, in a democracy, in a division of tasks between various bodies of government and in general principles of decent government. In short, government operates in the context of a constitutional state. In this context, a juridical approach concerns criteria such as the legality principle, the protection of fundamental human rights, the commitment of government to justice, government's monopoly over the use of the means of violence (army, police, court, taxation), the duty to maintain law and order, the independence of the judiciary, and so forth. In interacting with society, the general principles of decent government (representation and support, impartiality, equitable treatment) influence decision making and procedures (for instance, reasonable waiting periods, carefulness, proper arguing) as well as the content of these decisions (equality, no preferential treatment, the use of authority only when it is called for, a fair weighing of interests). The government's conformity to these principles is supervised by various public bodies such as the judiciary and the National Ombudsman. In general, government action – and thus administrative capacity – has to meet the juridical demands of due process, fairness, equality, etc., before the law.

Economic-Managerial Approach The economic approach of governance capacity has to be related mainly to the effective execution of public tasks. Examples of demands in this approach are necessity, effectiveness, efficiency, implementation capacity, maintainability, simplicity. Although these have attracted much attention under the label NPM since the second half of the 1980s, they are not new. Thomas Woodrow Wilson, the father of modern public administration, has already coined the slogan, "government should be run like a business" (Schafritz and Hyde, 1992). Subsequently, schools of thought such as 'scientific management' and 'scientific administration' also reinforced these ideas. All efforts of government had to be geared to enhancing productivity. *Taylorism* is the classical example of this *managerial approach.* NPM provided this approach with new momentum. It resulted, among other things, in a government that is increasingly evaluated for its output by using accountability norms and 'hard' performance indicators. In addition, it should be noticed that under the dominance of neo-liberal political thought in western politics during the last decades, economic managerial criteria are often not only used as a means to improve government, but also as a goal of government in itself. Furthermore, these criteria are not only used to determine the success or failure of government in retrospect. Also, performance measurement is used as an *ex ante* mechanism to shape future public action. Efficiency and effectiveness notions often result in discussions about similarities and differences between the public and the private sector.

Political and Civic Approach This approach highlights values in the structure and culture of democracy itself. One can think of such issues as representation, accountability, distribution of authority, oversight and control, openness, accessibility, participation. A conclusive definition of democracy has not yet been found, but there is consensus about a number of formal characteristics: periodic elections, multiparty system, free press, protection of human rights, freedom of political activity and organization, independent judiciary, a recognized role for civil society – societal organizations such as trade unions, non-governmental interest and pressure groups – and transparent economic policy, where the state holds no monopoly. In a variety of countries, the presence of such democratic institutions is neither a guarantee for democratic government (calling someone to account for actions without the fear of persecution) nor for *good governance* (transparent decision making; competent civil servants; accountability; absence of corruption, clientelism and nepotism).

The elaboration of the JEP-triangle so far has emphasised the criteria attributable to the corners of the figure (i.e. to the different logics). However, in policy practises the ribbons of the triangle are of special interest. In specific cases the characterisation of the tensions between the three dimensions will demonstrate the hard core of governance capacity. While the economy needs flexibility (in capital, labour and knowledge), the juridical dimension requires legality, certainty and predictability. While the market needs autonomous decision-making (exclusion) and free access of suppliers, the political dimension urges collective decision-making (inclusion) and authoritative value-allocation (political primacy). While the political dimension requires responsiveness to all those social problems which are legitimately recognised, the juridical approach requires involvement under conditions of accountability, trust and truth, security and maintenance. Logically, the characterisation of each of the three ribbons does not give the complete picture. It is the three ribbons together that construct the quality of the governance capacity in a particular context.

REFLEXIVE EVALUATION

In the previous section, we introduced the governance capacity approach (GCA) in its original design. In this and the next section, we proceed by linking this GCA to the policy arrangement approach (PAA) more explicitly. In doing so, we will introduce an additional tool – besides the JEP triangle – to evaluate the institutional governance capacity of policy arrangements. While the JEP triangle is a fine instrument to assess the performative governance capacity of policy arrangements, it is in our view less adequate to account for the institutional side of the story. Therefore we will elaborate on the concept of *congruence*, already introduced as an analytical tool in the previous chapter (Liefferink, this volume), to make it more relevant to our evaluative perspective.

Indicative Governance Capacity

When considering the indicative governance capacity of a certain policy arrangement, the key question is whether its architecture is such that we can expect a 'capacity to govern' in the near future. This means, for example, that there are enough resources available, that the key policy actors are involved, that the rules of the game do not prohibit appropriate (change) behaviour, that the dominant policy discourse is (to some extent) shared, etc. In other words, indicative governance capacity means that the different dimensions of a policy arrangement do not contradict each other (too much). To theorise about this prerequisite, we borrow the concept of *congruence* from Boonstra (2004).

Boonstra introduces the concept of congruence to theorise about the prerequisites for the *institutionalisation* of policy arrangements. We however use it to assess the *indicative governance capacity* of policy arrangements. These references are not similar, although strongly related. Without at least some institutionalisation, one cannot expect policy arrangements to exhibit potential governance capacity, in the sense that policy and administrative problems will be (partially) solved, while the norms and values of the democratic state are taken into account.

Boonstra distinguishes three types of congruence: *strategic, structural-internal* and *structural-external.* The first type refers to the extent to which policy actors share policy discourses and common interests when deploying their strategic actions. The second type, structural-internal congruence refers to the extent to which the dimensions of a policy arrangement are coherent. An example might be the backing of certain policy goals by adequate resources and appropriate rules. The third type of structural-external congruence refers to the extent to which the policy arrangement as a whole is embedded in the wider institutional context. It refers, for example, to the coherence between the structure of a policy arrangement on the one hand and the conventions of the democratic constitutional state on the other. Congruence in these three types thus means 'sufficient coherence' among respectively (1) the policy views of the different actors; (2) the dimensions of a policy arrangement; and (3) the policy arrangement and its wider institutional context. The assumption is that a certain level of congruence – strategic and structurally, internally as well as externally – is needed for any policy arrangement to perform (and, in contrast, that a lack of congruence implies governance failure). What 'a certain level of congruence' means, by the way, is hard to say in general terms and remains an empirical question to be specified in any research.

However, a number of reservations about the notion of congruence should be made before continuing our analysis. Firstly, congruence does not mean full consensus (in the case of strategic congruence) or full consistency (in the case of structural congruence), as Grin et al. (2004) also argue. There is room for contradictions, dialectics and counter-movements. Nonetheless, as Boonstra (2004) rightly argued, a certain level of congruence is needed for the institutionalisation of any emerging policy arrangement. We argue that the same holds for a policy arrangement to perform any governance capacity. Secondly, congruence should not be equated with a 'functional fit' of agents in institutions and of institutions in the wider context. Here again, one should read congruence in terms of the duality of structure. This means that there is room for agents to reflect upon and change institutions. It also means that institutions do not unilaterally determine the 'best fitting' actor constellation and the 'best fitting' policy solution. Thirdly, congruence should not be considered a static concept, as people's preferences, social institutions and structural processes may change. As a consequence, optimal coherence within and outside a policy arrangement at T0 might be different compared to optimal coherence at T1. Therefore the concept of congruence should also include flexibility. If policy actors and social institutions are not able to accommodate change or the need for change, then a situation of congruence can be easily lost.

Performative Governance Capacity

In the above it is claimed that the indicative governance capacity of policy arrangements can be assessed on the basis of the notion of congruence: the more congruence, the more (potential) governance capacity. However, this only says something about the institutional capacity of policy arrangements, nothing about performance, let alone about good governance. In order to be able say something about these latter aspects, an agency-oriented or strategic policy evaluation should be conducted. Here the focus is on policy actors, their strategies and outcomes as well as on a judgement of these. Such a judgement can be based on the JEP-triangle, as presented in the previous section. Applying this triangle means, amongst others:

1. Defining what 'good governance' in a certain situation is;
2. Determining what administrative logics of action are, or should be, involved – juridical, economic and/or political – and how these can be balanced the best way possible;

3. Determining what evaluation criteria need to be involved (efficiency, effectiveness, adequacy, legitimacy, democracy, clarity, legality, legal security, justice, etc.) and how these can be balanced the best way possible;
4. Assessing to what extent these criteria are met by the performances of policy actors, in terms of procedures (processes), plans (outputs) and problem solving (outcomes) (depending on what the research questions are as well as the nature of the evaluation: *ex ante, ex nunc, ex post*).

Given the premises on 'reflexive evaluation' dealt with in the above, such a multi-criteria evaluation should be conducted in dialogue with and in interaction with stakeholders. How this should be done – for example through the three phases of variation, selection and retention – was already discussed above.

To conclude this section, two types of governance capacity are to be distinguished: the indicative and performative ones. The first is defined as institutional capacity and is assessed on the basis of (strategic and structural, internal and external) congruence of a policy arrangement. We also refer to this type of analysis as an evaluation at *institutional* level. The performative capacity of policy arrangements is defined as good governance and assessed on the basis of the JEP-triangle. We also refer to this second type of analysis as *strategic* evaluation.

REFLEXIVE DESIGN

In this section on policy design, we again make a distinction between *institutional* and *strategic* analyses, based on the notions of indicative and performative governance capacity. The first relates to strategies for enhancing congruence – strategic and structural, internal as well as external – in policy arrangements, the second to improving the outputs and outcomes of policy arrangements in terms of good governance criteria.

Enhancing Congruence

As far as strategic congruence is concerned, deliberation and mutual learning among those involved in policy practices are very important strategies to enhance coherence among different discourse and interest coalitions. Yet one should realise that these processes take a long time and generally transcend the time frame of normal policy projects and processes (Grin et al., 2004; Hajer and Wagenaar, 2003). This is also close to what is called 'interaction and perception management' in the network literature (Kickert et al., 1997). There exist many techniques and tools for deliberation and learning, such as (accumulative rounds of) workshops, ateliers, digital labs, decision-making support models, scenario-building sessions, etc. (Grin et al., 2004).

Secondly, internal-structural congruence can be increased by what is called 'institutional management' in network literature or 'rule-altering design' in reflexive policy making (Kickert et al., 1997; Pestman and Van Tatenhove, 2001). The idea is that key actors and their policy discourses and interests should show sufficient coherence with the structures of rules and resources in policy arrangements, and vice versa. This can be achieved by inclusion or exclusion of certain actors, the extraction from or the adding to the policy arena of certain policy resources, and a change of the rules of the game, e.g. interaction, participation and decision making rules. These kinds of changes are more difficult to imagine than those for strategic congruence, however, as they seem to presuppose a central steering actor, with control over a policy arrangement as a whole, a perspective that became problematic in our late-modern society. Moreover, these manipulative techniques might quite easily clash with certain policy values, such as legal security (in case of changing rules or extraction of resources) and democracy (in case of the exclusion of certain actors). Yet such structural strategies are not impossible either, given the re-styling of public participation, public decision making and the re-direction of public funds in politics and administration the last couple of decades (Nelissen et al., 1999, 2000). Also, certainly in situations of so-called 'institutional voids', policy arrangements can and will be (re)built by the stakeholders themselves, without involvement of a formal, central, unitary political actor (Hajer, 2003).

Reflexive design for external-structural congruence is even more difficult to imagine. After all, a deliberate change strategy for entire policy arrangements or, even more ambitious, for societies as a whole can hardly be thought of. Although structures are shaped by human agencies, they exhibit a long and wide 'time-space frame', so that they appear as autonomous entities, which cannot be influenced. Yet structural change is the aim of what has been called 'transition management' or 'third generation' strategies in environmental politics (Grin, 2004; Ministerie van VROM, 2001). Although it is elaborated upon in a rather technocratic fashion so far, it nonetheless aims at systemic innovations for sustainable development, such as a shift from the carbon-economy to a society based on sustainable energy. This shift implies a technological and socio-economic revolution indeed and cannot be thought of as to be realised in a couple of years. Instead, the focus is on 2050. The idea is that certain key actors and key technologies may induce such change in the longer run, which nonetheless implies policy action today (political deliberation, research & development, restructuring of certain industrial sectors, etc.). Transition management is a way of thinking from the 'here and now' at the micro level to the 'there and then' at the macro level, from the perspective of certain policy ambitions and goals.

However, one can also work the other way around, taking structures and structural transformation processes as 'given' and reflexively design policy recommendations. For example, in Arts et al. (2001) recommendations, formulated at strategic level, on strengthening the organic farming sector in the Netherlands were judged in the light of structural processes, such as Europeanisation, ecological modernisation, post-materialisation, and the like (see next section). With that, some of the initial recommendations, which seem sensible at first sight, became obsolete, as they were likely to clash with certain encompassing political transformation processes. Hence, external-structural design in a reflexive fashion can mean two things: (1) redesigning structures in the long run, starting with the here and now and with small steps, and (2) judging here and now policy recommendations in the light of large scale processes of structuration and transformation processes.

Applying the JEP Triangle

Finally, before turning to the case study, a few words should be spent on *strategic* design, based on notions of good governance and the JEP-triangle. To proceed from evaluation to design, a negative value judgement of a certain policy arrangement is turned into its opposite: a strategy for improvement, based on a similar value. Reflexive design then means an interactive construction of sensible and credible values, an interactive assessment of these and an interactive formulation of a route map to policy change. This does not exclude a privileged role for the policy researcher, as explained in the above. For example, a felt lack of legitimacy may produce recommendations to enhance this value, e.g. through increased information exchange with citizens. Or a lack of legal security may prompt policy makers to stick more to given rules and resources in the policy arena concerned. Such an actor-based design needs to be reflexive for another reason too, as the different values, logics and criteria exhibit internal tensions and trade-offs. Any choice for a certain balance of rationalities and criteria will definitely produce negative externalities and unanticipated effects elsewhere, so that the decision making process for policy change should be recursively reflected upon. Of course, in a truly reflexive design, all levels – strategic and structural congruence as well as values for good governance – are brought together, as sensibly and comprehensively as possible. But here again, trade-offs, externalities and unanticipated effects are simply unavoidable.

ORGANIC FARMING IN THE NETHERLANDS

Reflexive Evaluation

As indicated, we turn now to our empirical case. Not to assess it in a context of encompassing structural transformations, nor to analyse its policy arrangement and the strengths and weaknesses thereof. We now deal with Dutch organic farming from a reflexive evaluation perspective.

Although the number of organic farms, their land area as well as their turn-over have more or less doubled in the Netherlands in the period 1997-2003, the Dutch organic farming sector is still small compared to other countries in Europe (Biologica, 2004). About 2,2% of the total Dutch agricultural area concerns organic farming, while comparable figures in Austria and Switzerland rise to 13% and 10% respectively. Moreover, recent figures show a decrease of growth figures. For example, the number of organic farms is even decreasing in the Netherlands today (Biologica, 2005).

Although the sector itself is quite old (1920s), policy interventions by the state are of recent date (1990s). It was only in 1996 that the first Action Plan on Organic Farming was published, focusing on improving market access for organic products and on stimulating consumers to buy these. State subsidies to strengthen the sector were introduced (Biologica, 2004, 2005). The second Action Plan was subsequently published in 2000. It aimed at: (1) professionalisation of the sector, (2) transparency in the production chain and (3) growth of production figures, while heralding more of a market philosophy than its predecessor. As a consequence, some state subsidies – for example for conversion from mainstream to organic agriculture, a legacy of the first plan – were phased out. The central aim of the action plan has nonetheless been to realise a 10% share of organic farming in Dutch agriculture areas in the year 2010. As today's share is about 2,2% and in view of current growth rates, however, it is not very likely that this objective will be achieved in the next 5 years. The effectiveness of the policy arrangement can therefore be questioned (as can other aspects of its governance capacity). Below we will go into the background of this.

As Liefferink (this volume) set out in the previous chapter, the Dutch organic policy arrangement is characterised by the dominance of mainstream agricultural organisations. They consider organic farming as an interesting niche market for those farmers who cannot or will not survive in mainstream agriculture. With that, 'conversion' and 'assimilation' are the main policy themes in the arrangement. Also, the state endorses a market philosophy, facilitating the sector at best, while refraining from direct intervention. At the periphery of the arrangement, however, we find the most organic organisations, with *Biologica* being the most important. These propagate a more ecocentric and holistic discourse and strategy, which in fact challenge mainstream agriculture. The governance discourse which is supported also differs from the mainstream one. Instead of supporting a market philosophy, the need for active state intervention in the sector is emphasised in order to overcome structural inequalities between both sectors. These views and strategies however clash with the ones of the traditional agricultural organisations as well as with those of the Dutch state. As a consequence, the arrangement is rather fragmented, both in terms of organisations and substance. This is even strengthened by the fact that *Biologica* and other organic organisations have different views on organic farming among themselves: they exhibit anthroposophist versus ecological views, various opinions on agriculture-in-conversion, and different views on large-scale application of organic farming.

Given the above characteristics of the organic farming policy arrangement, 'strategic congruence' can be considered rather low. There exist different views on what organic farming is all about, as well as on the role of the state within the sector among the stakeholders involved. Also, ambitions and goals of the different players vary widely. Whereas organic farming is *the only* sustainable future for Dutch agriculture according to some, it will and needs to remain a niche market for a limited number of producers and consumers according to others. 'Structural congruence' seems low too. And as Liefferink (this volume) illustrated, the four dimensions of the policy arrangement, actors, rules, resources, discourses are not very coherent. Moreover the official goal of a substantive growth of the sector from a 2% share today up to a 10% share in 2010, is not backed by sufficient and enabling networks, rules and resources in the field. The sector is even characterised by a deadlock: the state facilitates conversion at a rather (too) low level and subsequently waits for the sector to govern itself towards growth, while many organic farmers wait for the state to develop and implement more effective policies that directly intervene (eco-tax, R&D subsidies, direct subsidies for organic farmers, regulatory relief for organic farming, boosting of the EKO label, etc.). As a consequence, not so much happens. Here a more active state as well as a more active sector seem prerequisites to improving this situation, as the Danish case makes clear (Liefferink, this volume). Ambitions are one thing, a serious policy programme and strategy that support these another.

External structural congruence, in other words the embeddedness of the Dutch organic farming policy arrangements in its wider institutional context, is quite problematic as well. Mainstream law and regulations, both from the EU and the Dutch state, seem to constrain the organic farming sector in most cases. For example, organic farmers have to obey mainstream manure policies, which is quite costly, while their overall impact on the environment is less than the one of mainstream farmers. In contrast, current organic policy measures mainly favour those mainstream farmers who have planned to convert and go organic. This may be called 'the organic farming policy paradox': mainstream agricultural policy constrains the sector, while organic farming policy mainly enables the mainstream sector. Also, structural processes such as Europeanisation and liberalisation seem not to favour the organic sector. So far, the sector is too weak to compete with mainstream agriculture or even with organic farmers from abroad, e.g. Germany. Therefore some kind of protectionist policy – at least temporarily – seems necessary for the Dutch organic sector to flower in the near future. However, this is a curse in the current neo-liberal wave of economic policy.

Given this lack of strategic and structural congruence in and of the Dutch policy arrangement on organic farming, it is no surprise that its governance capacity is limited. In terms of the normative criteria of the JEP-triangle, its effectiveness is rather low (low growth figures) as is its efficiency (subsidies do not optimally foster the sector itself). Also, legal security and justice can be questioned, as some subsidies were immediately phased out after the introduction of the second Action Plan, for example, and organic farmers generally feel discriminated against by policy makers, particularly compared to their mainstream colleagues. In addition, their influence on and participation in policy making is limited, given the peripheral position of organic farming organisations in the policy arrangement. Hence, in terms of democracy, the arrangement does not perform very well either.

Reflexive Design

In case one would like to reverse this downward trend in Dutch organic farming, an ambitious policy programme should be designed and implemented. But before any sensible measure could be thought of, a more basic prerequisite for any governance capacity should be taken care of. This is the creation of at least some common basic understanding within the policy arrangement on matters such as the nature and shape of organic farming in Dutch, European and global contexts, the position and role of organic farming in Dutch agriculture as well as in the economy as a whole, the formulation of overall policy ambitions and goals and the role of the state, market and civil society in realising these.

The last two points also relate to what good governance in the organic sector is all about, according to the stakeholders involved. To create such a common understanding, the organisation and facilitation of a political, societal and sector-specific deliberation process on these issues seems necessary and useful, given the current fragmentation of the policy arrangement, both in terms of organisation and substance. Such an initiative seems not easy to realise, but it could be very well embedded in an initiative which already exists: the current transition debate in Dutch environmental policy, which also focuses on sustainable agriculture (besides energy and biodiversity; see Ministerie van VROM, 2001). Besides the search for a common basic understanding, such a deliberation process could also realise trust and coalition building among stakeholders. These aspects are to a large extent lacking in the current policy arrangement.

The above is a plea for realising at least some basic strategic congruence within the current organic farming policy arrangement before turning to any concrete policy measure. This is, by the way, not identical to full consensus, as noted before, as a certain diversity of views will always exist and, even more so, is a prerequisite for any meaningful reflexive policy making itself. Yet some basic commonality is also needed to push a certain sector into a new direction. Having said that, in case a deliberation process in the agricultural sector indeed produces clear and sensible policy ambitions and goals and a shared view on good governance, then one might think of taking some next steps. If such a common basic understanding is however not achieved, then one might even think of refraining from taking *any* next steps. This would imply that Dutch organic farming policy will then maintain its fragmented nature and that 'muddling through' would be the situation in the near future. In that case, it might be even better to entirely phase out current organic farming policy and leave the further development of the sector to the market alone, as current policies have hardly any positive effects. However, in case the opposite is true, namely that a deliberation process produces shared views on policy and governance, then next steps – in terms of structural congruence and concrete policy measures – can be thought of.

Structural congruence first of all means that the internal structure of a policy arrangement is made as coherent as possible (for as far as this is manageable and realisable). This means that in case the sector chooses for clear, sensible and legitimate ambitions and goals (discourses), a next step would be to think about the optimal policy arrangement structure to realise these. This implies the 'tuning' of actors, rules and resources with policy ambitions and objectives as well as with governance values and norms. More practically, it means that enough resources to finance certain initiatives are reserved; that law, regulations and action plans seriously address and build upon these ambitions and goals and focus on the right addressees. This might also mean fewer rules or some regulatory relief for certain target groups. It also means that key players who should implement these strategies and execute these tasks can participate in the policy making concerned. In terms of more concrete policy measures, internal structural congruence might imply the design of special policies and subsidies for converters on the one hand and existing organic farmers on the other, maybe including some regulatory relief from mainstream regulations. And it implies the extra funding of research on organics.

However, structural congruence also means that the policy arrangement *as a whole* is well embedded in its wider institutional context, in Dutch, European and global (agricultural) politics. From the above, we learned that this type of structural congruence is also low for Dutch organic farming. This implies that – in order to increase the governance capacity of the sector – the wider institutional context should be less constraining and/or more enabling for the sector than before. However, in management terms, this is hard to achieve, if not impossible. It is not easy to imagine how for example the needs of Dutch organic farmers might change European regulations. Yet if we decide, as Dutch society, as a consequence of the transition debate, that we have 'real' policy ambitions and goals regarding organic farming in the Netherlands, then both governmental agencies as well as societal organisations should seriously put pressure on Dutch mainstream agriculture, on Europe as well as on international organisations such as FAO and WTO to change those rules that are detrimental to organic farming. Instead one should design new ones that enable the sector. An example might be the overall internalisation of environmental costs in the market, e.g. through eco-taxes.

Though this instrument is being debated in both the EU and the WTO, it is controversial, as it might distort market competition. Yet, if we wish to change the uneven market opportunities for sectors which do and do not internalise their environmental costs, then such instruments should be discussed and – ideally – adopted.

Enhancing the level of strategic and structural congruence is meant to increase the indicative governance capacity of a policy arrangement in generic terms. In other words, congruence potentially increases the capacity to govern of a policy arrangement, because people's policy and governance views are converging, rules and resources seem to match, and the wider institutional context enables the policy sector as a whole. However, such a situation of congruence is no guarantee for actual performance nor for actual good governance. There are many variables that intervene between policy *outputs* (programmes, plans, subsidies, etc.) and policy *outcomes*, including effects in terms of growth, democracy, legality, justice, etc. In addition, views on good governance, both in terms of plans and outcomes, of insiders and outsiders, e.g. of policy scientists, might differ. This situation calls for a continual process evaluation: Are we still on the right track? How to deal with unexpected or unanticipated events? And it calls for a continual dialogue between insiders and outsiders. Therefore the deliberation process with which we started in the above is not just an initial phase of policy making, but a continuous one.

CONCLUSION

In this chapter, we added a normative framework for policy evaluation and design to the Policy Arrangement Approach (PAA), based on the Governance Capacity Approach (GCA). Together, these frameworks call for a reflexive approach, which tries to establish a middle-ground between rational-instrumentalist measurement models on the one hand and social-constructivist negotiation models on the other. Given this position, various logics of action, normative criteria and insiders' and outsiders' views are taken into account in policy evaluation and design. With that, the policy scientist becomes a sort of judge to balance these logics, criteria and views. In order to do so, two 'tools' were presented in this chapter: the JEP-triangle and the concept of congruence. The JEP-triangle offers various normative criteria to value policy making, which stem from different traditions in public administration, and facilitates reflection not only on how these values might be mutually supportive, but also on how these might conflict in policy practices. The concept of congruence, next, helps to reflect on policy evaluation and design in more institutional terms. It is not about good intentions, but about how these intentions relate to various stakeholders with different positions on the one hand (strategic congruence) as well as to the direct and wider institutional context on the other (structural congruence). To show how these tools can be applied in a practical case, the Dutch organic farming sector was taken as an example. This (short) analysis showed, besides the applicability of the PAA/GCA-model designed in this chapter, that this sector is suffering from a lack of governance capacity. There is low strategic and structural congruence and scores in terms of the JEP-triangle are quite low too. As a consequence, some ideas for reflexive design were presented.

REFERENCES

Abma, T. (2001), Variaties in beleidsevaluaties: meten, beoordelen en onderhandelen, in: T. Abma and R. in 't Veld (eds.), *Handboek Beleidswetenschap: perspectieven, thema's, praktijkvoorbeelden*, Boom, Amsterdam, pp. 311-320.

Abma, T. and R. in 't Veld (eds.) (2001), *Handboek Beleidswetenschap: perspectieven, thema's, praktijkvoorbeelden*, Boom, Amsterdam.

Arts, B., M. Bruns, P. Leroy, D. Liefferink and J.P.M. van Tatenhove (2001), *Biologisch groeien?! Een multi-actor analyse van het beleidsarrangement biologische landbouw (2000-2020)*, Katholieke Universiteit Nijmegen, Nijmegen.

Biologica (2004), *Eko-Monitor: Cijfers en trends, Jaarrapport 2003,* bron: www. biologica.nl.

Biologica (2005), *Eko-Monitor: Cijfers en trends, Jaarrapport 2004,* bron: www. biologica.nl.

Boonstra, F. (2004), *Laveren tussen regio's en regels: verankering van beleidsarrangementen rond plattelandsontwikkeling in Noordwest Friesland, de Graafschap en Zuidwest Salland*, Koninklijke Van Gorcum, Assen.

Denhardt, R.B. (2004), *Theories of public organization*, Thomson Wadsworth, California.

Dunn, W.N. (1994), *Public policy analysis: an introduction*, Prentice Hall, New Jersey, London.

Edelenbos, J. and M. van Eeten (2001), The missing link: processing variation in dialogical evaluation, *Evaluation*, Vol. 7, no. 2, pp. 204-210.

Fischer, F. (1995), *Evaluating public policy*, Nelson-Hall, Chicago.

Giddens, A. (1984), *The constitution of society,* Polity Press, Cambridge.

Grin, J. (2004), *De politiek van omwenteling met beleid*, Vossiuspers UvA, Amsterdam.

Grin, J., F. Felix and B. Bos (2004), Practices for reflexive design: lessons from a Dutch program on sustainable agriculture, *Int. J Foresight and Innovation Policy*, Vol. 1, no. 1-2, pp. 126-149.

Hajer, M.A. (2003), Policy without polity? Policy analysis and the institutional void, *Policy Sciences*, Vol. 36, no. 2, pp. 175-195.

Hajer, M.A. and H. Wagenaar (eds.) (2003), *Deliberative policy analysis: understanding governance in the network society, theories of institutional design*, Cambridge University Press, Cambridge.

Kickert, W.J.M., E.H. Klijn and J.F.M. Koppenjan (eds.) (1997), *Managing complex networks: strategies for the public sector,* Sage, London.

Ministerie van VROM (2001), *Een wereld en een wil: werken aan duurzaamheid* (NMP4), 's-Gravenhage.

Nelissen, N.J.M., M. Bemelmans-Videc, A. Godfroij and P. de Goede (1999), *Renewing government: innovative and inspiring visions*, International Books, Utrecht.

Nelissen, N.J.M., H. Goverde and N. van Gestel (2000), *Bestuurlijk vermogen: analyse en beoordeling van nieuwe vormen van besturen*, Coutinho, Bussum.

Nelissen, N.J.M., P. de Goede and M. van Twist (2004), *Oog voor bestuurskunde, een beknopte geschiedenis van de bestuurskunde*, Elsevier, 's-Gravenhage.

Osborne, D. and T. Gaebler (1992), *Reinventing government: how the entrepreneurial spirit is transforming the public sector*, Plume, New York.

Pestman, P. and J.P.M. van Tatenhove (1998), Reflexieve beleidsvoering voor milieu, ruimtelijke ordening en infrastructuur? – Nieuwe initiatieven nader beschouwd, *Beleidswetenschap,* Vol. 12, nr. 3, pp. 254-272.

Shafritz, J.M. and A.C. Hyde (1997), *Classics of public administration*, Harcourt Brace College Publishers, Fort Worth (4th edition).

Snellen, I. (1987), *Boeiend en geboeid: ambivalenties en ambities in de bestuurskunde*, Samson, Alphen aan den Rijn.

Swanborn, P.G. (1992), Verschillende opvattingen over theoriegebruik, in: G.J.N. Bruinsma and M.A. Zwanenburg (eds.), *Methodologie voor bestuurskundigen*, Coutinho, Muiderberg, pp. 157-175.

Swanborn, P.G. (1999), *Evalueren: het ontwerpen, begeleiden en evalueren van interventies – een methodologische basis voor evaluatieonderzoek*, Boom, Meppel.

Van de Graaf, H. and R. Hoppe (1992), *Beleid en Politiek: een inleiding tot de beleidswetenschap en beleidskunde*, Coutinho, Muiderberg.

Van der Meer, F. and J. Edelenbos (2002), *Evaluation in multi-actor policy processes: accountability, learning and cooperation*, Paper prepared for the 2002 EES Conference, Sevilla.

Van Tatenhove, J.P.M., B. Arts and P. Leroy, (eds.) (2000), *Political modernisation and the environment: the renewal of environmental policy arrangements*, Kluwer Academic Publishers, Dordrecht.

Chapter 5

The Institutional Dynamics of Water Management in the Low Countries

Mark Wiering and Ann Crabbé

INTRODUCTION

'Institutionalisation' refers to ongoing processes of both renewal and stabilisation of policy practices. From this angle, water management is particularly interesting, because of its history – it is one of the oldest community-based tasks in the Low Countries – and because of its dynamics in recent times. Water institutions are both deeply rooted in historical traditions and contested in the last few years. In this chapter we want to describe and interpret the institutional dynamics, by means of comparing the water policy arrangements in the Netherlands and Flanders.

The central empirical question in this chapter is: what impact does 'integrated water management' (IWM), as a new element in the discourse on water policy, have on the organizational dimensions of water policy arrangements? In both countries IWM was introduced, but the impact and the usage of the concept differ. Further, this empirical question is linked to theories of institutional change: what circumstances explain a different reception of IWM in both countries? Why do some of the dimensions of the policy arrangement show stability in time while others are more dynamic? And, are the institutional changes to be considered shallow or deep?

The water policy arrangements are analysed on the level of the sector based, national policy arrangements, whereby Flemish policy replaces the Belgium level of governmental interference because of the country's federal structure. We could have chosen underlying aggregation levels, e.g. only water quality issues or only flooding management, and reach far more detail. For purposes of international comparison however, and to relate our findings to 'systemic' institutional changes, it is better to focus on the national level.

After explaining our theoretical framework in the first section, the second section will 'set the scene' with a description of the characteristics of Flemish and Dutch water policy arrangements in the early 1990s.

B. Arts and P. Leroy (eds.), Institutional Dynamics in Environmental Governance, 93–114.

Section three focuses on the concept of IWM entering the policy stage. Sections four and five analyse the reception of the concept in the Netherlands and Flanders, and goes into the nature of changes, and their magnitude. The chapter winds up with our conclusions and we briefly reflect on the possibilities of combining the policy arrangement-approach with theories of institutional change.

POLICY ARRANGEMENTS AND INSTITUTIONAL CHANGE

The dimensions of policy arrangements can be functional in reconstructing where and in what order institutional changes take place, but this type of analysis does not, in itself, explain why policies change, nor does it touch upon the magnitude of these changes. Therefore, we supplement the basic elements of the policy arrangement-approach with three fundamental issues relating to transition in policy arrangements: the forces (or impetus) of institutional change, its nature and magnitude.

Forces of Change

In policy analysis a distinction is made between forces of change endogenous to the policy domain and exogenous forces (Arts and Leroy, 2003; Bressers, O'Toole and Richardson, 1995; Dudley and Richardson, 1996; Marsh and Rhodes, 1992; Sabatier and Jenkins-Smith, 1993; Smith, 2000). However, framing developments as 'internal', 'endogenous' or 'inside' versus 'external', 'exogenous' and 'outside' implicates certain (strict) boundaries of policy arrangements. Such boundaries are often difficult to draw (for a similar discussion on boundaries of networks: Bressers, O'Toole and Richardson, 1995, p. 211). In our view, exogenous forces are not strange entities from the outside. They are changing patterns of action and behaviour, changing discourse elements or changes in vocabulary that are processed through actor and structure patterns (Giddens, 1984).

The (perception of the) poor functioning of the policy domain can be a dominant endogenous force of change. A policy arrangement can evolve in such a way that it cannot deal sufficiently anymore with the problems it faces, i.e. its governance capacity is low. It is labelled inefficient (the economic argument), it loses political legitimacy (the political argument) or it is seen as too complex and non-transparent (the institutional and juridical argument).

Exogenous forces of change can spring from other policy domains or from long-term societal processes influencing policy arrangements. With long-term societal processes we refer to the discussion on political modernisation in chapter 2 of this volume. Societal change is reflected in: (1) the emancipation of citizens and processes of individualisation; (2) changes in the scale of societal interactions; and (3) the ongoing differentiation of societal structures and – at the same time – the need for coherence and integration. These evolutions are summarised as respectively the multi-actor, the multi-level, and the multi-sector trend.

Finally, stimuli can also take the form of shock waves in society, such as a sudden disruption of the physical environment (flooding; tsunami) or a political event (political murder). Shocking events can trigger and stimulate existing institutional changes, and can cause rapids (but also congestions), in the ongoing institutional development of policy domains.

The Nature of Change: Indicators of Change in Policy Arrangements

The impact of IWM on the dimensions of water policy arrangements in Flanders and the Netherlands will be described with different indicators of institutional change. *Policy discourse* can be further differentiated in definitions of reality or 'paradigms' wherein actors live (ontological layer of discourse), the desirable situations they strive for (normative layer), and the 'route' they foresee in reaching desirable situations (instrumental layer). As far as the dimension *rules of the game* is concerned, we will look at (changes in) legislation (formal rules), procedures (informal rules) and political culture (political rules of the game). In the *actors and coalitions*part the focus is on the constellation of actors and change in patterns of their interaction. Finally, changes in *power balance* are interpreted through shifts in resource constellation and changes in power relations. But, to be clear, our focus is more on the impact of discursive changes on the arrangement as a whole, and less on the other possible entrances of the arrangement (power, rules or actor-coalitions).

The Magnitude of Institutional Changes

The magnitude of policy change is, amongst others, discussed by Dudley and Richardson (1996), and Hall (1993). Hall makes a distinction between first, second and third order change. We can think of first order change when certain events lead only to incremental changes within routine decision making, such as adjusting budgets to new circumstances. Second order change involves the development of new policy instruments and goals, which means that the policy domain makes bigger adjustments to its policy environment. First and second order change can be viewed as adaptation strategies of a policy arrangement seeking for continuity, where the 'policy core' stays the same, to express it in terms of the Advocacy Coalition Framework (Sabatier and Jenkins-Smith, 1993). Third order change entails a paradigmatic shift in the core values and perceptions (of the majority) of actors in the policy domain, such as the switch from Keynesianism to monetarism (Dudley and Richardson, 1996, p. 65).

In other words, we can think of institutional transitions as relatively shallow in nature, stemming from 'normal' adaptations of a policy domain, or deep and revolutionary, bringing the policy arrangement to a different phase or in the realm of a different paradigm. Our hypothesis is that deep, third order change requires both radical changes in the discourse dimension and the triggering of changes in all other dimensions (e.g. new legislation, new coalitions, and new power resources).

SETTING THE SCENE OF DUTCH AND FLEMISH WATER MANAGEMENT

In this section Dutch and Flemish policy arrangements for water management are described. We go into the constellation of public actors involved in water management and we portray the division of resources and power between them. Further, we discuss the prevailing rules of the game in both policy arrangements and, finally, we focus on some remarkable parallels and differences between Dutch and Flemish water management. Our main intention here is to 'set the scene' in which the concept of integrated water management was introduced from the mid 1980s onwards.

Constellation of Public Actors

In the Netherlands four governmental layers are responsible for water management. Besides the three general layers, the national government, provinces and municipalities, there is a fourth, relatively autonomous layer of specialised public administrations, the regionally operating water boards. Another important policy actor is the Directorate-General for Public Works and Water Management (*Rijkswaterstaat*), which is part of the Ministry of Transport, Public Works and Water Management, and operates at the national level, but with regional departments. In general, the activities of the Directorate-General concern the main state water system of large rivers, canals, coastal waters and estuaries (and its infrastructure), while the powers of the water boards are geared towards the regional water management, both water quantity (such as maintenance and enforcement of dikes, dunes and embankments) and water quality (surface water pollution; waste water treatment). Exemptions to this are the navigable regional and the local waters, which fall under the jurisdiction of the provinces and municipalities respectively. The latter two also have specific tasks in water management. The provinces are responsible for groundwater management and the planning aspects of regional water management, and the local authorities for urban water management and sewerage networks (Kuks, 2004, pp. 84-85). Because the water boards are also concerned with water quality (environmental) issues and waste water treatment, the role of the Dutch Ministry of Housing, Spatial Planning and Environment is less prominent, compared to the Flemish constellation (Figure 5.1).

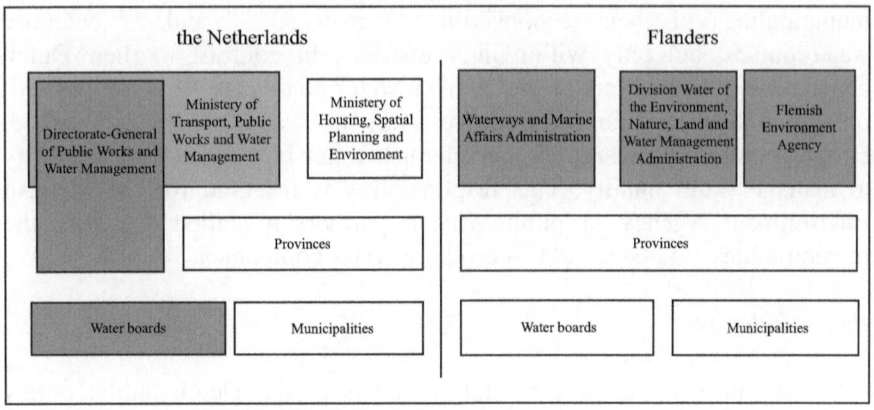

Figure 5.1. Constellation of public actors in Dutch and Flemish water management.

Since the Belgian state reforms of 1980 and 1988, the regions (Flanders, Wallonia and Brussels) are responsible for determining and implementing water policy. The national (Belgian) government hardly kept any legal powers in that policy domain, with the exception of the management of coastal waters. Within the Flemish regional government, the competences for water policy are divided amongst several public services. The Waterways and Marine Affairs Administration is rooted in the former national ministry of public works. It is responsible for the management of the navigable waterways and canals, and executes this task with a mainly technical-economic approach. In contrast to its Dutch equivalent (the Directorate-General), the Waterways and Marine Affairs Administration has no dominant influence on water management in Flanders. It shares steering power with at least two relatively strong Flemish administrations for the environment. The Division Water of the Environment, Nature, Land

and Water Management Administration is entitled to manage the unnavigable watercourses of the so-called 1st category (watercourses with drainage areas that cover more than 5.000 ha) and it is responsible for preparing and formulating ground water policy. The Flemish Environment Agency, a so-called parastatal organization, has the competency to monitor water quality and to programme public works for water purification infrastructure.

Besides the administrations of the Flemish region, there are also other public actors involved in the Flemish policy arrangement: municipalities, provinces and water boards. None of them has a dominant influence on (local) water management. The provinces are competent to take care of middle-sized unnavigable watercourses of the 2nd category. Municipalities are in charge of the ditches and the small unnavigable watercourses of the 3th category. Water boards relieve the provinces and municipalities of their responsibility to manage 2nd and 3th category watercourses, but only within their districts. In contrast to their Dutch counterparts, the districts of the Flemish water boards are very fragmented: only in polders and in river source areas are water boards established. Furthermore, it is remarkable that Flemish water boards have no authority to manage water quality. This responsibility is reserved for the Flemish Environment Agency, a public-private partnership called Aquafin, the municipalities, and (since 2005) drinking-water companies.

Power Relations

When we turn to the powers and resources of the Dutch public policy actors, we must stress the influential role of the 200-years-old Directorate-General which was mainly responsible for the preparation and formulation, as well as the execution, of Dutch water policies. Together with the water boards, the Directorate-General forms the heart of Dutch water management. An important power resource of these administrations is their impressive 'engineering' knowledge, fostered by the strong epistemic community of hydraulic engineering at mainly the technical universities (Disco, 2002).

When it comes to power relations in Flanders, we see that the available resources lie scattered around. No single Flemish regional actor has managed to grow into a dominant player in Flemish water policy. The Waterways and Marine Affairs Administration and the Flemish administrations for the environment actually appear to be countervailing powers, with their own expertise and methods of working (i.e. a technical/economic approach versus an ecological approach). On the local level, the provinces have relatively more power than the municipalities and the water boards. The provinces derive that authority from their position as a higher government, the larger scale on which they work and their ambition to be a relevant player in the policy arrangement. The water boards have fairly limited powers to steer. They have executive and practical tasks, and are financially dependent on municipalities, the provinces and the Flemish region. A similar conclusion applies for the municipalities. They lack organizational capacity and the interest of local politicians, which makes them relatively weak water managers.

Rules of the Game

Dutch water management is differentiated by a tight web of rules, to be found in e.g. the Water Management Act, the Groundwater Act, the Embankment Act, the Pollution of Surface Waters Act and the Pollution of Sea Water Act. Besides these substantive laws, there are procedural, constitutional rules about the jurisdiction and competencies of the water policy agencies. The legislation is difficult for outsiders to penetrate, and because of this complexity authorities often rely on informal agreements about division of tasks.

The Dutch political culture with regard to water management can be described as follows. Firstly, water management is (still) predominantly the responsibility of the public domain (Dicke, 2001; Kuks, 2004), although there are public-private interrelations, mainly concerning surface water (pollution) and ground water. Because of this hegemony of the state, the Dutch policy arrangement can be characterised etatist (Liefferink, this volume). Secondly, the water management agencies generally workrather autonomously and in isolation. Their position is not controversial since they enjoy the confidence of the Dutch population. The implementation of large and world-famous water works have certainly contributed to that. Thirdly, water management is technocratic in nature and not primarily concerned with considerations about the claims of other policy fields. This is fostered by a specific epistemic community that traditionally focuses on 'hydraulic engineering' (Disco, 2002).

The Flemish rules of the game are also numerous. Legislation can be found in laws, decrees and many implementing orders. Recent legislation on water management nearly always touches upon issues of water quality. The management of water quantity mainly operates on national laws, dating back to the 1950s-1960s. A characteristic informal rule of Flemish water management is that public services rarely come to informal agreements on division of tasks. Public services react very defensively towards attempts of others to reshuffle management tasks, mainly because they want to prevent their position from being weakened.

With regard to the political culture of Flemish water management, we distinguish three dominant characteristics. Firstly, public concern for water management is rather limited. Only in critical circumstances, when water problems are a threat for public safety, water management gets a more prominent place on the political and societal agenda. Secondly, there is a gentle evolution towards the mobilization of (semi)private actors in Flemish water management. Even though water management is predominantly a responsibility of the public domain, the Flemish region started to experiment with public-private partnerships in the beginning of the 1990s. Thirdly, Flemish water management has less the image of a technocratic arrangement of civil engineers. An important explanation is the division of powers between technical and environmental administrations. Both have their specialties, but neither has succeeded in creating an epistemic community that is able to dominate public discourse on water management.

Remarkable Parallels and Differences

For both countries we observe that coordinated policy-making is everything but obvious, given the amalgam of organizational structures, institutional rules and the range of different (not always compatible) policy approaches. But we do also see some remarkable differences, for example in the role of the water boards and environmental administrations.

While water boards are a dominant actor in Dutch water policy, the Flemish water boards have relatively limited powers to steer. We explain the relatively weak position of the Flemish water boards by referring to the fact that they pertained to private law until the 1950s, whereas the Dutch water boards already became public institutions round 1850 thanks to constitutional reformer Thorbecke (Van de Ven, 2004). Moreover, since the 1950s the organic laws of the Flemish water boards were not (or scarcely) brought up to date, while Dutch water boards managed to grow into big, rationally-conceived public organizations.

In reverse, the environmental administration in the Netherlands has a relatively small part to play in comparison to its Flemish counterpart(s). We ascribe the relatively weak position of the Dutch environmental administration to the dominance of the Directorate-General: a 'state within the state' with deep-rooted authority in Dutch society (Disco and Van der Vleuten, 2004; Van der Ham, 1999).

THE CONCEPT OF INTEGRATED WATER MANAGEMENT

Until the 1960s, the traditional hegemonic discourse in water management came down to 'the battle against water' (TeBrake, 2002; Van de Ven, 2004; Van Steen and Pellenbarg, 2004). Water was seen as a threat to society, and policy strategies were installed to protect people and economic life against the water. This discourse resulted in a policy in which land was conquered from the sea and the rivers, enclosed and cultivated. It also led to the streamlining of rivers, closing creeks and small streams, and replacing natural watercourses by canals.

In the 1970s the tasks of water management were supplemented with the issues of water quality, especially with the responsibilities for surface water pollution and waste water treatment (Van Leussen, 2002). But it took until the 1980s and 1990s to reach an 'ecological turn' in the discourse on water management (Disco, 2002). In that period environmental scientists and others started pleading for an alternative way of managing water. The underlying idea was that water systems, if left alone, shape the landscape, regulate water supply and create nature in their own way.

In the realm of water policy, this ecological turn in water management was accompanied by the introduction of the (policy-) concept of integrated water management. The concept of IWM offered a new frame of reference. In its ecological dimension, it stands for sustainable development of the entire water system. In the literature on public administration, IWM was put forward as an alternative for existing coordination problems (Grijns and Wisserhof, 1992). Public administration experts in fact pleaded for optimized coordination: between water managers, between water managers and neighbouring policy domains (such as spatial planning, nature conservation and land development planning), and between policy makers, target groups and interested citizens.

In recent years the concept of integrated water management is supplemented by the concept of river basin management (RBM). "[RBM] is the process of co-ordinating conservation, management and development of water, land and related resources across sectors within a given river basin, in order to maximise the economical and social benefits derived from water resources in an equitable manner while preserving and, where necessary, restoring freshwater ecosystems" (Jones et al., 2003). A river basin approach is very gradually being institutionalised, at different levels and geographic scales. It effects both international coordination and co-operation regarding the European rivers and local and regional policy for sub-river basins. The objectives and strategies have been formalised in the

EU Water Framework Directive 2000/60/EC, published 22 December 2000.

To be sure, the dominant discourse of the 'battle against water' is not entirely replaced by a more ecosystem based integrated water management discourse. Momentarily, there exist two discourses next to each other: 'the battle against water' and the 'accommodating water' – or 'living with water' – discourse, with the recommendation to give more space to the rivers (Van Stokkom et al., 2005; Wiering and Immink, forthcoming).

CHANGES IN DUTCH WATER MANAGEMENT

In this section we focus on the impact of integrated water management (IWM) on the institutions of Dutch water management. As IWM affects all water issues (flooding risks, drought, salt water intrusion, pollution, etc.) it is difficult to summarise the developments in these domains. The main projects of contemporary water management are the national spatial planning key decisions about 'Space for the river', which is about creating space for the main rivers to reach the safety goals and improving the spatial quality of the river areas. A second major discussion is about emergency measures concerning water safety, if the regular policy would not be sufficient. Another set of activities is focused on addressing the ambitions of the Water Framework Directive. We start with the context of relevant forces of institutional change. Thereafter, the nature of changes is discussed, while applying the policy arrangement approach. And finally, we discuss the magnitude of these changes.

Forces of Change

Both endogenous and exogenous forces influence developments in Dutch water management. Endogenous forces manifest themselves, mainly, in the idea of failure of the traditionally dominant 'battle against water' discourse, and the need to move towards a 'living with water' or 'accommodating water' policy. This is especially explicated in governmental plans (e.g. Ministry of TPW, 2000). The existing focus on reinforcing dikes as an answer to any new water challenge has been characterised as the 'control paradox' (Remmelzwaal and Vroon, 2000): defence by dikes creates a feeling of safety and thus encourages a more intensive land use behind the dikes. When an incident occurs, people are not at all prepared and the damage is great. This causes an urgent situation and a desire to raise and reinforce the dikes again, which leads to a new feeling of safety, that causes new land use, with new risks, etc. (Remmelzwaan and Vroon, 2000; Van Stokkom et al., 2005; Wiering and Immink, forthcoming). Other endogenous forces in the water policy domain are also relevant. The complex water legislation, referred to in the above, is viewed as problematic in terms of efficiency and transparency (Memorandum, 2004).

Long term societal trends are clearly affecting Dutch water management. The multi-actor-trend is visible in today's discussion in public administration, which is about the lack of democratic structures of (functional) water management and its low public accountability. Other exogenous forces are the discussions on climate change, and the measures which are being taken to reverse it, and the multi-level governance instigated by both international flooding management and the European Water Framework Directive (WFD), which will influence future policy practices in water quantity and quality. It is of course difficult to draw exact lines between exogenous and endogenous forces. Governance (multi-actor) issues are stemming from both the desire of water management itself to become a more integrated part of the Dutch community – and thereby create more public sensitivity for water issues – and the societal call for water management to better inform people on water issues and make them more involved (Ministry of TPW, 2000).

The multi-level trend alters the policy landscape, in the sense that it stimulates both internationalisation and regionalisation of water management. Both in flooding management and in water quality issues, integrated water management is taken more seriously and a river basin approach is promoted, with new responsibilities for the regional water boards and the provinces. In both policy issues the multiple level character of water management is stressed, which is demonstrated by the call for cross border co-operation and the new responsibilities for the region.

To close off the identification of forces of change, we mention the near-flooding events of 1993 and 1995, during which there were long periods of high water levels in the large rivers (the Rhine branches and Meuse). Especially the event of 1995 can be characterised as a shocking event in Dutch society. In January 1995 the water rose to the highest levels since 1926, and continued at these high levels for an extraordinarily long period, so the dikes were put to the test. In precaution almost 250,000 inhabitants of the river basins were evacuated. The event was recalled in almost every governmental note on flooding risks for many years since. Although it initially strengthened the traditional 'battle against water' discourse and was used to speed up the planned reinforcement of the dikes, it also became part of a counter-discourse in which the existing water policy was a *cul-de-sac* and had to be replaced by a new perspective (Wiering and Driessen, 2001).

The Nature of Changes

What impact did the concept of IWM have on the rules of the game of Dutch water management? We already stated that the water legislation was complex and that its efficiency and transparency was questioned (see next section). As a consequence, the issue of redesigning the Dutch water legislation has arisen often. In 2002 a Committee was set up to give advice on legislative redesign and on the direction of possible institutional changes. Very recently, the Dutch government has confirmed that redesigning is indeed necessary, and has set the path towards an Integrated Water Management Act (Memorandum, 2004). In the context of our analysis the legislative Committee used several interesting arguments. In their view a change of legislation was necessary, because of the lack of internal coherence and transparency, and because of the implementation of the European Water Framework Directive. Thus, endogenous and exogenous forces together legitimised an institutional intervention, which is grounded on the umbrella-like concept of IWM.

Another sign of institutional change is to be found in the available policy instruments of water management in relation to neighbouring policy domains. An exponent of new procedures, in relation to multi-sector governance (as discussed above), is the process induced by the 'water test' (*watertoets*). This policy instrument requires governmental authorities to judge the water-related aspects in all relevant spatial plans, by means of obligatory advice of the water manager (mostly the regional water boards) and a separate section on water issues in the explanatory policy document (e.g. the land use plan). This procedure is a form of 'water impact assessment'. It is expected to considerably change the interrelations between water management and spatial planning in the Netherlands (Wiering and Immink, forthcoming). The test is about both water quantity issues (impacts on retention and storage capacity, risks of flooding, drought, groundwater level) and water quality issues (surface- and groundwater pollution, water sanitation or biodiversity issues). It is yet another 'materialized' exponent of the ideas behind IWM.

Has the introduction of IWM resulted in new actors entering the policy stage? We doubt this. Although it is now far more common to work on water projects in joint action with engineers, ecologists, hydro-biologists and environmental scientists, we find no important new administrative structures. In water quantity issues, the proposal of the WB21 Committee led to a 'National Administrative Agreement on Water' that made clear that new policy responsibilities can be taken up *without* changing the organisation of water management. This demonstrates that the authorities cling to the existing organisational order and division of tasks among municipalities, provinces, water boards, the Directorate-General and the Ministry.

Although we do not expect important shifts in the actor constellation as such, there is a change in interaction patterns, more specifically, a move towards decentralising responsibilities and towards the empowerment of the regional authorities. In the policy process of the 'Space for the river' procedures the provinces have an essential voice and are strongly represented in the advisory steering committees (Meijerink, 2004). Both the WB21 policies and the WFD have stimulated territorial shifts towards the region and sub-river basins. In sum, the actors stay the same, but the interactions between the different governmental layers are being intensified and we see more co-operative and horizontal interrelations.

Finally, we have asked ourselves if there are changes in resource constellation (new or more resources) or power relations (important reallocation of resources). In the past decade, the financial resources available for water management have indeed been increased, to anticipate climate change, to meet new risk norms in water safety and to implement the Water Framework Directive. The concept of IWM has also increased the variety of knowledge production, which is now more differentiated and includes disciplines such as hydrobiology, policy analysis and environmental sciences. This has also influenced the means for the knowledge infrastructure. New research programs are being developed, and the scope of these research programs has been broadened: more attention is paid to ecological research, social science research, policy analysis and socio-economical research. However, we can not confirm a real reallocation in resources and power relations. As was made clear before, the organisational structure of Dutch water management has remained rather stable so far. We observe the same key players in policy and science, and we observe (more or less) similar power relations, as the new resources have also strengthened those already 'in power' (Wiering and Arts, forthcoming).

The Magnitude of Dutch Institutional Changes

How can we interpret this range of institutional changes in Dutch water management? Do we understand them to be merely incremental, limited adaptations of today's water management, or are institutional changes more fundamental? To summarize our findings on the organisational part of the Dutch arrangement, we mainly see changes in the rules of the game and in the interrelations between actors, but not so much in the actor constellation and in power relations. We do find that Dutch water management is swiftly adapting to its environment and, the other way around, Dutch society is increasing its 'sensitivity' for water issues. The proposition of the autonomous, technocratic, closed policy arrangement is no longer valid and water management is becoming a more integrated part of Dutch society. The (cautious) changes in the democratic structures of water boards illustrate this. We also see a serious start of a redesign of the water legislation towards integrated water management and a further 'horizontalisation' of interrelations between the relevant authorities. These are indications of second order institutional change, in which goals (normative discourse) and instruments (route-discourse) are changing. But we do not have indications of 'paradigmatic' institutional change, because the core values of the policy community and the underlying ontological discourse remain intact and resource – and actor constellation as well as power relations remain stable over time.

CHANGES IN FLEMISH WATER MANAGEMENT

Just as we did for the Netherlands, we will discuss the 'forces of change', the 'nature of change' and the 'magnitude of change' for Flemish water management.

Forces of Change

Discontent with the results and the organization of Flemish water policy was an important stimulus inciting institutional change. While billions were spent on the installation of sewers and waste water treatment plants, surface water quality remained below standard, and frequent problems with local flooding made people conclude that Flemish water management had failed (Crabbé and Leroy, 2004). As a consequence, environmental action groups, members of parliament, and even public servants of environmental administrations publicly criticised the lack of cooperation between water managers, the inadequate financial management, and the poor attention for water related ecology. This negative discourse gradually spread and became dominant. In their search for solutions, policy makers picked up the concept of integrated water management.

Besides this general discontent with water management as it was, trends of political modernisation increased the (exogenous) pressure on Flemish water management. In that matter, the growing influence of multi-level governance is a tangible evolution since the 1990s. The internationalization of water policy, and particularly the European Water Framework Directive, has increasingly incited Flanders to 'download' river basin management to Flemish catchments and sub-catchments. Further, a growing awareness of the need for multi-actor policy making characterizes Flemish water management. Transparency and consultation of stakeholders is considered important, mainly because the support of societal actors is an important condition for policy's legitimacy.

Nature of Change

Since the concept of integrated water management was introduced in Flemish water policy, it has had an effect on the rules of the game, on the the constellation of actors involved in policy making, and – to a limited extent – on the division of resources and power.

In the beginning of the 1990s, the Flemish government started preparing a decree on integrated water management. The process of political decision-making regarding the decree took more than 10 years. The obstacles were numerous. For example, there were many discussions on the idea of closing down the water boards in order to replace them by new 'integrated' organizations for local water management. In the period from 1999 till 2004, when ministers of the green party held office, there was a breakthrough in the political discussion on the decree. The necessary implementation of the European Water Framework Directive and the political need to answer (then recent) problems of flooding were important incentives to speed up the legislative process. In the summer of 2003, the decree on integrated water management was finally accepted by the Flemish parliament. The intention of the then minister was to subsequently prepare additional decrees: to link 'old' legislation on water management to the new framework decree, and to update outdated regulations. But, since a new minister took office in 2004, the political enthusiasm to start new legislative processes has diminished, mainly because there are other (socio-economic) priorities on the political and societal agenda.

The decree on integrated water management anchors the main principles of integrated water management, and it also launches some new policy instruments. Firstly, the decree requires water managers to develop policy plans on three levels: at the level of the international river basin districts of the river Scheldt and the river Meuse, at the level of Flanders'

11 river basins, and at the level of 103 sub-basins. Policy planning is perceived as an essential step in developing integrated visions on water management. Secondly, the decree introduces juridical instruments to develop river banks ecologically: the right of pre-emption, the statutory obligation of buying up land etc. The demarcation of river banks for ecological development is an exercise that is done in the framework of the numerous policy planning initiatives. Thirdly, the decree offers a policy instrument to prevent future problems with flooding in residential areas: the 'water test' (*watertoets*). The water test implies that governments must obtain expert advice of authorized water managers before granting construction permits. In contrast to the water test in the Netherlands whereby water interests are imposed on adjacent fields, the water test in Flanders is strictly a means of coordinating expert advices of water managers in permitting procedures.

The political culture of water management in Flanders has certainly changed since the concept of integrated water management was introduced at the end of the 1980s. We see the rising of a 'participatory reflex' in Flemish water management: consultation of societal actors has gradually become self-evident in preparing new water policy, whereas water management used to be a relatively closed arrangement. Moreover, water management has opened up towards other policy domains. For example, the 'water test' has improved relations between water management and spatial planning. However, all these changes in political culture are unstable. Even though most principles of integrated water management are generally accepted, some strategic discussions remain topical. Public servants and politicians do not always agree on what options are best for water policy. For example, the dominance of ecological values in water management is somewhat contested, especially since green, ecologically inspired policy is associated more and more with regulations that hinder economic life and individual freedom.

In contrast to the Netherlands, Flanders has actually created new administrative structures for integrated water management. In the 1990s the first consultative bodies were established on an informal basis. Water managers then were invited to gather for three-monthly meetings, in which all relevant Flemish administrations and local governments participated. In the beginning ad hoc water problems of the river basin appeared on the agenda, but from 2001 onwards the discussions during the meetings are mostly linked to the development of river basin policy plans. The decree on integrated water management (Decree IWM, 2003) institutionalized these new policy practices. Since the Flemish minister for water management has issued the first implementing order on the decree on integrated water management (2005), new formal administrations have been established: one for each of the 11 Flemish river basins, and organizations for (clusters of) the 103 sub-basins.

With regard to patterns of interaction, regular meetings of water managers have improved personal relations and stimulated the transfer of information. The meetings resulted in more frequent and more effective cooperation between water managers of the Flemish region, but the participation of local water managers (of provinces, but particularly of municipalities and water boards) remained relatively modest. A plausible explanation is that the rather abstract discussions on river basins go beyond the concerns of local water managers.

Furthermore, there are indications of increasing co-production between water managers and target groups. Policy planning for river basin management is an opportunity for Flemish water managers to proceed to interactive, participatory policy making. In the framework of policy planning activities, interest groups are actively involved: they are invited to think along with water managers about the future of water policy. On the other hand, this evolution towards more multi-actor governance must be nuanced. Many water managers still have doubts on the eventual surplus of all their participatory policy planning efforts. They do not have confidence in the possibility of reconciling conflicting interests, such as the interests of nature conservationists (who prefer higher water levels for ecological reasons) and farmers (who have specific needs concerning water levels).

When it comes to resource constellation, we see that the Flemish government has invested extra resources for integrated water management between 1999 and 2004. In the framework of a project that stimulates river basin management, financial means and personnel were invested in order to develop river basin policy plans. This extra organizational capacity is important in paving the way towards river basin management.

Concerning power relations in the arrangement of Flemish water management, we do not see many changes. Since the 'old' regulations remained unaffected, all water managers kept their legal competencies, and for that reason power relations remained rather stable. Moreover, the new formal administrative structures on the level of the river basins and sub-catchments still lack institutional capacity to play a relevant part. To empower those new structures, there is a need for extra personnel and financial means. But since the Flemish government has cut down public expenses from 2004 onwards, there are only limited means to make the new public organizations for integrated water management operational. Furthermore, the water managers themselves do not advocate changes on the existing power relations. As stated above , they react very defensively towards initiatives that could potentially lead to a reshuffle of their responsibilities.

If any changes in power relations will occur in the near future, they are to be expected from outside the policy arrangement. In 2006 a massive reorganisation of Flemish government will have as a consequence that the Division Water of the Environment, Nature, Land and Water Management Administration will be absorbed by the Flemish Environment Agency, a 'parastatal' organization (Figure 5.1). This merger will certainly influence power relations. At this moment, however, it is difficult to forecast to what extent power relations will change.

Magnitude of Change

From the description of the nature of change, we conclude that Flemish water management is institutionally adapting itself towards more integrated water management. In terms of Hall, we witness institutional change of the second order. As a consequence of the introduction of the concept of integrated water management, new policy instruments have been developed, consensus structures have been installed, and even a framework decree for integrated water management has been adopted. All these indicate institutional changes that go beyond a limited, incremental adaptation to changing circumstances. However, we do not see a paradigmatic shift. The existing discourse of 'the battle against the water' is not replaced by the new discourse on integrated water management. In fact, both discourses co-exist. And while the first discourse is firmly rooted and institutionalised, the second one is on its way to institutionalising, although with an uncertain future.

In short, we see changes in some but not all dimensions. In the discourse dimension, it is notable that Flemish water policy has been enriched with ideas on river basin management, ecological development of river banks and so on. These ideas have incited the creation of new coalitions: between water managers, with other policy domains and with interest groups. Even though cooperation between them is not always obvious, they feel interrelated and mutually dependent, particularly since the decree on integrated water management has legally anchored cooperation in new administrative structures. In the rules of the game dimension, the new decree embedded the main principles of integrated water management, and it put new policy instruments in place. For that reason, we conclude that the new discourse has had an influence on Flemish water management regulations. The only dimension in which we do not witness much change is the 'power and resources'-dimension. Power relations turn out to be rather stable.

CONCLUSIONS

In both the Netherlands and Flanders the introduction of the concept of integrated water management has incited institutional changes, although they are stemming from a different mixture of endogenous and exogenous forces. The different ingredients of the Dutch and Flemish water policy arrangements show important alterations. In both countries we see a profound, but not paradigmatic, shift towards more integrated, ecologically inspired water management.

In the Dutch institutional context the introduction of integrated water management evolved gradually, from 1985 (*Omgaan met water*) until the present day. Although we saw pressure from both endogenous forces (the control paradox) and exogenous forces (climate change, the WFD), and triggering events such as the near-flooding of 1995, the water agencies, together with their knowledge infrastructure, have a relatively firm grip on their policy environment and are not willing to give up their hegemony in water management. They resist change in administrative structures and resource constellation. On the other hand, the gradual evolution towards integrated water management is expected to lead to new formal rules (redesign of legislation), in which integrated water management is functioning as a key concept. And we actually see changes in interaction patterns, mainly in the tendency towards decentralisation. But on the whole, considering the continuation of the existing actor constellation and its power and resources, these changes must be put in perspective. There are certainly indications of second order institutional change, in which goals and instruments are changing, but this can not be interpreted as 'paradigmatic' institutional change, in which core values and the underlying ontological discourse are at stake.

In Flanders the leading endogenous force of change is the efficiency argument, i.e. the long lasting dissatisfaction with the fragmented and poorly operating organisation in water management. We conclude that the Water Framework Directive functioned as a strong impetus that was utilised to bring the discussion on integrated water management (that already started in the early 1990s) to another stage. The efficiency discussion and the exogenous forces were melded together to create a context in which integrated water management could become a leading concept. Since the 1990s, integrated water management affected interaction patterns, the constellation of actors, and the rules of the game (new legislation, new procedures and a gradually changing political culture). But the power balance in Flemish water management stayed rather stable. As in the Netherlands, institutional changes were significant, but not paradigmatic in nature.

Considering our analysis in both countries, we come to a hypothesis on the sequence of institutional change under circumstances of shifting discourses. We hypothesize that there are different thresholds for each of the four dimensions, in such a process of institutional change. The first threshold is the problematic rising of a new, counter-storyline, opposing the existing and hegemonic discourse. The acceptance of the new discourse is, of course, easier when the ideas on the existing policy are disputed in the societal and political sphere. A second threshold is the creation of an actor-coalition that puts the new ideas into practice, with sufficient independent resources to enforce its ideas. The third threshold is anchoring the new (until then informal) policy practices into formal legislation or political rules of the game. For that matter, adding new rules is often easier than adapting existing rules, because the latter will alter the power balance to a greater extent. Changing power relations is the fourth, the last and the most difficult threshold to pass. Changes in power relations require a combination of strong counter-coalitions (that weaken existing coalitions), with strong storylines, new rules of the game, redistribution of resources and the (strategically used) help of endogenous and exogenous 'forces of change' that make policy makers susceptible for fundamental institutional change.

We think that the approach of policy arrangements and the theories of institutional change are supplementary. The policy arrangement-approach gives mainly the lexicon to describe, both precisely and comprehensively, the nature of institutional changes and can be used in combination with general propositions in institutional theory. It can also be helpful in describing the magnitude of changes, because of the differentiation of dimensions (and further differentiated in change–indicators). But it is obvious that the concepts of forces, nature and magnitude of change still need more sophistication to be part of a coherent institutional theory.

REFERENCES

Arts, B. and P. Leroy (eds.) (2003), *Verandering van politiek, vernieuwing van milieubeleid: klassieke en post-moderne arrangementen*, Nijmegen University Press, Nijmegen.

Bressers, J.Th.A., L.J. O'Toole and J.J. Richardson (eds.) (1995), *Networks for water policy: a comparative perspective*, Frank Cass, London.

Crabbé, A. and P. Leroy (2004), *Op weg naar vernieuwd lokaal waterbeleid: tussentijdse analyse en beoordeling van de ontwikkeling van waterbeheerplannen op deelbekkenniveau*, University of Antwerp, Antwerp.

Decree on Integrated Water Management (2003), published in: Belgisch Staatsblad, 14 November 2003, pp. 55038-55058.

Dicke, W. (2001), *Bridges and watersheds: a narrative analysis of water management in England, Wales and the Netherlands*, Aksant Academic Publishers, Amsterdam.

Disco, C. (2002), Remaking nature: the ecological turn in Dutch water management, *Science, technology and human values*, Vol. 27, no. 2, pp. 206-235.

Disco, C. and E. van der Vleuten (2004), Water wizards: reshaping wet nature and society, *History and technology: an international journal*, Vol. 20, no. 3, pp. 291-310.

Dudley, G. and J. Richardson (1996), Why does policy change over time? Adversarial policy communities, alternative policy arena's and British trunk roads policy 1945-95, *Journal of European Public Policy*, Vol. 3, no. 1, pp. 63-83.

Giddens, A. (1984), *The constitution of society*, Polity Press, Cambridge.

Grijns, L.C. and J. Wisserhof (1992), *Ontwikkelingen in integraal waterbeheer, verkenning van beleid, beheer en onderzoek*, Delft University Press, Delft.

Hall, P.A. (1993), Policy paradigms, social learning and the state: the case of economic policymaking in Britain, *Comparative Politics*, Vol. 25, no. 3, pp. 275-95.

Jones, T., B. Phillips, C. Williams, J. Pittock, and T. Davis (eds.) (2003), *Conserving rivers: lessons from WWF's work for integrated river basin management,* WWF, Gland, Switzerland.

Kuks, S. (2004), *Water management and institutional change*, University of Twente, Enschede.

Marsh, D. and R.A.W. Rhodes (eds.) (1992), *Policy networks in British government*, Clarendon Press, Oxford.

Meijerink, S.V. (2004), Rivierbeheer als leerproces: een tussentijdse evaluatie van het procesontwerp voor de PKB Ruimte voor de Rivier, *Bestuurswetenschappen*, Vol. 58, nr. 5, pp. 406-427.

Memorandum (2004), *Parliamentary paper 29694*, No. 1, Integratie van Waterwetgeving, Le Hague.

Ministry of Transport, Public works and water management (2000), *A different approach to water, water management policy in the 21st century*, [English version 2001] http://www.verkeerenwaterstaat.nl.

Remmelzwaal, A. and J. Vroon (2000), *Werken met water, veerkracht als strategie*, RIZA, report nr. 2000.021, Lelystad.

Sabatier, P.A. and H.C. Jenkins-Smith (eds.) (1993), *Policy change and learning: an advocacy coalition approach*, Westview Press, Boulder.

Smith, A. (2000), Policy networks and advocacy coalitions: explaining policy change and stability in UK industrial pollution policy, *Environment and Planning, Part C, Government & Policy*, Vol. 18, no. 1, pp. 95-114.

TeBrake, W.H. (2002), Taming the waterwolf: hydraulic engineering and water management in the Netherlands during the Middle Ages, *Technology and Culture*, Vol. 43, no. 3, pp. 475-499.

Van de Ven, G.P. (2004), *Man-made lowlands: history of water management and land reclamation in the Netherlands*, Matrijs, Utrecht.

Van der Ham, W. (1999), *Heersen en beheersen: rijkswaterstaat in de twintigste eeuw*, Europese Bibliotheek, Zaltbommel.

Van Leussen, W. (2002), *Leven met water, vermaatschappelijking van het waterbeheer – consequenties voor de civiel ingenieur en voor waterbeheerorganisaties*, Inaugural lecture University of Twente, Enschede.
Van Steen, P.J.M. and P.H. Pellenbarg (2004), The Netherlands in maps: water management challenges in the Netherlands, *Tijdschrift voor Economische en Sociale Geografie*, Vol. 95, no. 5, pp. 590-598.
Van Stokkom, H.T.C., A.J.M. Smits and R.S.E.W. Leuven (2005), Prospects of living with flood in the 21st century: flood defense in the Netherlands: a new era, a new approach, *Water International*, Vol. 30, no.1, pp. 76-87.
Water Framework Directive (2000/60/EC), published in: Official Journal (OJ L327), 22 December 2000.
Wiering, M.A. and P.P.J. Driessen (2001), Beyond the art of diking: interactive policy on river management in the Netherlands, *Water Policy*, Vol. 3, pp. 283-296.
Wiering, M.A. and B. Arts (forthcoming), Discursive shifts in Dutch river management: 'deep' institutional change or adaptation strategy?, *Hydrobiologia* [approved].
Wiering, M.A. and I. Immink (forthcoming), When water management meets spatial planning, a policy arrangements -perspective, *Environment and Planning, Part C* [conditionally approved].

Chapter 6

High Noon in the Low Countries: Recent Nature Policy Dynamics in the Netherlands and in Flanders

Dirk Bogaert and Jaap Gersie

INTRODUCTION

This chapter analyses nature policy in the Netherlands and Flanders based on the policy arrangement approach. The institutionalisation of the nature policy area occupies centre stage, and the chapter also looks at the most important adjacent policy areas of spatial planning and agriculture. The analysis deals in the main with national policy as far as the Netherlands is concerned, but as nature policy in federal Belgium has been more or less fully devolved to regional level since the nineteen-eighties, the discussion focuses on the administrative level of Flanders.

The start point of the analysis is 1970 and the end point is 2005 for both countries. Although both countries did have a nature policy before 1970, 1970 is generally accepted to be the beginning of a new period of government intervention with environmental issues and nature in north-western Europe (Bogaert and Leroy, 2004). In particular, the first European Year of Nature Conservation, 1970, acted as a boost to nature conservation policy in several countries in Europe. 1989 is the second key date. This year was a kind of 'High Noon' in the institutionalisation of nature policy in both countries, as it was the year in which the first nature policy plans appeared in both the Netherlands and Flanders. The publication of these policy plans coincided with a significant new element in the discourses: more and more advocates at international level for a system of nature reserves based on island theory (Gersie, 1987). It was argued that large nature reserves, possibly subject to different protection regimes, linked together by landscape elements that could function as migration corridors, would considerably increase the viability of wildlife. The creation of such networks would mean the replacement of the defensive strategy of nature protection by an offensive strategy of 'nature development'. At European level this resulted in the concept of Natura 2000, in the Netherlands it was

B. Arts and P. Leroy (eds.), Institutional Dynamics in Environmental Governance, 115–138.

developed into the National Ecological Network (EHS), and in Flanders it was developed into the Green Main Structure (GHS) and later the Flemish Ecological Network (VEN).

The main question addressed in this chapter is how the new discourses about ecological networks affected the institutionalisation of nature policy in the two countries and how, for all their similarities, the differences between the Netherlands and Flanders can be explained. It examines where these new discourses did or did not lead to the involvement of new actors, and to new resources and rules of the game. What stands out is that there really were both parallel and divergent processes of institutionalisation going on. In Flanders, for example, quite a lot of attention had been given to the issue of societal support and legitimacy since as long ago as 1989 (at least in discourses) (Bogaert, 2004). In the Netherlands, attention to winning public support for nature conservation policy started only around 2000. In conformity with the policy arrangement approach, explanations for these and other forms of convergence and divergence are sought in the interaction between the distinguished dimensions (discourses, power, actors and rules of the game), in structural developments, and in developments in and reciprocity between the two. One important structural development is the fact that in the period under consideration, Belgium evolved from a unitary to a federal state, as a result of which nature policy was pretty well fully devolved to regional level. The diverse phases of this reform of the state were accompanied by high levels of vitality in institutions, in sharp contrast with the relative institutional quietude in the Netherlands during this period. In developing its relatively new nature policy, Flanders imported policy concepts from abroad, especially from the Netherlands. The GHS and later the VEN can be seen as an example of policy transplantation (De Jong et al., 2002) and of the difficulties that are associated with copying policies in a different institutional context.

This chapter describes the institutionalisation of Dutch nature conservation policy followed by Flemish policy. These developments are then compared proceeding from the dimensions distinguished in the policy arrangement approach: discourses, power, actors and rules of the game. Finally, explanations are offered for the differences and similarities between the nature policies of the two countries.

NATURE POLICY IN THE NETHERLANDS

1970-1989

In 1970 the Dutch nature conservation movement was a small but close-knit coalition dominated by private and public owners of nature reserves. The most important private association, the Society for the Preservation of Nature in the Netherlands (NM) and a number of regional NGOs together owned about 50,000 hectares of woodland and other nature reserves at the beginning of the 1970s. The state of the Netherlands, represented by the Dutch National Forest Service, owned about 100,000 hectares, including a large proportion of the woodland in the country. These public and private actors still coordinate their purchases. In 2005, the NM and its regional partners owned 180,000 hectares and the National Forest Service had 230,000 hectares. This land, spread over the whole of the country, currently accounts for about 70% of the land given over to nature in the Netherlands (MNP, 2005) and remains to the present day an important source of power and influence for the Dutch nature conservation movement. In addition to the landowners, the arrangement around 1970 also included a number of scientific institutes, the advisory body the Council for Nature Conservation, and a small government bureaucracy for distributing grants and implementing the 1968 Nature Conservation Act.

Nature policy was given a significant boost in the 1970s as a result of increasing public concern about the quality of the environment. The nature policy discourse was made more profound with the input of ecological grounds for nature conservation. On the one hand, the loss of species was an indicator of environmental degradation; on the other hand, living nature had to be conserved in order to stabilise and clean up the damaged environment. The founding of the Netherlands Society for Nature and Environment in 1972 typified the growing coalition with the 'new' environmental movement, in which a large number of old and new actors cooperated. They took joint action against the encroachment of urban sprawl and infrastructure upon nature reserves. In addition, there was growing interest in nature and the environment outside nature reserves: wildlife-rich areas which had not yet been purchased and wildlife on agricultural land (meadow birds, agricultural wetlands, hedgerows). Here, however, the nature conservationists ran up against the boom being enjoyed by their old enemy and challenging coalition, Dutch agriculture. In 20 years (1970-1990), the Netherlands had grown to become the second agricultural superpower in the world (10% of world exports; US 14%). While it is true that a government policy document to regulate the relationship between agriculture and nature conservation (the Relationship Document) had set out detailed rules in an attempt to improve that relationship (subsidies for nature-friendly extensive agriculture: Ministries of Agriculture and Fisheries, Housing and Spatial Planning, and Culture, Recreation and Social Work, 1975), these rules were rarely used before 1990.

Nature policy at that time had few instruments of its own to work with outside the reserves. The interests of the natural world were, until 1990, represented by spatial planning and environment policy, two rapidly growing policy areas that had been incorporated into the Ministry of Housing, Spatial Planning and the Environment since 1982. The modest scale nature policy could only keep up with this development by linking up with these stronger partners. The policy area of spatial planning, in particular, led the way by being the first to introduce a system of strategic planning in the Netherlands, and to create a legal system for regional and local planning. These regulations controlled the urbanisation of the Netherlands, enabling building on many nature reserves to be prevented. Environmental policy from the 1980s onwards also developed its own planning system. Outside the nature reserves, however, even spatial planning and environmental policy were unable to stand up to agriculture and the growing power of the Ministry of Agriculture and Fisheries. Encroachment upon the nature reserves by surrounding intensive agriculture was able to continue unabated until the 1990s.

The Ministry of Housing, Spatial Planning and the Environment published the 'Structure Scheme for Nature and Landscape Conservation' in the 1980s, a national strategic plan *avant la lettre*, aimed at protecting all the remaining nature reserves in the Netherlands. This ambitious aim resulted in many regional conflicts between agriculture and nature conservation. The power of the agricultural lobby reached its maximum expression in 1982, when the Departments for Nature Conservation and Open Air Recreation were moved from the Ministry of Cultural Affairs to the Ministry of Agriculture and Fisheries. As a consequence of this transfer, the power of agriculture as the dominant policy actor in rural areas increased still further at the expense of spatial planning. Nature policy was in danger of being separated from its old coalition partners, spatial planning and environment, and swallowed up in the then neo-corporatist arrangement of agricultural policy.

The discourse of nature policy, its discursive underpinning by concepts and insights from natural sciences, also changed in the 1980s. The old discourse with its emphasis on the conservation, protection and management of separate nature reserves was supplemented by two new, related concepts: 'nature development' and 'ecological networks'. Nature development is about expanding the existing area of natural habitats. Deploying the policy of nature development mainly to expand existing nature reserves and connect them up with each other allows the creation of ecological networks which give plants and animals a better chance of survival. This change of discourse stemmed from developments in ecological sciences and, together with the organisational incorporation into agricultural policy, it led to a close-knit coalition of professional scientists and policy-makers, at the expense of relationships with actors in the nature policy field who are more influenced by social considerations.

1989-2005

Based on the new ideas about nature development and ecological networks, the Ministry of Agriculture and Fisheries (later Agriculture, Nature Management and Fisheries) published the Nature Policy Plan (1989). The adjacent policy fields also published new plans during this period, such as the National Environment Policy Plan and the Fourth Policy Document on Spatial Planning. The most important policy concept from the Nature Policy Plan was the EHS, a network of the largest, existing nature reserves, new nature development areas and corridors connecting them. With the network as goal and nature development as means, the new nature policy was presented as offensive, in contrast with the old defensive policy of conservation and protection.

The new discourse and the EHS won a lot of support in society, not only among professional conservationists but also among the political and governing classes in the Netherlands. Scientific knowledge and financial resources were mobilised successfully. Regulations were introduced to allow implementation at provincial level and government bodies with responsibilities for implementing the policy, such as the Government Service for Land and Water Management, were given more scope. Nature policy strengthened its image and acquired, through the EHS of all things, a definite place in Dutch environmental policy. Successful realisation of the EHS by 2018 seems, therefore, to be assured.

The success of the nature policy in the 1990s was not only due to a well-chosen new discourse. The point of departure was also favourable. The EHS could be achieved with established actors and under existing rules. The traditional large-scale landownership of nature conservation organisations in the Netherlands was an important resource, as the greater part of the 700,000 hectares destined for the EHS consisted of land already protected to a greater or lesser degree by nature conservation measures.

The implementation of the EHS also benefited from the weakening of two competing policy fields: spatial planning and agriculture. As explained earlier, the incorporation of nature conservation into the Ministry of Agriculture and Fisheries from 1982 resulted in spatial planning losing power in rural areas. However, the position of spatial planning weakened generally in the 1990s due to the rise of internal, strategic planning in various policy areas: water, traffic and transport, environment and economy. Conflicts between these areas were frequently settled between themselves without the intervention of spatial planning. The EHS itself, being a compromise between agriculture and nature conservation, is a typical example of this.

Although taking over nature conservation policy may have given the Ministry of Agriculture, Nature Management and Fisheries an even stronger position in rural areas, agriculture, which had been so dominant up until the end of the 1980s started to decline from that time (Van Tatenhove, 1993). Due to the incorporation of nature policy, the Ministry could no longer focus exclusively on agriculture, but had to serve more general public ends and come up with its own solutions for the agriculture-nature question. The economic and institutional power of agriculture also decreased in the 1990s, as a result of the gradual reduction in the considerable EU support and problems with manure, animal welfare and animal disease.

Despite these favourable circumstances, problems arose with implementing the EHS policy in the 1990s. Rising land prices made it difficult to purchase as much land for nature conservation purposes as was originally intended, and the land that was eventually bought was still highly fragmented. It proved difficult to realise the aim of large connected areas, partly because agriculture had insisted on the sale of farm land being voluntary. There was no funding available to purchase the connecting corridors, and other instruments turned out to be too weak to make these zones happen. Furthermore, the agricultural lobby at regional and local level tried to drive back the scale of the proposed nature development areas (Horlings and Gersie, 1995) and also to limit the number of hectares given over to farming for nature management, partly because this scheme caused the land price to fall. They failed to cooperate by entering into voluntary management contracts with the government and nature conservation organisations as much as had been hoped. In short, the Dutch nature policy came up against the limits of its capacity. On the one hand, agriculture turned out to be a more powerful lobby than expected; on the other hand, the funding and instruments for nature conservation policy were insufficient to bring the offensive strategy to a successful outcome.

Since 1995, diligent efforts have been made to find solutions. A new national policy document, 'Nature for People, People for Nature' (Ministry of Agriculture, Nature Management and Fisheries, 2001) presented two new strategies. The first involved strengthening the network philosophy of the EHS, the second involved winning and developing public involvement and interest in nature policy.

The new EHS strategy meant that extra efforts would be made to tackle the still fragmented national nature network. Purchasing would now be concentrated in the Large Units, areas of the EHS with the largest and most concentrated fragments of natural habitats. The policy has been to link these large units together with a number of what are known as robust corridors, new corridors that are broader and longer than their predecessors under the Nature Policy Plan. It was accepted that these robust zones could only be achieved by purchasing land, which meant an extra claim on the limited financial resources available.

It was also recognised that the gradual 'scientification' of the policy's discourse and content, and the increasing professionalisation of the pursuit of policy had resulted in nature policy becoming isolated from the general public. Nature policy in the Netherlands was confined to government actors and resources. Apart from the traditional nature conservation organisations, ordinary citizens and market parties felt little involvement in and responsibility for nature. As a result, nature policy has been vulnerable to political change and cut-backs in government spending. The strategy of winning public involvement and interest aimed at boosting political support and consistent input of government funding. In particular, non-government actors were to be asked to take on part of the responsibility for the conservation and development of nature and to make a financial contribution to this (Leroy and Gersie, 2004).

Up to now both the attempts to strengthen the EHS and the attempts to win public support for nature have had little success. The forging of new coalitions with social organisations and market parties has been more difficult than anticipated. Despite projects targeting health care, recreation and tourism and the building industry, all of which have something to gain from a high-quality natural environment, it has proved to be difficult to get these parties to put in their own resources. Studies of what all kinds of groups in society (city dwellers, children, ethnic minorities) want in terms of the natural environment has not up to now brought the strongly science-biased EHS discourse any closer to the people.

At the same time, the imminent loss of political support and financial resources has become reality. In 2002, the new government, a coalition of Christian Democrats and Liberals, blocked all grants for the purchase of nature reserves, something which had not been done since the Second World War. While it is true that the measure was reversed a year later, the intended economies were still largely achieved by the decision not to purchase 50,000 hectares of farmland for wildlife management but to leave the farmers to manage it themselves. In the spring of 2005, the Dutch parliament passed motions to investigate whether the planned robust corridors really did need so much new land to be purchased and so much extra government money.

Urged on by a number of active Dutch NGOs working for nature conservation, the European Birds and Habitats Directives were implemented in the Netherlands from the end of the 1990s. The Dutch found that EU nature policy was stricter than what they were accustomed to. Several building and infrastructure projects were halted, not so much due to the possible extinction of plants and animals but because procedures had not been followed correctly. There was some consternation at first among road builders and the leisure industry ('the Netherlands is closing down') but society seems to be learning fast how to live with the EU nature policy. An important factor is that the land to be designated as Special Protection Zones (SPZs) is often land that already enjoys protected status under national nature policy.

An opportune institutional starting position and accommodating social developments in the 1990s allowed Dutch nature policy to realise some of its objectives from 1989. With an attractive discourse, a limited number of actors who are on the same wavelength and tried and tested regulations, the best possible use has been made of the public resources mobilised to safeguard much of the remaining natural habitat in the Netherlands. In 2005 this arrangement seems to have reached the limits of its steering capacity. The EHS discourse is showing signs of wear, partly because it is still an uphill battle establishing the planned network. Government support can no longer be taken for granted, new coalitions are difficult to get off the ground and extra resources are hard to obtain.

NATURE POLICY IN FLANDERS

1970-1989

The origins of nature conservation policy in Flanders can be traced back to the mid-19th century, with antecedents going even further back in time (Ponting, 1992; Van der Windt, 1995; Van Hoorick, 2000). It was only in the latter decades of the 20th century, however, that government started to develop policy to protect nature and the landscape. Before 1970, nature reserves comprised only a few small projects, and in the early 1970s there were only 3.600 hectares given over to nature reserves (Noirfalise et al., 1970), and 5.238 hectares in 1988 (Kuijken et al., 2001). These figures have to be compared with the 28,059 hectares (or 2.1% of the territory of Flanders) in 2004 (Dumortier et al., 2005) and with the Dutch figures (50.000 hectares already in the 1970s, as stated above).

Nature conservation policy in Belgium was given an important boost in 1970 when the Council of Europe designated that year as the first European Year of Nature Conservation. Diverse actors – nature conservation societies, scientists and some government departments – started at that time to focus on the precarious state of the natural environment in Flanders and have maintained that interest since then. This coalition, mainly comprising nature conservationists and scientists, tried to get nature onto the policy agenda, resulting in 1973 in the Belgian Nature Conservation Act. While this Act has been a milestone in the development of nature conservation as a policy sector, it was not enough to counteract the degeneration of nature and landscape in Flanders. This was partly due to inadequacies in putting the law into operation and the failure of implementation decrees to materialise for a long time.

Regional autonomy gave nature policy another boost, when the powers relating to nature conservation were pretty well fully devolved to regional level. Flanders not only got its own Minister for the Environment (including nature), but also its own Department of Spatial Planning and Environment and its own advisory bodies (including the Flemish Council for the Environment, the Flemish Advisory Council for Forestry and the Flemish Advisory Council for Nature Conservation). In addition to this, the Institute for Nature Conservation was set up in 1985 to carry out scientific research. The powers relating to nature conservation were entrusted to the Flemish Minister for the Environment, while agriculture policy remained almost entirely in the hands of the federal government until 2001. This not only implied a significant transfer of powers from the federal to the Flemish policy level but also the uncoupling of nature conservation policy and agriculture policy.

The period from 1970 to 1989 was therefore characterised by the early stages of institutionalisation: the Nature Conservation Act had introduced sector-specific rules of the game, which was now gradually followed up by policy preparation, consulting, implementation and scientific underpinning. The protection of nature and the landscape developed as a policy sector in this period. The fact that it was a sectoral policy in the main was due both to the administrative context in which this institutionalisation took place and the dominant discourses about nature conservation at that time. The administrative context in this period was characterised by policy areas developing side by side and, as in the Netherlands, spatial planning and environment policy developed in parallel in Flanders. The fact that nature policy also developed as a sectoral policy was therefore typical of that time. In addition, a discourse in which 'nature' was treated as an independent policy area was dominant during this period. Important shifts had taken place in that discourse in earlier decades from a mainly visual approach to an ecosystem approach, and from protection of nature and the landscape to management and care of natural habitats and landscape. Nevertheless, nature policy in Flanders, as elsewhere, remained solely bent on nature conservation in the strict sense for a long time (Van der Windt, 1995; Van Hoorick, 2000). Until the mid-1980s, the protection of species and nature reserves prevailed over a more holistic vision incorporating concern for, for instance, the quality of the environment and spatial planning.

Gradually the same new scientific insights and international developments that had inspired nature conservation policy in the Netherlands also penetrated Flanders. Because both the quality and quantity of natural environments had degenerated further in Flanders, conservationists and scientists pressed for a stronger nature conservation policy. The earlier shift in discourse from protection of nature and the landscape from protection of nature and the landscape to management and care of natural habitats and landscape was not enough for an effective nature policy. Nature policy needed a 'more offensive' approach, summed up by the term 'nature development'. This discourse was fed not only by scientific insights (island theory, see section above), but equally by international developments. Frequent reference was made to examples abroad, where nature development had been put into practice successfully. The examples cited most frequently were the Oostvaardersplassen and the Stork Plan in the Netherlands. Flemish policy-makers were also advised that these new ideas from abroad had also been translated into various inspiring policy documents, not least the Dutch Nature Policy Plan (Ministry of Agriculture, Nature Management and Fisheries, 1989). Developments in international nature policy also offered opportunities for embedding in cross-border networks. The 1971 Ramsar Convention and the Birds Directive (79/409/EEC) were cited as examples. Changing European agriculture policy (Regulation 797/85; Regulation 1760/87) also offered important prospects for nature development.

1989-2005

Spurred on by the NGO *Natuurreservaten* (now: *Natuurpunt*) and a number of scientists, the concept of 'nature development' was adopted in the first Flemish policy plans: the MINA-2000 plan (Kelchtermans, 1989) and the more extensive Environmental Policy and Nature Development Plan (Kelchtermans, 1990). This represented a discursive turn in Flanders away from a policy that tended to emphasise preservation (nature conservation) to a more offensive policy for nature (nature development). As mentioned, the policy plans were inspired to a great extent by the Dutch Nature Policy Plan. Flemish nature policy is self-evidently copied from Dutch policy, both in its definition of the problems and in the approaches to a solution. The network idea, for example, was translated in Flanders by analogy with the Dutch EHS into the concept of the Green Core Structure (GHS).

In Flanders this new discourse also resulted in shifts in resources, rules and actors. Many new instruments appeared within a short period of time and were sometimes uncoordinated. For example, in addition to the GHS, Municipal Nature Development Plans, Ecological Action Areas and Regional Landscapes were launched as policy instruments. That mobilised enthusiasm and led to new forms of cooperation. However, the new instruments also had their problems: as they usually remained informal and without legal foundation, they contributed to the growing legal uncertainty. To the extent that they called upon local authorities to act, they led to questions about competence and to capacity problems. Furthermore, as new actors became involved (farmers, landowners, anglers, holiday-makers, guardians of culture and others), nature policy got involved in new and sometimes competing discourses.

The first Flemish policy plans not only involved innovative ideas on the concept of 'nature development', but also emphasised (at least at the level of discourse) the concept of 'societal support'. As nature policy became increasingly institutionalised, that concept, unlike 'nature development', failed to be translated into resources or rules to any significant extent if at all, and later interest in it waned. This is a paradox, because since the launch of the GHS more and more people had been confronted with the consequences of the (still often sectoral) nature policy.

Realisation of the GHS got bogged down due to lack of coordination with the new rules of the game and constraints that could be traced back to the adjacent policy area of agriculture. Against the background of economic trends on the one hand – an international and European debate about the future of agriculture focused on the GATT negotiations – and stricter environmental regulations for agriculture partly imposed by Europe on the other hand, the manure problem was critical in Flanders. A great deal of social and political turmoil, and lengthy negotiations mainly between farmers' representatives and representatives of nature conservation organisations ultimately led to the Manure Decree and the Manure Action Plan. Disagreement still remained on three essential points: the standards for fertilisation – and therefore: for manure spreading , the site specific tightening up of those standards, and the control of this manure spreading. It was no accident that all three clashed head-on with the offensive strategy of the nature policy. A coalition of farmers and sympathetic politicians challenged the supporting coalition of scientists and nature conservationists and opposed the GHS, especially the spatial and ecological claims being made for it. This heralded in a turbulent period, in which the agricultural sector opted for conflict and some even resorted to violence at local level. That resulted initially in the postponement of the GHS, on the grounds that the new policy plan for spatial planning (the Flanders Structure Plan) would weigh up the pros and cons of the GHS, as a sector plan for nature policy, alongside other sector plans. In the end though the GHS disappeared from the policy agenda. At the same time, new international obligations on nature conservation policy were imposed upon Flanders by, for instance, the Habitats Directive. The GHS may have been allowed to disappear because of lack of support but the idea of ecological networks still had to stay on the agenda in Flanders in view of Natura 2000.

In the second half of the 1990s, various new formal rules of the game in and in connection with Flemish nature policy came into existence. Three of these are crucially important: the Decree on the General Provisions regarding Environmental Policy, the Flanders Spatial Structure Plan and the new Nature Decree. The Decree on the General Provisions regarding Environmental Policy introduced a more systematic and integrated policy on nature and the environment, with reporting on nature and nature policy planning. The new Environment Policy Plan, the MINA-plan 2, the Flanders Structure Plan and, of course, the Nature Decree all provided for a statutory and structured embedding for the 'natural structure', now called the Flemish Ecological Network (VEN), the equivalent of the former GHS. Despite the promised integration, policy was still formed along two separate lines: the Nature Decree for nature policy, and the Flanders Structure Plan for spatial planning. Coordination between the two was poor, as became clear from the different terminology and planning horizons. This led to growing legal uncertainty among the various actors from the start, especially among those actors who felt they had been excluded from the consultations on the Nature Decree, which had only involved two groups, nature conservation organisations and agricultural organisations. A new coalition, made up of owners and residents of homes located in areas not designated as residential, such as nature reserves, residents of weekend homes, anglers and hunters, was formed to challenge the policy.

Just as poor coordination between nature and agriculture policy had led to conflict around the GHS at an earlier date, similar problems between nature policy and spatial planning now created serious problems for the implementation of nature policy, in this case the VEN, and for winning public support. Once again, nature policy seemed to be ill-equipped to deal with conflicts with neighbouring policy areas. After much debate, two important aspects of nature policy were eventually modified in a political agreement in the Flemish government (summer 2002). First, spatial planning was officially given precedence over nature policy: demarcation of the VEN (1st phase) was only possible within the 'green areas' already designated within the Flanders Structure Plan. Second, the rules of the game for participation were significantly changed. A classic public enquiry would define all the planning areas (including the green areas) for the 1st phase of VEN. This thwarted earlier, more ambitious forms of participation, and delayed decision-making and implementation (Leroy and Bogaert, 2004).

The objections submitted to the public enquiry on the VEN bore witness to the mobilisation of organised resistance. This culminated, in May 2003, one week before the federal parliamentary elections, in an anti-VEN demonstration, organised by a special coalition of anglers, hunters, property owners and farmers. Even though the VEN is a Flemish matter, and so did not formally have anything to do with the federal elections, the timing of the demonstration was chosen to have maximum strategic effect. The Green Party lost all its members of parliament in one fell swoop at the elections, including the Minister for the Environment and Nature. One year later, with a new name, it would just survive in the Flemish elections. In the new Flemish government, the environment and agriculture portfolio went to the Christian Democrats (CD&V), while spatial planning remained with the Liberal Party (VLD).

If the policy remains unchanged, it will be impossible to achieve the objectives of VEN, either in terms of surface area or quality objectives (Dumortier et al., 2005). Furthermore, the new government has scaled down the increase in human and financial resources for nature policy (2005). It was precisely this increase in resources from the late 1990s that resulted in the professionalisation and strengthening of the nature policy of government and NGOs, and the expansion of the area of land managed for nature. In the year 2005 Flanders is still far from achieving a connected ecological network.

NATURE POLICY IN THE LOW COUNTRIES: LOOKING THROUGH THE TETRAHEDRON

For our comparison of developments in and around Dutch and Flemish nature policy, we used the approach outlined by Liefferink in chapter 3 of this book. This approach examines the four corners of the tetrahedron, which symbolise the interrelationships between the four dimensions of a policy arrangement. Taking each dimension in turn as a starting point, we focus on its relationships with the other three dimensions. We look at discourses first, because the crux of our analysis is the different effect of a largely similar discursive High Noon. We then go on to analyse the perspectives of actors, rules of the game and resources. Finally, we present our conclusions based on this four dimensional analysis.

Discourses

The 1970s saw a revival of discourses about the relationships between nature, the environment and society in both Flanders and the Netherlands. Increasing concern about nature and the environment led to interest in the extinction of species, which was connected with the ecosystem approach stemming from the then rapidly developing science of ecology. Environmental and nature conservation organisations attempted to exploit this increasing concern and knowledge to get the authorities to pay more attention to nature. The governance discourse of that time also reserved a prominent role for government. Right into the 1980s the dominant discourse in the Netherlands and Flanders aimed at protecting species and land by safeguarding reserves.

There were nevertheless important differences between the two countries. The Flemish arrangement developed in isolation until 1989 and this contributed to the stabilisation of this traditional nature conservation discourse, whereas the Dutch arrangement was developing in closer association with society 'outside the reserves'. In the conflict with agriculture and the coalition with spatial planning, a more holistic discourse developed which included concern for the quality of the environment and nature outside nature reserves. An example of this is the introduction of the management of agricultural land for nature through the Relationship Document (Ministries of Agriculture and Fisheries, Housing and Spatial

Planning, and Culture, Recreation and Social Work, 1975). Despite the fact that these regulations were rarely used until the 1990s, they still helped to focus attention on the poor quality of the environment and nature in and around agricultural areas. Conservation and protection were of little use in these areas, the poor situation demanded targeted intervention to restore old qualities or create new ones.

This is where the idea of ecological restoration came from (Londo, 1997; Van Andel and Grootjans, 2006), which would also be used within reserves to counter encroachment. During the 1980s, partly under the influence of views of nature coming from international nature conservation organisations (such as WWF), a more extreme variant of nature restoration, called 'nature development' emerged. It referred to the retreat from large areas of existing land use, especially farmland, to allow the development of a genuine wilderness with minimal intervention.

Although the Flemish guise of 'nature development' was less 'wild' than the Dutch one, it was mainly this kind of 'new nature'-discourse that lent both the Dutch and Flemish nature policy plans of 1989, the High Noon, their offensive image. In combination with thinking about ecological networks and the idea of a national (regional in Flanders) green infrastructure, the age of merely protecting fragments of natural habitat seemed to belong to the past. Both plans presented a connected network, that does better in a 'national plan' than a collection of fragmented nature reserves.

For all the points of agreement, partly connected with the copying of Dutch ideas by Flanders, the different effects of the plans (support in the Netherlands, conflict in Flanders) also have discursive roots. The offensive nature development presented affected less than 10% of the EHS area in the Netherlands, as the greater part of the EHS, 60%, consisted of areas of natural beauty or wildlife habitats that were already protected by ownership or other instruments. Improving the quality of wildlife and habitats in existing nature reserves, agricultural land managed for nature, and connecting zones, was not presented as nature development. At first there were not even any targets for the number of hectares for the new connecting zones. The fact that the EHS was the culmination of a traditional Dutch discourse of spatial separation of agriculture and nature in a rough mosaic of monofunctional land use also played a role in its development and public acceptance.

That contrasted sharply with the fine-scaled interweaving of urban areas, agriculture and natural habitats in Flanders. Furthermore, whereas farmers and other land-users in the Netherlands had little to fear from the EHS, this was not the case at all in Flanders. 40% of the GHS was land for nature development and 30% was land for connecting corridors. Of the remaining 30% of core nature territory, only part was actually being managed as nature reserves. In other words, the GHS was much more offensive, and for many rural land users was their first acquaintance with possible restrictions for the sake of nature. That, together with the lack of cohesion between policy and regulations *and* the interwoven land use, explains the enormous resistance.

Recent discursive developments in both the Netherlands and Flanders mainly concern the governance discourse. In an age of redefinition of the state's role, resulting in its decreasing role in some domains, in the liberalisation of some formerly public domains etc., there are concerns in both countries about the future of government aid and support for nature. In Flanders this concerns the debate about societal support that has been going on since the early years of the GHS, which bore witness to an early awareness of its weak position. In the Netherlands, because of the consensus in the early years, this awareness only came later, when implementation of the EHS stagnated and cutbacks and loss of political legitimacy threatened. It proved difficult, however, to develop a discourse that appealed to the new actors. In the Netherlands, it may be possible to explain the problems around recruiting support in part by the fact that requests to become involved were almost always coupled with requests for financial contributions. However, neither country has succeeded in developing a discourse that links the scientific discourse of ecological networks with the discourse of the new actors. What may be needed here is an expansion of the images of nature deployed in nature policy, with less emphasis on cognitive, mainly scientific, aspects and more emphasis on ethical and aesthetic aspects (Keulartz et al., 2000; Swart et al., 2001).

Actors

The nature policy arrangement is very much dominated by a small number of actors in both the Netherlands and in Flanders. The main support for the arrangement comes from the competent government bodies and NGOs, the Netherlands' *Natuurmonumenten* and the Flemish *Natuurpunt.* Driven on by a relatively strong discourse coalition, land purchase was used much earlier in the Netherlands than in Flanders, with the government providing the resources in the form of grants to the societies purchasing the land. In this way a resource-driven interdependence between the two actors was created.

The way in which consultation between government and NGOs is arranged gives the nature policy arrangement a closed neo-corporatist character in both countries (Liefferink, this volume). There is little active involvement of other actors. In the Netherlands this has led to the realisation that further development of the nature arrangement requires greater societal involvement and public support, which implies a search (with little success up to now) for engagement from new actors from the leisure industry, from health care and elsewhere. In Flanders the closed character of the nature policy arrangement has led to consecutive conflicts with two adjacent policy areas: agriculture and spatial planning. At two occasions agencies from these fields enter the nature policy arrangement, but they do so in a defensive way, provoked as they are to defend themselves against what they perceive as a threat to their particular interests. The disparity in the speed of institutionalisation of nature policy, 10 years in Flanders versus decades in the Netherlands, is one explanatory factor for the uneasy way Flanders deals with outsiders. The difference in scale of the private interests that feel threatened, due to differences in land use patterns, is without doubt a second. Furthermore, these two factors are connected: in view of the long-running institutionalisation of Dutch nature policy, 'nature development' was mainly introduced as a strategic concept; in the younger Flemish nature policy, 'nature development' was mainly an agenda-setting – and therefore provocative – concept. That also explains why the Dutch EHS was able to be implemented in reasonable harmony with spatial planning, while Flemish spatial planning put up a set of game rules to oppose first the GHS and then the VEN. In Flanders, various actors felt threatened by the nature policy, by their lack of involvement, the speed with which the policy was introduced, and especially by its extraordinary and offensive spatial claims. That produced a coalition of opponents, not unlike the Countryside Alliance in England. While the Dutch EHS fulfilled a peace-making role between traditional, part waning, interests, the Flemish GHS and VEN led to conflicts between many established and one new and offensive spatial interest.

Rules of the Game

An important difference between the institutionalisation of nature policy in the Netherlands and Flanders is the time aspect. In the Netherlands, institutionalisation has been gradual over decades, in Flanders it has been an explosive process over a short period of time. While the respective policy documents from 1989 did indeed mean that the new discourses on nature policy and nature development were translated into policy in both countries, with their associated rules of the game (and resources, see next section), the significance of that High Noon of 1989 was very different in the two countries. This is because in the Netherlands it was mainly about consolidating and reinforcing existing rules of the game. Hardly any new rules of the game were introduced and they were, at most, concentrated within the EHS. Outside the EHS, farmers were largely free of the restrictive rules of the nature policy. Despite the offensive image of the EHS, in terms of rules of the game it is in fact a defensive policy concept, as the restrictive nature policy has been pulled out of other parts of the country and concentrated in the EHS, as a last green bastion. Viewed in this way, the EHS is still mainly a peace-making instrument for keeping nature and agriculture in their own separate zones in the Netherlands.

In Flanders, however, the new policy plan implied the introduction of many new rules of the game. The initial lack of an adequate legal basis for at least some of them, and the lack of clarity and complicated nature of others, created a perception of legal uncertainty. Herein lies an important difference with the Netherlands, where the EHS was more clearly delineated spatially, and was also guided by longstanding familiar rules of the game. By concentrating these rules within the EHS and withdrawing them from the rest of the country, the EHS in the Netherlands actually contributed to the removal of legal uncertainty.

In both countries it became more and more difficult to use the classic game rule in nature policy, land purchase, because of rising land prices and constant pressure on land. At the same time, people were increasingly realising that other rules of the game, such as delineation of areas as protected for nature and management agreements were not powerful enough to really protect nature. In Flanders especially, there were discrepancies between the rules of the game of the young policy area of nature conservation and those of the adjacent areas of agriculture and spatial planning. It was not only these discrepancies that provoked problems, but also the fact that the ambitious game rules of nature policy were prepared with little transparent consultation.

This difference in levels of tension had also partly to do with the different speeds with which the rules of the game were developed and introduced. In the Netherlands, the rules governing the relationship with agriculture had been laid down for the most part in the Relationship Document of 1975. In Flanders, this relationship was only addressed for the first time after 1990, with the Manure Decree and the Manure Action Plan.

Finally, both countries were affected by the fact that international rules of the game are increasingly becoming the benchmarks and mandatory. Europe is playing an important role in this. The Birds and Habitats Directives, for instance, require Member States to designate special protection zones. These measures have compelled both countries to revise not only their own laws on nature conservation but also their compliance and enforcement. However, the accumulation of measures has meant that the European rules have tended to offer additional rather than new protection for many valuable natural assets. All the same, NGOs especially are increasingly seizing upon these European rules to alert their national governments to their international obligations. In both the Netherlands and Flanders this has resulted in the suspension of major infrastructure projects (port expansion, railway tracks), mainly on account of failures to follow procedures correctly. NGOs operate at both national and local levels as importers of the game rules of international nature policy, both in defining areas to be protected and in tapping into European resources (e.g. LIFE-Nature).

Resources and Power

In 1970, private landownership and government grants for the purchase of land constituted the most important basis of power for Dutch nature conservation policy. The policy domain of nature conservation and those involved have been important actors in issues of land use for decades in the Netherlands. In Flanders, on the other hand, there was no power base in the form of land and money for nature policy at that time.

In the Netherlands, financial relations with the government provided a good starting point for the development of the policy organisation and regulations during the period of accelerated institutionalisation in the 1970s. In addition to the purchase of more land and government grants, the Dutch nature arrangement strengthened its position through the rules of the game governing its relations with spatial planning and agriculture. Here too, agriculture proved itself to be a counterforce. The set of instruments for managing farmland for nature from 1975 was hardly used until the 1990s. They only started to be used when the traditional resources for agriculture, income from the sale of products on the market and EU subsidies, dried up. Because of the rules of the game developed earlier, the subsidies for managing farmland for nature could be quickly deployed as a new resource.

The discursive persuasiveness of the national policy plans of 1989 have not only their scientific basis to thank but also, as explained earlier, the suitability of the infrastructure and network concepts for developing into a strategic plan. They also turned out to be useable to strengthen the position of other actors. In the Netherlands, the Ministry of Agriculture, Nature Management and Fisheries entered the arena of national planning with the Nature Policy Plan, thereby strengthening its role as dominant policy actor in the countryside. In Flanders, the MINA-plan as the first regional environment plan certainly contributed to strengthening the new Flemish identity.

Differences in established rules of the game and available resources determined the completely different positions of Dutch and Flemish nature policies in 1989. The greater part of the Dutch EHS had already been realised with existing reserves. Tried and tested instruments were in place where the policies overlapped with spatial planning and agriculture and were ready for use. It was possible to react quickly and effectively to the reallocation of funding and land through the new EHS discourse. In Flanders, both the large areas of nature reserves and the institutional framework were absent. The land allocations for the GHS , later the VEN, therefore involved an attack on existing positions, rights and power relationships in the countryside by an as yet unthreatening, or even unknown, adversary.

Apart from these different starting positions, the dynamics in the positions of power of adjacent policy areas also played a part in determining the divergent implementation of the EHS on one side, and the GHS and VEN on the other side. By 1989, both agriculture and spatial planning were past their peak in the Netherlands. In Flanders, spatial planning was in the process of establishing a position of power in the throes of the construction of the Flemish administration. Agriculture, however, was not run at regional but at federal level, which complicated a possible dialogue between the two sectors. In fact the agricultural sector felt free to attack freely. The young and ambitious Flemish nature policy arrangement with its modest resources was no match for this.

Where there have been some successes in Flanders despite this, they have been mainly due to the classic instrument of government grants. Prosperity in the 1990s meant that there was sufficient money available in both countries. As living standards are stagnating and the government has wanted to cut back on public spending since the late 1990s, continuity of funding for nature policy has become a matter of concern. Thinking about other sources of funding, apart from the EU, has scarcely got off the ground in Flanders. In the Netherlands, while the idea of recruiting support from other societal groups has been under discussion for five years, the actors to whom appeals have been made have been unwilling to make much of a financial contribution if any to nature policy. The only party that has put itself forward in the Netherlands and Flanders, and is naturally against paying, is agriculture. Over the last few years nature policy has increasingly been funded through schemes for managing farmland for nature with money intended for the purchase of reserves. This form of societal support is certainly not what the founding fathers of this concept intended.

CONCLUSIONS

Between 1970 and 2005 nature policy developed into a recognised area of government concern in the Netherlands and Flanders. Modest but discernible nature policy arrangements came into being in both countries but there were important differences between the Dutch and Flemish arrangements in the period leading up to 1989. Dutch nature policy at that time already showed the characteristic features of an institutionalised arrangement with a tradition of resources (land, people, knowledge), rules of the game (legislation and instruments), actors and coalitions. Flemish nature policy, on the other hand, showed typical features of early institutionalisation as it had limited resources, had yet to develop rules of the game and only a few actors were involved. Flemish nature policy subsequently not only developed over a shorter period of time but in a radically changing institutional context. Regional autonomy resulted in the development of a regional Flemish nature policy alongside other Flemish policy sectors that were also developing rapidly at this time.

The area of greatest similarity in this period was the discourses employed, which were highly scientific both in their definition of the problems and in their approaches to solutions. Furthermore, only a small number of actors were actively involved in the arrangements in the two countries, resulting in closed policy arrangements with a neo-corporatist character.

An important discursive revival occurred in both arrangements in the late 1980s with the introduction of ecological networks and 'nature development'. Inspired by scientific insights, this discourse appeared to suit the new national (regional in the case of Flanders) strategies for nature policy, with the Netherlands becoming a model for Flanders. The limited steering capacity of Flanders, in terms of experience, expertise, funding and human resources, was a factor that contributed to Flanders' copying problem definitions, approaches to solutions and strategies but, of course, Flanders could not take over the institutional context, resources and rules of the game that existed in the Netherlands because of historical factors.

The national (regional) nature policy plans published in the two countries held out the prospect of consolidation (the Netherlands) or expansion (Flanders) of resources and rules of the game, heralding in a High Noon for nature policy in the Low countries. Central to both policy plans was the achievement of ecological networks: the EHS in the Netherlands and the GHS in Flanders. However, while the discourse seemed to be offensive in both countries, our analysis appears to show that this was especially true in the case of Flanders, where, unlike the Netherlands, they had yet to make a start on land purchase and the development of strategies and instruments. Partly because of this, the implementation of the EHS and the GHS proceeded very differently. In Flanders, implementation produced two crises, in the face of fierce border conflicts with adjacent policy fields of agriculture (1995) and spatial planning (1998-2001). In the Netherlands, there was support at national level and problems with implementing the policy were confined to local incidents. Institutional unrest resulting from devolution of powers to the regions in Belgium versus the relative institutional quietude in the Netherlands is one explanation. In addition, the relative power of adjacent sectors and policy fields differed markedly: strong in Flanders, in the fervour of regionalisation; on the wane in the Netherlands, mainly because of the declining power of agriculture and spatial planning. As a result of this, the implementation of nature policy was facilitated by the adjacent sectors and policy fields in the Netherlands, while those same sectors and policy fields were obstructive in Flanders. In the meantime, both the physical and institutional scope for implementing the VEN has been so restricted that it is reasonable to question whether a cohesive VEN will ever be created. In the Netherlands, the EHS has been given some space up to now, but the limits are in sight and it is debatable whether the plans as intended in 1989 can be fully implemented.

These matters have played out against the background of similar structural trends in the two countries: a worsening economy, a political culture placing a lot of emphasis on reducing state intervention and increasing the involvement of other stakeholders in society, and a social culture in which nature and the environment are no longer the greatest priority. The dominant strategic and financial role of government in nature policy is much less taken for granted and there is definitely less focus on nature. It is uncertain how nature policy arrangements will develop further in this climate, respectively to what extent larger changes in the state-market-civil society relations might affect nature policy.

REFERENCES

Bogaert, D. (2004), *Natuurbeleid in Vlaanderen, natuurontwikkeling en draagvlak als vernieuwingen?*, Dissertatie, Radboud Universiteit Nijmegen/Instituut voor Natuurbehoud, Brussel.

Bogaert, D. and P. Leroy (2004), Het Vlaamse natuurbeleid, de institutionalisering van een beleidsveld, *Landschap*, Vol. 21, nr. 4, pp. 185-198.

De Jong, M., K. Lalenis and V. Manadouh (eds.) (2002), *The theory and practice of institutional transplantation: experiences with the transfer of policy institutions*, Kluwer, Dordrecht.

Dumortier, M., L. De Bruyn, M. Hens, J. Peymen, A. Schneiders, T. Van Daele, W. Van Reeth, G. Weyemberh and E. Kuijken (2005), *Natuurrapport 2005, toestand van de natuur in Vlaanderen: cijfers voor het beleid,* mededelingen van het Instituut voor Natuurbehoud, nr. 24, Brussel.

Gersie, J. (1987), Geografie voor wilde dieren: ecologische infrastructuur en de natuurbescherming in Nederland, *Geografisch Tijdschrift*, Vol. 21, nr. 4, pp. 338-353.

Horlings, L.G. and J. Gersie (1995), Agriculture and nature in ecological networks in the Netherlands and Europe, *European Environment*, Vol. 5, pp. 7-12.

Kelchtermans, T. (1989), *MINA-plan 2000: analyse en voorstellen voor een vernieuwd Vlaams milieu- en natuurbeleid*, Ministerie Vlaamse Gemeenschap.

Kelchtermans, T. (1990), *Milieubeleidsplan en natuur-ontwikkelingsplan voor Vlaanderen*, voorstellen voor 1990-1995, Beleidsbrief, stuk 296, nr. 1 van de Vlaamse Raad, zitting 1989-1990, 14 februari 1990.

Keulartz, F.W.J., J.A.A. Swart and H.J. van der Windt (2000), *Natuurbeelden en natuurbeleid: theoretische en empirische verkenningen*, NWO Ethiek en Beleid, nr. 00/1, Den Haag.

Kuijken, E, D. Boeye, L. De Bruyn, K. De Roo, M. Dumortier, J. Peymen, A. Schneiders, D. Van Staaten and G. Weyembergh (2001), *Natuurrapport 2001, Toestand van de natuur in Vlaanderen*, Instituut voor Natuurbehoud, Brussel.

Leroy, P. and D. Bogaert (2004), Het Vlaams Ecologisch Netwerk als natuurconflict: verwarde beleidsvoering en georganiseerde hindermacht, *Landschap*, Vol. 21, nr. 4, pp. 211-224.

Leroy, P. and J. Gersie (2004), Een historisch tegendraadse ambitie: de vermaatschappelijking van de natuurbescherming in Nederland, in: G. Overbeek and S. Lijmbach (eds.), *Medeverantwoordelijkheid voor natuur*, Wageningen Academic Publishers, Wageningen, pp. 23-44.

Londo, G. (1997), *Natuurontwikkeling*, Deel 6 Bos- en Natuurbeheer in Nederland, Bakhuys Publishers, Leiden.

Milieu- en Natuurplanbureau (2005), *Natuurbalans* 2005, RIVM, Bilthoven.

Ministerie van L&V (1989), *Natuurbeleidsplan, Beleidsvoornemen,* 's-Gravenhage.

Ministeries van L&V, VRO and CRM (1975), *Nota betreffende de relatie tussen landbouw en natuur- en landschapsbehoud*, 's-Gravenhage.

Ministerie van LNV (2001), *Natuur voor mensen, mensen voor natuur*, 's-Gravenhage.

Ministerie van de Vlaamse Gemeenschap (1997), *Vlaams Milieubeleidsplan 1997-2001*, Brussel.

Noirfalise, A., J. Hublé and W. Delvingt (1970), *De natuurreservaten van België*, Ministerie van Landbouw, Bestuur van Waters en Bossen, Brussel.

Ponting, C. (1992), *Een groene geschiedenis van de wereld,* Amber, Amsterdam.

Swart, J.A.A., H.J. van der Windt and J. Keulartz (2001), Valuation of nature in conservation and restoration, *Restoration Ecology* Vol. 9, no. 2, pp. 230-238.

Van Andel, J. and A.P. Grootjans (2006), Concepts in restoration ecology, in: J. Van Andel and J. Aronson (eds.), *Restoration Ecology: the new frontier*, Blackwell Publishers, Malden/Oxford, pp. 16-28.

Van der Windt, H. J. (1995), *En dan: wat is natuur nog in dit land? Natuurbescherming in Nederland 1880-1990*, Boom, Amsterdam/Meppel.

Van Hoorick, G. (2000), *Juridische aspecten van het natuurbehoud en de landschapszorg*, Intersentia, Antwerpen-Groningen.

Van Tatenhove, J.P.M. (1993), *Milieubeleid onder dak? Beleidsvoeringprocessen in het Nederlandse milieubeleid in de periode 1970-1990, nader uitgewerkt voor de Gelderse Vallei*, Pudoc, Wageningen.

Chapter 7

Dynamics in Nature Policy Practices Across the European Union

Mariëlle van der Zouwen

INTRODUCTION

This chapter provides an analysis of change and stabilisation in nature policy practices in three areas in the European Union since the late 1980s: Yorkshire Dales (UK), Doñana (Spain) and the Veluwe (the Netherlands). In one way or the other, (part of) these areas traditionally have a formal status as designated nature sites: the Yorkshire Dales and Doñana are 'national parks', while the Veluwe is a 'national landscape'. Consequently, nature policy practices in these more 'traditional' areas are well established in terms of discourses and rulings.

Over the last decade, however, nature policy practices across Europe generally show a high degree of innovation. This basically comes down to a horizontal and a vertical development. Increasingly nature policy is a matter of interplay between actors from state, market and civil society. In many European countries, national and regional authorities or even environmental NGOs facilitate the establishment of committees or commissions of public and private parties to formulate and implement nature policy for specific areas. Furthermore, nature policy is not only formulated at national level, but also and increasingly at regional and international level. The growing influence of, for instance, the EU Birds and Habitats Directives and regional authorities on national nature policies shows that contemporary nature policy is characterised by the interplay between several governmental levels. National government increasingly has to share its role with either supra- or sub-national actors. Academics refer to the before mentioned horizontal shifts as 'governance' (e.g. Rhodes, 1997; Kooiman, 2000; Pierre, 2000) and to the vertical shifts as 'multi-level governance' (Hooghe and Marks, 2001). These two terms are my operationalisation of the concept of political modernisation.

Next to organisational trends also substantive developments occurred. In various countries as well as at the EU level concepts such as

B. Arts and P. Leroy (eds.), Institutional Dynamics in Environmental Governance, 139–159.

ecosystems and ecological networks have emerged in addition to or to replace species protection and habitat preservation policies (Bogaert and Gersie, this volume). Furthermore, next to ecological values, also functions such as recreation and agriculture are increasingly addressed in nature policy processes.

Given the before mentioned changing character of nature policy on the one hand and rather stable nature policy practices in traditional nature areas on the other, the aim of this chapter is to describe, explain and compare how nature policy practices in traditionally designated nature areas have evolved over time, and whether these practices reflect a shift towards governance and multi-level governance. Therefore, I proceed in considering nature policy practices in the Yorkshire Dales, Doñana and the Veluwe by addressing three questions:

- How can change and stabilisation in nature policy arrangements be characterised?
- How can change and stabilisation in nature policy arrangements be explained?
- To what extent do the nature policy arrangements reflect a shift towards governance and multi-level governance practices?

Before I address these three questions, the next section links the concepts of 'governance' and 'multi-level governance' to the policy arrangements approach. On the basis of these two concepts, I formulate expectations for the emergence of 'governance' and 'multi-level governance' characteristics in nature policy practices in each of the four dimensions of a policy arrangement. This enables a nuanced answer to the third question in the remainder of this chapter. After this conceptual section, two sections follow which respectively deal with the characterisation and explanation of change and stabilisation in nature policy arrangements. After that, the next section addresses the emergence of governance and multi-level governance practices in the cases. Finally, I deal with all questions in a brief and concluding manner in the last section.

GOVERNANCE AND MULTI-LEVEL GOVERNANCE

In the policy arrangement approach encompassing, structural processes are captured by the concept of political modernisation (Arts and Van Tatenhove, this volume). As stated in the introduction I operationalise this concept in terms of 'governance' and 'multi-level governance'. I opt for elaborating on these concepts, because these generally reflect the changing role of the nation state and therefore the horizontal and vertical shifts in contemporary policy processes described in the introduction.

Governance

Many scientists have pointed towards the emergence of the term 'governance' as a buzzword. Indeed, anyone who casts a first glance on governance literature is confronted with a wide variety of definitions and usages of the term, as well as with different viewpoints on the role of the state. Especially in the 1990s and beyond, the use of the term 'governance' in academic literature multiplied. Despite the exploded number of conceptions, scholars in governance literature seem to agree that there is a development towards an increasing involvement of non-governmental actors in policy making. Additionally and consequently, the boundaries between state, market and civil society become blurred, policy processes are increasingly situated outside the classical institutions of the nation state and decision making processes increasingly take place in networks in which both governmental and non-governmental actors are involved. For this study I perceive governance as a structural process which affects contemporary nature policy arrangements across the EU through:

- the blurring of boundaries between state, market and civil society (Pestman and Van Tatenhove, 1998; Van Twist, 2002);
- shifts in the locus of nature policy making towards more informal practices (Hajer, 2003);
- the emergence of network like structures in which governmental as well as non-governmental actors interact (Rhodes, 1997).

Multi-Level Governance

The example in the introduction of the increasing interplay between various governmental levels can be associated with a particular issue in the governance debate, namely that of 'multi-level governance'. This concept has been developed to study governance in the EU and specifically in the empirical field of regional policy and the structural funds. It provides an alternative to state-centric or intergovernmental approaches towards European integration. These latter approaches underline the still powerful position of the state or national government in EU policy processes (Moravcsik, 1994). Multi-level governance scholars take another stance and indicate that the concept of multi-level governance points towards the dispersion of decision making power among actors at different territorial levels (Hooghe and Marks, 2001). They also acknowledge the increasing involvement of governmental and non-governmental actors in policy processes. In that respect, multi-level governance can thus be seen as an elaboration of a specific issue within the governance debate. Concerning the emergence of multi-level governance, Hooghe and Marks (2001) indicate two specific driving forces: European integration and regionalisation. European integration has resulted in the transfer of authority from national states to EU institutions, whereas regionalisation processes have resulted in the shift of responsibility from national states to sub-national, regional and local government. The multi-level governance concept is thus directly linked with European integration, EU policy making and implementation processes. My study emphasises nature policy practices in three specific nature areas and therefore does not necessarily focus on policy making at EU level alone. Nevertheless, insights from the multi-level governance perspective are helpful as Hooghe and Marks (2001) picture distinctive characteristics of which two are relevant for this study:

- decision making power is not solely in the hands of national governments, but shared by actors at different levels;
- the interconnectedness of political arenas: actors have their playing field at different levels at the same time and they connect these levels through their interactions.

Expectations

From this brief illustration of the concepts of governance and multi-level governance we can conclude that these shifts manifests themselves in:

- blurring boundaries between state, market and civil society, as well as an increasing interconnectedness between EU, national, regional and local levels of policy making;
- shifts in the locus of nature policy making towards more informal practices;
- the emergence of network like structures in which public as well as private actors from different territorial levels interact.

In order to allow for a more detailed understanding of the emergence of governance and multi-level governance practices in nature policy, I link these governance characteristics with the four dimensions of a policy arrangement: actors and coalitions, power and influence, rules of the game and discourses (Liefferink, this volume), while formulating expectations for change. These expectations are listed in Table 7.1.

Table 7.1. Expectations for nature policy practices

Dimensions	Governance	Multi-level governance
Actors and coalitions	increase in governmental and non-governmental actors and coalitions composed of actors of governmental and non-governmental origin	increase in local, sub-national and EU actors and coalitions composed of actors from various territorial levels
Power and influence	increase in power and influence of non-governmental actors	increase in power and influence of local, sub-national and EU-actors level
	increase in actors' mobilisation of informal resources	increase in actors' mobilisation of resources from local, sub-national and EU level
Rules of the game	increase in informal and negotiable rules	increase in importance of local, sub-national and EU rules
Discourses	increase in discourses which challenge the dominant discourse	increase in discourses stemming from local, sub-national and EU-level

CHANGE AND STABILISATION CHARACTERISED

In this section I present for each case (1) the characterisation of nature policy arrangements in the three cases as well as (2) the explanation for change and stabilisation of these arrangements. For each case I describe these two issues since the late 1980s until the first years of the 21st century. I label the arrangements in terms of:

- which *actors* are playing a role: governmental actors or non-governmental actors or both; in case of both type of actors I use the term 'mixed';
- which *discourse* on nature is dominant (for instance 'ecological coherence' or 'natural beauty').

The focus on these two dimensions is a choice for coherence in the naming of the arrangements. Interviews with representatives from organisations involved in nature policy for the area and content analysis of (policy) documents and minutes of meetings provided the basic material for the empirical research. I first uncovered so-called 'turning points' in nature policy in the cases. From there I reconstructed change and stabilisation in nature policy processes in the three cases (for a further methodological account: Van der Zouwen, 2006).

Yorkshire Dales – UK

From the late 1980s and the early 1990s, I distinguish two separate policy arrangements in Yorkshire Dales' nature policy: the *governmental natural beauty arrangement* and the *governmental preservation arrangement*. The foundation for these arrangements is the presence of two dominant co-existing discourses on nature: the 'natural beauty' and the 'species and habitats preservation' discourse. These discourses institutionalised at the national level in the late 1940s, when policy for national parks and nature substantively and organisationally took shape. For the preservation of species and habitats English Nature was set up, being the national governmental nature conservation body (then named the Nature Conservancy). Policy on natural beauty (the appearance and enjoyment of the landscape) was taken up in national park policy by the National Parks Commission, predecessor of the Countryside Commission. This substantive and organisational separation is referred to as 'the great divide' (Winter 1996). The divide is reproduced in the Yorkshire Dales National Park where English Nature's local team is focusing its efforts on the preservation of species and habitats in nature reserves, while the National Park Authority deals with the protection of natural beauty. Both arrangements cover another discourse and traditionally very few contacts between actors advocating those discourses existed. Nevertheless, some similar characteristics are present in both arrangements. This is for instance clearly visible in the application of the stewardship rule in which farmers are perceived as stewards of the Dales' countryside. This rule partly stems from EU agricultural policy and provides payment to farmers by agri-environmental schemes. Both English Nature and the National Park Authority separately developed their own rules concerning these schemes.

In the *governmental natural beauty arrangement*, the National Park Authority – belonging to North Yorkshire County Council – is the dominant actor which initiates and directs activities concerning nature. Since the creation of the national park in 1954 the authority has been acting as a coalition, consisting of more or less the same actors. Since the late 1980s, seventeen out of the total number of twenty six members of the National Park Authority are regional and local authorities. Nine members are non-governmental and are participating to care for the so-called 'national interest'. In terms of power, resources and influence, the position of all members is based on the 1949 National Parks and Access to the Countryside Act and the 1972 Local Government Act. Often the 'national interest' members have connections with interest organisations, such as the Ramblers' Association, the Council for the Protection of Rural England and the Yorkshire Dales Society, and they are strong advocates of public access and nature conservation interest. Regarding financial resources, these flow from the ministry of the Environment and the North Yorkshire County Council. However, the national park was not really perceived as a priority by the latter, which had consequences for the allocated budget. The North Yorkshire County Council is clearly quite powerful, because it controls resources and constrains the National Park Authority in doing so. Another powerful position is held by the landowners, which for the greater part are farmers. They hold the key in the protection of natural beauty and their cooperation is on a voluntary basis. The rules result from the National Park Authority structure in which the members function. This means that the National Park Authority itself takes initiatives, but is restricted in their implementation by the North Yorkshire County Council. Actors outside the National Park Authority do not have direct access to decision making.

The *governmental preservation arrangement* is the realm of the national governmental nature conservation body English Nature. Its position as such in the field of the preservation of flora, fauna and the conservation of nature areas is based on formal, legal rules (for instance the 1949 National Parks and Access to the Countryside Act and the 1981 Wildlife and Countryside Act) and its scientific expertise of species and habitats. However, the few financial and personnel resources in the late 1980s and early 1990s have made English Nature a rather weak actor. Furthermore, the fact that English Nature was highly dependent on the co-operation of landowners (mostly farmers) has contributed to this formally strong, but in practice weak, position.

The great divide and juxtaposition of two arrangements were stable characteristics until the early 1990s. Factors accounting for this are the deeply institutionalised boundaries between the two arrangements, the limited budget for the elaboration and implementation of nature policy in the two arrangements, and the initial hostile attitude towards nature policy measures from landowners.

Since the 1990s, the two arrangements partially overlap. Driving forces for these dynamics are exogenous and diverse. An exogenous change concerns the emergence of the 'partnership rule' which prescribes the formation of coalitions consisting of a diversity of actors to tackle environmental problems. The introduction of this rule has flown from a number of national and international calls. At national level, organisations like English Nature and the Countryside Commission felt the need to cooperate more on rural affairs since the late 1980s. Nature is one of those issues for which these organisations saw the possibilities to tune their efforts. At global level, the 1992 Rio Summit and the Agenda 21 programme have set the scene for the involvement of local actors. Together, these national and international calls have driven the entrance of the rule of partnership in the Yorkshire Dales' nature policy. Both English Nature and the National Park Authority have implemented the rule in the area's nature policy in respectively the formulation of a Natural Area Profile and the Local Biodiversity Action Plan. Within the *governmental natural beauty arrangement*, the partnership rule has made the access for other actors than those represented in the National Park Authority easier. The same goes for the *governmental preservation arrangement*. But still, the National Park Authority or English Nature remain the initiator.

Apart from developments at global and national level, also other exogenous and endogenous changes stimulated the emergence of the partnership rule. The independence of the English National Park Authorities through the 1995 Environment Act has enforced the Yorkshire Dales National Park Authority to actively seek partnerships with others, for instance for obtaining EU funded projects. In some cases this resulted in temporary, project-driven coalitions. Furthermore, endogenous financial shortages stimulated the National Park Authority to create the Yorkshire Dales Millennium Trust. Through the trust several short term projects are carried out which practically all run through cooperation between a variety of governmental and non-governmental actors. Nature policy has thus become a more project-driven activity in which time and time again partnerships between the various actors have to be formed.

Also a discursive development occurred in the 1990s: the introduction of the 'biodiversity' discourse. It basically stems from the 1992 Rio Summit and the Convention of Biological Diversity. Developing a Natural Area Profile for the Yorkshire Dales is English Nature's way of implementing the convention. The National Park Authority did so by creating the Local Biodiversity Action Plan. This has not fundamentally changed the substance of nature policy in either arrangement. Rather, the vague term of biodiversity gave room to the two traditional discourses and acts as a bridging element between the two arrangements. The bridging potential of both the partnership rule and the biodiversity discourse have thus been very important.

Doñana – Spain

In the late 1980s there was one arrangement in the Doñana case: the *governmental protection arrangement*. It is characterised by the dominance of the Ministry of Agriculture, Fisheries and Food and formal rules on participation and responsibilities. The ministry's formal responsibility and the expertise which it had developed in the field of park management account for its dominance. Besides the ministry, also the Estación Biológica de Doñana (Biological Station of Doñana; belonging to the Ministry of Education and Science) has been able to be influential in this arrangement. Extensive scientific research and monitoring enabled the Estación to stimulate the Ministry of Agriculture, Fisheries and Food to develop a strategy on the regeneration of Doñana's hydrological system. Discursively, the ministry advocated a specific discourse which aimed at the protection of the national park area and specifically the management of the national park's water system. Therefore I termed this discourse 'territorial water management'. It got increasingly challenged at the end of the 1980s, when a coalition of WWF and the IUCN openly questioned its legitimacy claiming that it was not based on sound scientific data. Besides, the Spanish Ornithological Society had been pushing the ministry to seriously address the protection of the national park by mobilising the EU Birds Directive and issuing complaints to the European Commission. Neither actions, however, resulted in changes.

Since the late 1980s, following the devolution of nature policy competencies to the regional level, the *governmental protection arrangement* slightly changed. The creation of a regional nature park next to Doñana national park in 1989 brought the regional authority Junta de Andalucía as a new actor. Ever since, the Junta de Andalucía has challenged the dominant rules for the formal responsibility for the national park. However, its success has remained limited for many years. This lasted until 1999 when the responsibility for the national park became a joint national-regional governmental matter. This change was enforced by broad opposition from all Spanish regions to the sole reigning of the Ministry of the Environment in Spain's national parks (this ministry has been responsible for nature policy since 1996). The Constitutional Court judged in favour of the regions, which resulted in setting up of a mixed commission for each region in which national and regional authorities were jointly responsible for national parks. Despite this organisational change, the regional and national authorities were still worlds apart. When in April 1998 a disastrous mining spill occurred which polluted a large part of Doñana, both the ministry and the Junta developed their own restoration programmes and accompanying committees for 'their' parts of the Doñana area (respectively the 'Doñana 2005' and the 'Corredor Verde' project).

Since the early 1990s, a new arrangement has taken shape: the *governmental sustainability arrangement*. It is characterised by the Junta de Andalucía's efforts to develop the larger Doñana's area in a sustainable manner. Discursively, the wider Doñana area is perceived as a resource for sustainable development. While in the *governmental protection arrangement* issues like the management of the national park area were important, the struggle for the real protection of the national park took place outside this arrangement and thus also literally outside the national park's territory. The *governmental sustainability arrangement* emerged out of the intensified clashes between nature conservationists on the one hand and those aiming at the socio-economic development of the Doñana area on the other. The tension between nature conservation and socio-economic development has been an issue since the first ideas for the conservation of Doñana in the 1950s. The clash between these two interests peaked when plans for a tourist urbanisation project (Costa Doñana) were developed in the late 1980s. Additionally, the interference of the European Commission through NGOs complaints and the political momentum created by the regional elections stimulated the Junta de Andalucía to establish an international commission of experts which had to advise on the sustainable development of the Doñana area. Apart from the Junta's leading role, the arrangement is characterised by a broad coalition of actors, both governmental and non-governmental and originating from various sectors. As far as resources are concerned, the 75% EU funding for the implementation of the Sustainable Development Plan of Doñana (1993) is an important prerequisite of the existence of the arrangement.

As just noted, the mining spill initially showed that the formally institutionalised cooperation between the Junta de Andalucía and the ministry of the Environment was overshadowed by still separate organisational performance of both governmental actors. However, after the worst pollution in the area was dealt with, several changes in the *governmental protection arrangement* occurred. First, both in the Doñana 2005 and the Corredor Verde project a new discourse was introduced, addressing the larger water system and ecosystem of Doñana. For the national park and the Ministry of the Environment, this replaces the territorial water management discourse. As far as the Junta de Andalucía is concerned, the Corredor Verde project for the first time introduced a strategy for Doñana's nature policy based on an ecosystem approach. Both innovations broaden the discursive dimension of the arrangement. The mining spill has thus triggered both the Ministry and the Junta to develop new substantive strategies. In the slipstream of the discursive innovation a coalition took shape between the Junta de Andalucía and the ministry of the Environment. Not initially, but after repetitive calls for better cooperation between the two projects from (international) scientists and nature conservationists, a coordination commission was created in Autumn 2001.

Apart from these calls, the appointment of a new general coordinator for the Doñana 2005 project has also driven the coordination between the national and regional authorities. Continuing along this line, both projects also gradually involved other actors in their plans, such as environmental and nature conservation NGOs and agricultural organisations. This particularly goes for the Corredor Verde project. As far as the environmental and nature conservation NGOs are concerned, a first innovation is the re-entrance of WWF/Adena in Doñana's nature policy scene. Furthermore, the coalition between Ecologístas en Acción, SEO, WWF/Adena and temporary Greenpeace has increased NGOs' influence in Doñana's nature policy. Because of these two major changes, I now re-label the policy practices in the governmental protection arrangement as the *mixed ecosystem arrangement*. Highly important for particularly WWF/Adena's position is the budget this NGO has at its disposal. Despite these innovations, coherent nature policies for the (wider) Doñana area remain very difficult and national-regional tension are still omnipresent.

Veluwe – the Netherlands

In the late 1980s one arrangement in Veluwe nature policy existed: the *mixed landscape arrangement*. Herein, the province Gelderland acts as the directing pivot. The province advocates a 'landscape' discourse: nature is considered an integrated part of the Veluwe landscape and one of the issues which has to be addressed in Veluwe policy. The province had actively pushed itself forward right from the moment that the Ministry of Culture, Recreation and Social Work introduced its policy for national landscapes in the mid 1970s. The province had thus placed itself at the centre of the *mixed landscape arrangement* and was able to develop rules which had become rather fixed since then. Due to internal financial cut backs the ministry played a less imminent role in Veluwe policy in the course of the 1980s, while the province's role as director of the policy process was strengthened.

Right from the first steps towards a further elaboration of the national landscape idea in the late 1970s, the province tried to involve other actors in Veluwe policy. Earlier experiences with consultation regarding the first land use plan for the Veluwe, and the final dissatisfaction of local people about the limited effect of their involvement, had made the province aware of the creation of a regional coalition. Not only other governmental actors found their place within a new participatory body. Also larger private landowners and interest organisations, such as recreation entrepreneurs, agricultural, nature conservation and environmental organisations and local people, were part of this body. Furthermore, characteristic for the Veluwe is the emphasis on the participatory process and the development of consensus among the parties involved. Here, the importance of landownership as a resource comes to the fore. Actors possessing large parts of the Veluwe, like the State Forest Service, the NGO Natuurmonumenten and owners of large estates could make their own rules concerning the management of their sites. With the province lacking sufficient budget and manpower, this situation could continue to exist. This has resulted in the fragmentation of management of the Veluwe as a nature area. In fact – from a nature management perspective – the Veluwe thus consisted of a large number of properties with distinctive rules. To cope with this situation, the province Gelderland purposely put forward the rule that Veluwe nature policy was based on the *existing* natural values in the distinctive properties. Realising that cooperation from the property owners was essential for a successful national landscape policy, the province herewith confirmed the powerful position of the individual NGOs and private estate owners. This rule has prevented substantive change within the regional arrangement. Nature policy focused on the maintenance of the status quo.

Within the *mixed landscape arrangement* the focus on the landscape discourse and the participatory process continues in the first half of the 1990s. This also happens when the province's national landscape policy formally ends in 1994. It is then succeeded by policy on 'valuable cultural landscapes' of the ministry. The enlargement of the eligible Veluwe area for this new policy category hardly has any consequences regarding the substance and organisation of the policy process. Again – as was the case in the late 1980s – the limited budget available hinders changes from emerging. The province Gelderland formally remains the leading actor in the arrangement in the first half of the 1990s. This is, however, more than a continuation of the earlier practice. This role of the province now matches the trend in Dutch rural policies for more region-oriented approaches and as such this approach is thus resulting in a stabilisation of the reign of the province in the arrangement.

At the same time, a new arrangement came to light: the *governmental ecological coherence arrangement*. Informally, and outside the existing *mixed landscape arrangement*, the ministry and the province started a project on the development of an ecological vision in the early 1990s. This action was triggered by the publication of the first Dutch nature policy plan, which provided a new framework for nature policy in the Netherlands. In this plan the Veluwe is an important core area in the newly introduced Ecological Main Structure (Bogaert and Gersie, this volume). Furthermore, it is driven by the dissatisfaction among some employees of the respective organisations concerning the absence of a coherent ecological vision on the whole of the Veluwe. As the formulation of such a vision can not count on wide support, the project is implemented low-profile and informally by a coalition of employees from both organisations. Despite the low-profile and informal characteristics, at management level both the province and the ministry enforced the creation of a couple of interaction rules that had to guide the project. One of those rules is that a final ecological vision would not be an official policy document. The employees of the ministry and the province took the initiative to produce such a vision and involved a variety of actors, ranging from local authorities to private estate owners and from nature conservation NGOs to researchers. Although the project was low-profile and a final report did not have an official status, the production of the ecological vision lays the foundations for a more solid, but still informal coalition at staff level between the province and the ministry. Within this coalition, the ecological coherence discourse dominates.

After the publication of the report in 1997, the two arrangements continued to evolve separately. Media attention and positive responses from regional and local policy makers regarding the report stimulated staff members from the province to develop a plan for a more ecologically coherent Veluwe policy for each of the two arrangements. Interestingly, these staff members are the same as the ones taking part in the small *governmental ecological coherence arrangement*. The final plan, entitled Veluwe 2010, was discussed in the *mixed landscape arrangement* and perceived as a way to continue existing valuable cultural landscape policies, of which the end is in sight. When the Veluwe was designated as a rural reconstruction area, a reconstruction commission for the Veluwe was set up in February 2001. This practically is a continuation of the already existing structure under the valuable cultural landscape policy. The reconstruction commission also has the task to implement Veluwe 2010. The landscape discourse and the integrated approach towards nature in the Veluwe remain important discursive elements in this arrangement. So, apart from the change of the framework from valuable cultural landscape policy to reconstruction policy, the *mixed landscape arrangement* remains stable.

It turns out that new policy confirms the already existing substance and organisation of the arrangement.

Logically, as representatives from the province in the two arrangements partly overlap, the plan Veluwe 2010 also plays a stimulating role in the *governmental ecological coherence arrangement.* The informal interaction in the arrangement has stabilised and is further strengthened by the set up of a so-called 'Veluwe core team', consisting of an informal coalition of the ministry, the province and the NGO Natuurmonumenten and the State Forest Service (Staatsbosbeheer) which is now an independent (semi-)public body. For Natuurmonumenten, the active role it is playing in this coalition is resulting from the internal decision taken at national level to increase its involvement in Veluwe policy. Because of the increasing diversity of actors in the arrangement, I re-labelled it as the *mixed ecological coherence arrangement.* The core team remains fairly on its own in implementing the large projects designed to create an ecologically coherent Veluwe. We thus see a further institutionalisation of the new arrangement, which is characterised by the informal coalition between the province and the ministry, and later Natuurmonumenten and Staatsbosbeheer.

CHANGE AND STABILISATION EXPLAINED

The arrangements which were present in the late 1980s in the three cases have basically remained stable over the 1990s and the early 21st century. This goes for the *governmental natural beauty arrangement* and the *governmental preservation arrangement* in the Yorkshire Dales, the *governmental protection arrangement* in Doñana and the *mixed landscape arrangement* in the Veluwe. These arrangements find their origins in times long before the late 1980s. Only in Doñana, change of the *governmental protection arrangement* into the *mixed ecosystem arrangement* occurs in the late 1990s. This change is very much 'event and actor initiated'. After the 1998 mining spill, repetitive calls for better cooperation between the ministry of the Environment and the Junta de Andalucía and a new project leader for the Doñana 2005 project pushed these two governmental actors to start to organisationally and substantially develop a joint approach for Doñana's nature policy.

Changes of only part of the arrangement is a more common issue. In the case of the Yorkshire Dales the divide between the *governmental natural beauty arrangement* and the *governmental preservation arrangement* became so deeply institutionalised that a change of the two arrangements is highly unlikely. However, the introduction of the biodiversity discourse and the partnership rule, both easily fitting into each of the two arrangements, drove internal change in the two arrangements and made the two strongly institutionalised arrangements partly overlap. Apparently the National Park Authority and English Nature got themselves a new 'language' for interaction. Furthermore, the National Park Authority's functional and financial independence in 1997 and the need to cooperate with actors outside the initial arrangement for a sound financial basis opened the arrangement for other actors. The other occasion of change in an arrangement is situated in the Veluwe case, where the *mixed landscape arrangement* changed two times. When the Veluwe was designated as a valuable cultural landscape by the ministry, new actors (most notably farmers) and rules (e.g. new policy framework, namely valuable cultural landscape policy from the ministry) came in. This change took place in the context of an integration effort from the ministry and devolution of responsibilities from the national to the regional level in the field of rural and nature policy. However, since land owning actors still held their land as a powerful resource, substantive changes did not emerge. Another change of rules (again: a new policy framework) took place when the Veluwe got a new designation as reconstruction' area. Again, this did not really result in changes in other dimensions.

New arrangements turned up in both the Doñana and the Veluwe case, juxtaposed to existing ones. In Doñana the new *governmental sustainability arrangement* appeared next to the *governmental protection arrangement* in the early 1990s. This was triggered by continuous conflict between non-governmental environmental and nature organisations on the one hand and the Junta de Andalucía who also aimed at the socio-economic development of the Doñana area on the other. At the same time, the devolution process in Spain as well as the political opportunity of new elections and the publication of the advice of an international expert committee on Doñana's sustainable development provided the momentum for the new arrangement. In the Veluwe the *governmental ecological coherence arrangement* appeared next to the *mixed landscape arrangement* in the mid 1990s. It could originate from the good personal relationship between staff from the province and the ministry, both sides feeling the need to develop an ecological coherent perspective for the area. The actors in this arrangement interacted on an informal basis and did not interfere into policy processes within the traditional *mixed landscape arrangement*. In this context, they worked on ideas for a better ecological coherence of the Veluwe area and their ideas as well as their relationships with staff from other organisations could mature into a final ecological vision and a coalition with two major landowning actors (the NGO Natuurmonumenten and the State Forest Service).

The role of individuals for initiating new coalitions stands out in all cases, albeit in different points in time. In the Yorkshire Dales good personal relationships between staff from the national park and English Nature has surely contributed to the formation of coalitions over the boundaries of the *governmental natural beauty arrangement* and the *governmental protection arrangement.* For Doñana, the appointment of the coordinator for the Doñana 2005 project is a nice illustration in the *mixed ecosystem arrangement.* In the Veluwe such relationships have so far had the most far-reaching consequences, since these have contributed to the emergence of a new arrangement (first the *governmental ecological coherence arrangement* and later the *mixed coherence arrangement*).

The arrangements in the three cases are to a certain extent stable. In the Yorkshire Dales, the dominance of the natural beauty discourse on the one hand and the species and habitats preservation discourse on the other has driven this stability. In Doñana, stability of arrangements is clearly driven by governmental actors who mobilise formal rules in a fight over competences. Stability in the Veluwe seems more driven by a rather vast set of coalitions in which landowning actors are able to dominate. These findings concerning the high extent of stability, slight changes in arrangements and the emergence of new arrangements seem to comply with one of the assumptions of the policy arrangement approach that the new arrangements do not replace older ones, but rather emerge next to existing arrangements.

GOVERNANCE AND MULTI-LEVEL GOVERNANCE PRACTICES?

In the introduction of this chapter I made clear that nature policy for all case areas has existed for quite some time and therefore, no doubt, traditional characteristics like classical views on nature and the involvement of governmental actors could be recognised. To determine the extent to which governance and multi-level governance practices are emerging in these cases, which all possess a long history, I now take a closer look at the expectations I formulated earlier. There I presented expectations concerning changes in each of the four arrangement's dimensions. First, I briefly address these expectations and consequently the emergence of governance and multi-level governance practices in the three cases. For a detailed account, I again refer to Van der Zouwen (2006). After that, I deal with similarities and differences across the cases regarding governance and multi-level governance.

Emergence of Governance and Multi-Level Governance

In the Yorkshire Dales, my expectations concerning *governance* characteristics in the dimensions are partly met. Regarding actors and coalitions we see an increase in the involvement of non-governmental actors and the formation of temporary coalitions between them and the already existing actors (National Park Authority and English Nature). However, the involvement of these actors as well as their coalitions is of a temporary character. This also goes for the other dimensions. There is for example a temporary shift towards more power for local nature conservation groups, because they use their knowledge of the distribution of a certain species as input in the policy process. However, as soon as the project finishes, the chance to become permanently involved fades away. Because of the limited number of projects so far, it is hard to claim that these temporary practices are institutionalising. However, when temporary coalitions become a new mode of steering, these might very well institutionalise. The expectation concerning governance developments in the discursive dimension is not met. The existing 'natural beauty' and 'species and habitats preservation' discourses are not challenged by other discourses, but rather by one another.

Multi-level governance practices are partly present in terms of rules and resources: actors mobilise the EU stewardship rule and accompanying budget from the adjacent policy field of agriculture. This is not a new characteristic of nature policy in the Yorkshire Dales. It has been present since the late 1980s when the first agri-environmental schemes were introduced. The importance of the rule has, however, grown over the years. Multi-level characteristics are also present in the so-called partnership rule and the biodiversity discourse both stemming from the global and EU level. Thus, multi-level practices especially emerge in terms of resources, rules of the game and discourses and partly come from the adjacent EU agricultural policy field.

In Doñana a trend towards *governance* practices seems to set in, however, to date this development is very recent and only premature signs of such practices are visible. Governmental actors still dominate and have most power and actual influence. Furthermore, the use of formal rules such as legislative procedures by both governmental and non-governmental actors is an important characteristic in policy practice. In such a context, change towards governance might hardly institutionalise. Nevertheless,

WWF for instance has been able to enforce more participatory rules in both arrangements. This has increased the participation of other non-governmental actors. A discursive competition can not be discerned. Thus, recently introduced governance features can be recognised regarding all dimensions but discourses. The institutionalisation of these practices remains unsure so far.

The *multi-level governance* expectations are far more visible. In both arrangements, EU actors, rules and discourses emerged. EU nature policy has increasingly been mobilised by NGOs to enforce a better protection of the national park. The European Commission itself has also become actively involved in both arrangements, both in contributing budget for sustainable development policy and in enforcing EU nature policy in the area. In the *governmental sustainability arrangement* the regional Junta de Andalucía has successfully mobilised EU resources from the adjacent regional development policy field. Furthermore, both arrangements also show the increasing influence of the regional level of the Junta de Andalucía vis-à-vis the national ministry of the Environment.

At first sight, nature policy in the Veluwe shows clear characteristics of *governance*. In the 'mixed landscape arrangement', governmental and non-governmental actors are involved; non-governmental actors hold a rather strong position (for instance due to their possession of nature sites) and consensus and rather open access are important rules in the policy process. These governance-like characteristics have been present for a long time and reflect a typical policy making style in the Netherlands, rather than being exponents of the shift from 'government to governance'. Also, discourses are not really challenged in this case. However, the emergence of a new *mixed coherence arrangement* in itself can be regarded as challenging the existing landscape discourse. The latter arrangement is a clear example of an emerging governance practice. Here, informal rules, governmental and non-governmental actors, and informal resources such as trust and good personal relationships are important features. A shift towards more *multi-level governance* practices is not visible. Remarkably, the EU level is not part of either arrangement in terms of actors and coalitions, power and influence, rules and discourses.

Comparative Perspective

Comparing the cases regarding the emergence of governance and multi-level governance practices, the following observations stand out. First of all, governance practices slowly emerge in the Yorkshire Dales and Doñana. Governmental actors, rules, resources and accompanying discourses are strongly institutionalised here and are related to the historical background of nature policy. Therefore, challenging shifts have great difficulty in getting institutionalised. Consequently, governance practices in the Yorkshire Dales mainly emerge on a project and temporary basis.

Second, different from the Yorkshire Dales and Doñana, as a policy making style governance characteristics have traditionally been present in the Veluwe in the *mixed landscape arrangement*. Having said this, governance is thus not a new feature in Veluwe nature policy. Next to this, a new governance practice develops with the institutionalisation of the *mixed coherence arrangement*. Why could this arrangement develop itself relatively 'undisturbed'? I made clear that this was facilitated by the condition that new plans for the Veluwe had to have a non-binding status (as formulated by people from the province and the ministry at management level).

Third, multi-level governance practices emerge in the Yorkshire Dales and Doñana where domestic actors mobilise EU rules, resources and discourses. Rules and resources are mainly stemming from adjacent EU policy fields, rather than from EU nature policy. In Doñana the European Commission plays an active role. Thus, the rise of multi-level practices mainly proceeds along the lines of resources and rules from adjacent policy field at EU level. In the Veluwe multi-level governance is not clearly visible. Apparently, the long existing governance practice built by and around the province Gelderland is able to withstand that.

Fourth, domestic multi-levelness (the interplay between the national and regional/local level) appears in all cases. These processes are very much characterised by rivalry among the different governmental actors. The mobilisation of formal, legislative rules by the regional Junta de Andalucía has long characterised interactions in Doñana during the last decade. This has even led to the emergence of the *governmental sustainability arrangement* in Doñana. Devolution in Spain has driven the introduction of the regional Junta de Andalucía, resulting in a more powerful position for this actor in both the *governmental sustainability arrangement* and the *mixed ecosystem arrangement*. Next to that, the shock event of the 1998 mining spill and a new project leader for the Doñana 2005 project have also provided the basis for multi-level practices in terms of joint discourses in the *mixed ecosystem arrangement*. In the Yorkshire Dales and the Veluwe, the historical background of regional government's position in respectively the *governmental natural beauty arrangement* and the *mixed landscape arrangement* accounts for the strong position of regional authorities. The fact that domestic multi-level practices are emerging in the Yorkshire Dales is clearly a matter of interlinkages between the two existing arrangements which are either dominated by national or local governmental actors.

CONCLUSION

This chapter characterised and explained change and stabilisation in nature policy practices in the Yorkshire Dales, Doñana and the Veluwe. Furthermore, it addressed whether there has been a shift towards governance and multi-level governance characteristics. Each case shows nature policy arrangements which have been present for a long time and have largely remained stable over time. These 'traditional' arrangements are the *governmental natural beauty arrangement* and the *governmental preservation arrangement* in the Yorkshire Dales, the *governmental protection arrangement* in Doñana and the *mixed landscape arrangemen*t in the Veluwe. Consequently, contemporary practices strongly bear the stamp of earlier episodes in nature policy. At the same time, new arrangements have occurred next to the already existing ones. The analyses in these cases clearly confirm the assumptions of the policy arrangement approach concerning non-linearity and juxtaposition of traditional and new arrangements.

Change of entire nature policy arrangements hardly occurred in the three cases. Rather parts of nature policy arrangements changed over time. In Doñana and the Veluwe, new arrangements emerged. As demonstrated in one of the previous sections, such changes within arrangements as well as the rise of new arrangements can both be explained by endogenous and exogenous factors.

Governance and multi-level governance characteristics appear in all three cases. However, these only limitedly emerge in the long-standing, traditional arrangements or, as is the case in the Veluwe, have already been present for a long time.

REFERENCES

Hajer, M.A. (2003), Policy without polity? Policy analysis and the institutional void, *Policy Sciences*, Vol. 36, no. 2, pp. 175-195.

Hooghe, L. and G. Marks (2001), *Multi-level governance and European integration,* Rowman & Littlefield Publishers, Lanham.

Kooiman, J. (2000), Societal governance: levels, modes, and orders of social-political interaction, in: J. Pierre (eds.), *Debating governance: authenticity, steering, and democracy*, Oxford University Press, Oxford.

Leroy, P. and B. Arts (2003), De vernieuwing van het milieubeleid en de veranderingen in de politiek, in: B. Arts and P. Leroy (eds.), *Verandering van politiek, vernieuwing van milieubeleid*, Nijmegen University Press, Nijmegen, pp. 1-4.

Moravcsik, A. (1994), *Why the European Union strengthens the state: domestic politics and international cooperation*, Centre for European Studies Working Paper Series #52, Harvard University, Cambridge.

Pestman, P. and J.P.M. van Tatenhove (1998), Reflexieve beleidsvoering voor milieu, ruimtelijke ordening en infrastructuur? – Nieuwe initiatieven nader beschouwd, *Beleidswetenschap,* Vol. 12, nr. 3, pp. 254-272.

Pierre, J. (2000), Introduction: understanding governance, in: J. Pierre (eds.), *Debating Governance, authority, steering and democracy*, Oxford University Press, Oxford, pp. 1-10.

Rhodes, R.A.W. (1997), *Understanding governance: policy networks, governance, reflexivity and accountability*, Open University Press, Buckingham.

Van der Zouwen, M. (2006), *Nature policy between trends and traditions – dynamics of nature policy arrangements in the Yorkshire Dales, Doñana and the Veluwe*, PhD Dissertation Nijmegen University, Eburon, Delft.

Van Tatenhove, J.P.M., B. Arts and P. Leroy, (eds.) (2000), *Political modernisation and the environment: the renewal of environmental policy arrangements*, Kluwer Academic Publishers, Dordrecht.

Van Twist, M.J.W. (2002), *Dubbelspel: publiek-private samenwerking en het management van verwachtingen*, inaugurele rede Katholieke Universiteit Nijmegen, Lemma, Utrecht.

Winter, M. (1996), *Rural politics, policies for agriculture, forestry and the environment*, Routledge, London.

Chapter 8

Diffusion or Diversity in Cultural Heritage Preservation? Comparing Policy Arrangements in Norway, Arizona and the Netherlands

Sara de Boer

INTRODUCTION

This chapter involves a comparative analysis of three policy arrangements in the field of cultural heritage preservation. The aim is to analyse and explain the similarities and differences between contemporary preservation practices in different Western countries. 'Cultural heritage' could be defined as the customs, beliefs, art, way of life and social organisation that a society or group has had for many years, that are considered to be important characteristics of its culture and that it wishes to conserve and pass on to future generations (Hornby et al., 2000; Howard, 2003). In this chapter, the concept of cultural heritage only refers to the category of built heritage, which involves all spatial elements and structures that were constructed in the past and that are regarded as very valuable (Nelissen and Bogie, 2000).

Many different arguments are used for the preservation of the built heritage. It is often stated that it makes a positive contribution to our living environment and quality of life; that it provides material for research and education; that it is a source of inspiration for designers of new buildings, urban and rural landscapes; and that it generates income through recreation and tourism. Finally, many preservationists argue that some of the values of cultural heritage are absolute; that some kind of historic value is intrinsic to the whole notion of something being identified as truly old or 'authentic' (Cantacuzino and King, 1999; Clark, 2000; Mason, 2002; Nelissen and Bogie, 2000).

Nowadays, a considerable amount of cultural heritage in Western society (Europe and North-America) is being preserved by governmental actors. In most Western countries however, the very first initiatives to

B. Arts and P. Leroy (eds.), Institutional Dynamics in Environmental Governance, 161–181.

preserve cultural heritage typically came from the side of the intellectual elite. Only in the late 19th and early 20th centuries, governmental bodies were established with the explicit task of preserving the national heritage. Their work mainly consisted of listing significant historic buildings and protecting them through newly created preservation laws (Howard, 2003; Tyler, 2000). Today, most preservation policies are based on more or less similar principles and ideas such as: the obligation to perform research and documentation in order to generate and safeguard knowledge; the obligation to respect cultural heritage as a physical record of human activity; the obligation to safeguard the authenticity of historic buildings and sites; and the obligation to do no harm (Maturo, 2000). At the same time, current preservation practices still vary greatly: from minimal interventions and conservative repairs to artistic restorations and extensive adaptations according to the fashion of modern life (Jokilehto, 1999; Maturo, 2000).

Moreover, policy practices in the field of cultural heritage preservation are continually changing. At present, there appears to be a general trend that preservation policies are becoming broader in scope. Preservationists are moving away from the idea of designating individual sites to the idea that the whole of the landscape may have significance. Accordingly, cultural heritage preservation is becoming increasingly integrated with policy fields such as land use planning, urban renewal and nature management. Furthermore, although preserving the national heritage remains an important policy goal, many preservationists argue that in our age of globalisation, it should be complemented by efforts to safeguard regional and local distinctiveness. Consequently, local and regional heritage is receiving more attention and preservation tasks are being decentralised to local and regional government levels. Finally, there is a growing variety as to the policy actors that are involved in cultural heritage preservation. In many Western countries, the role of non-governmental organisations, historic property owners and private property developers in developing and implementing preservation policies is increasing (Cantacuzino and King, 1999; Clark, 2000; Goverde, 2000; Howard, 2003).

In order to analyse the similarities and differences between current preservation practices in Western society, I will compare three different policy arrangements in the field of cultural heritage preservation: the contemporary arrangements in Norway, the Netherlands and Arizona (since preservation arrangements differ considerably from state to state in the US, I concentrate on one of them and I can therefore not draw general conclusions). In accordance with the policy arrangements approach, the arrangements in Norway, Arizona and the Netherlands are analysed as the temporary stabilisations of the organisation and substance of cultural heritage preservation at national or state level.

The comparison between the three preservation arrangements is based on two hypotheses. On the one hand, these three policy arrangements have developed within very different historical, social-political and geographical contexts, which has led to the emergence of divergent policy discourses and policy practices. In this perspective, policy arrangements are interpreted as contingent responses to specific circumstances and specific policy processes. At the same time, I am fascinated by the question whether the three policy arrangements are increasingly growing alike along the lines of general developments that are taking place in the field of cultural heritage preservation. Accordingly, I will explore the extent to which a process of policy diffusion is proceeding and I will examine the factors that either stimulate or restrain this process in the three policy arrangements under study.

In summary, this chapter analyses and explains the similarities and differences between three different policy arrangements in the field of cultural heritage preservation against the background of (a) the specific contexts in which the policy arrangements have been (re)produced and (b) the process of policy diffusion that may be taking place. However, before I will analyse the three different policy arrangements, two different phases of cultural heritage preservation will be described. Furthermore, I will clarify my interpretation of the concepts 'policy discourses' and 'policy diffusion' and some remarks will be made on the applied research methodology.

TWO PHASES OF CULTURAL HERITAGE PRESERVATION

In the field of cultural heritage preservation, I distinguish two phases, characterised by specific connections between state, market and civil actors and specific discourses on cultural heritage issues (see Table 8.1). In the early phase of cultural heritage preservation, cultural heritage is mainly seen as a source of national pride and unity. It is valued for being historic, beautiful and/or created by a great artist. The focus in this phase of cultural heritage preservation is on protecting individual historic buildings or sites against unwanted developments. The predominant type of governance involves hierarchical steering by the central government. The state is responsible for selecting and preserving the national heritage. Civil society, typically in the form of a social-political and cultural elite, plays an agenda-setting role by promoting the protection of historic buildings and sites and by encouraging the government to make a greater effort. Market actors play no role of significance in this early phase of cultural heritage preservation.

Table 8.1. The two phases of cultural heritage preservation

Phase / Characteristic	Early phase	Late phase
Definition of cultural heritage	Objects that are historic, beautiful and/or created by great artist	The historic landscape as a whole
Value of cultural heritage	Source of national pride and unity	Source of local and regional identity, spatial quality, economic prosperity and social cohesion
Focus of preservation	Protecting individual objects against unwanted developments	Preserving a representative sample of local and regional heritage values
Actors involved	Social-political and cultural elite	All interested parties
Control over major resources	State actors	State, market and civil society
Prevailing rule of interaction	Hierarchy and advocacy	Deliberation and cooperation

In the late phase of cultural heritage preservation, cultural heritage is mainly valued as a source of local and regional identity. In addition, cultural heritage preservation is believed to contribute to spatial quality, economic prosperity and social cohesion. The focus is not only on individual objects but also on larger areas or landscapes, typically referred to as 'historic environments'. Preservationists believe that the whole of the landscape may have significance. Furthermore, the importance of decentralised, deliberative and transparent styles of governance is emphasised. State actors acknowledge the importance of participation by civil society (NGOs) and market actors in order to define and manage a representative sample of local and regional heritage values. Market actors are willing to invest in cultural heritage preservation because of the opportunities cultural heritage sites offer as tourist attractions and settlement factors.

A basic assumption in this chapter is that in today's field of cultural heritage preservation, discursive and institutional elements from the two different phases go hand in hand. In other words, the two phases should not be seen as two separate, consecutive worlds but as coexistent, juxtaposed modes, more precisely, policy arrangements of cultural heritage presservation. Clearly, the distinction between the two phases is related to the concept of political modernisation (Arts and Van Tatenhove, this volume). However, whereas political modernisation refers to general macro-sociological transformations (such as globalisation and individualisation) that affect and are affected by day-to-day policy practices, the two phases distinguished in this chapter represent different policy discourses and different policy practices that (co)exist within today's field of cultural heritage preservation.

Policy Discourses

In my view, policy discourses in the field of cultural heritage preservation first of all include ideas about the object of preservation. They involve notions about what cultural heritage is and why it is worth protecting. In addition, preservation discourses contain perspectives on the content of preservation: about the way in which cultural heritage should be preserved and how cultural heritage preservation should be funded. Finally, preservation discourses include ideas about the organisation of cultural heritage preservation: about what policy actors should be involved in the preservation of cultural heritage, what tasks and responsibilities they should have and what should be the rules of the game. In conclusion, in my operationalisation, policy discourses comprise notions about both the substance and the organisation of a policy arrangement.

Policy Diffusion

Policy diffusion can be defined as "(...) the international spread of ideas and approaches as well as concrete institutional innovations and policy outputs in a given policy area" (Jörgens, 2001, p. 123). Processes of policy diffusion are influenced by (a) the complex interplay of international developments, (b) national factors and (c) the characteristics of the policy innovations involved (Jörgens, 2001; Tews et al., 2003). First of all, the increasing globalisation of communication through international organisations, transnational advocacy networks and global scientific discourse encourages the diffusion of knowledge and perceptions of policy problems, policy solutions and 'best practices' across countries (Drezner, 2001; Tews et al., 2003). In the field of cultural heritage preservation, international organisations such as UNESCO, ICOMOS, and the Council of Europe and international media such as the Internet, international preservation conferences, and international publications on preservation play an important role in stimulating a process of policy diffusion.

At the same time, the political, economic, societal and institutional characteristics of a particular state serve as filters to the adoption of policy innovations. Administrative traditions, regulatory structures, policy styles and the legacy of past policies may lead to national variations in the design and implementation of policy innovations (Hoberg, 2001; Jörgens, 2001; Tews et al., 2003). The specific features of policy innovations may also play a role. An important factor that can either facilitate or hinder a process of policy diffusion is the compatibility of policy innovations with existing structures and practices (Tews et al., 2003). In other words, the characteristics of an existing policy arrangement may interfere with processes of policy diffusion. For example, a newly introduced policy discourse or policy practice may be incongruent with the existing rules of the game, the existing division of resources or the prevailing policy discourses in a particular preservation arrangement.

A Reflexive Comparison of Cases

The information presented in this chapter is based on the research that I conducted for my dissertation. My research methodology involved a reflexive or interpretative method of analysis. In order to reconstruct the discursive and organisational aspects of the three policy arrangements, I analysed the texts of laws, regulations, policy documents, websites, interviews, meetings, hearings and conferences. In these texts, I focused on explicit statements about and implicit references to: (a) the policy actors that are involved in cultural heritage preservation; (b) the formal decision making structures and the division of tasks and responsibilities between the different policy actors; and (c) the informal rules that implicitly determine the autonomy and dependency between the policy actors involved in cultural heritage preservation. In addition, I identified (d) the ideas policy actors have about the object, the content and the organisation of cultural heritage preservation (De Boer, forthcoming).

Based on this information, I compared the discursive and institutional aspects of the three different policy arrangements against the background of their specific characteristics, their specific contexts and the process of policy diffusion that may be taking place. This enabled me to determine: (1) the main similarities and differences between the policy arrangements; (2) the extent to which the policy arrangements can be seen as the contingent outcomes of specific circumstances and specific policy processes; (3) the extent to which the policy arrangements can be understood as the results of a process of policy diffusion; and (4) the factors that either facilitated or hindered a process of policy diffusion.

'KULTURMINNEFORVALTNING' IN NORWAY

Norway is a relatively young state. It was not until 1814 that it became independent from Denmark and the following union with Sweden was dissolved only a century ago, in 1905 (Allardt et al., 1981). As a consequence, the growing interest in '*kulturminneforvaltning*' (literally: cultural heritage management) in the 19th and 20th century was closely tied to the process of nation and identity building. Norwegian nation building, involving the emergence and growth of an independent nation, was most of all a political phenomenon, organized by the cultural elite and those who dominated the public sphere. Their national romanticism was based on a systematic cultivation of the origin and development of the Norwegian people throughout history (Burgess, 2001; Mangset, 2000).

Systematic preservation of cultural heritage in Norway started in 1844. In that year, the first (non-governmental) organisation in the field of cultural heritage preservation, *Fortidsminneforeningen*, was founded (Aasland et al., 2002; Mangset, 2000; Tschudi-Madsen, 2002). In its early years, *Fortidsminneforeningen* aimed primarily at the preservation of Norway's prehistoric and medieval monuments, such as the stave churches that were rapidly disappearing in the course of the 19th century. As of 1860, the organisation was granted an annual sum from the Norwegian government to cover the salary of a full-time official, a position that eventually became a permanent appointment within the national government. In the end, this led to the establishment of the Central Office for Historic Buildings in 1912, the forerunner of the existing Directorate for Cultural Heritage (*Riksantikvaren*). The Central Office was made responsible for the preservation of Norway's national cultural heritage (Fortidsminneforeningen, 2002; Vestfold Fylkeskommune, 2004). The first legislation regarding the legal protection of historic buildings in Norway was passed in 1920. On the basis of this legislation, protection orders could be issued for individual buildings of historic or architectural value that were older than 100 years (Mangset, 2000; Vestfold Fylkeskommune, 2004).

Although in Norway cultural heritage preservation was mostly a matter of the intellectual and cultural elite in central Oslo at first, the post-war years and especially the 1970s witnessed a strong growth in preservation efforts at local and regional level. From the mid 1970s, a comprehensive national programme for the registration of monuments and sites was put in motion and in 1978, the first Cultural Heritage Act (*Kulturminneloven*) was established, providing a strong protection against the disturbance, alteration or demolition of national heritage sites (Mangset, 2000). From the very beginning, the official work in the field of cultural heritage preservation has been linked to the wider task of environmental protection. Accordingly, it is the Ministry of the Environment that has the main responsibility for cultural heritage preservation in Norway (Riksantikvaren, 2003).

The organisation of Norwegian cultural heritage preservation is fairly centralised. The national government (i.e. the Directorate for Cultural Heritage) has the main responsibility, through strict laws and regulations, to select and preserve a representative sample of Norwegian heritage sites. Regional and local governments merely have an advisory task with regard to the selection and preservation of national heritage (European Heritage Network, 1998). One of the main objectives of Norwegian *kulturminne-forvaltning* is to take cultural heritage considerations into account in all planning processes, at all governmental levels. Especially the local governments have an important responsibility here, being the ultimate land use planning authorities in Norway (Miljøverndepartementet, 2003). However, most local governments in Norway lack competence and resources to develop autonomous preservation policies. Only the larger cities have sufficient know-how and expertise to apply their land use planing authorities for preservation purposes.

Private property owners in Norway hardly have any possibilities to prevent their properties from being officially listed and protected against unwanted developments. They can however pose a request for compensation of the extra costs that the preservation of their historic properties brings about (European Heritage Network, 1998). Finally, there are a limited number of non-governmental organisations involved in Norwegian cultural heritage preservation. *Fortidsminneforeningen* is the most influential. It has been closely connected to the Directorate for Cultural Heritage from the very beginning.

Basically, two competing policy discourses can be reconstructed in the Norwegian arrangement of cultural heritage preservation. On the one hand, there is a typically early phase discourse in which the focus lies on the preservation of individual cultural heritage sites representing the 'real Norwegian' culture, such as stave churches, Viking ships and farmhouses. Modern developments such as urbanisation, changing farming practices and the mass departure from Norway's rural areas are considered to be major threats against which the national heritage should be protected. As Norway is a very sparsely populated country with many small communities, a nationally coordinated approach is considered necessary. Therefore, this policy discourse emphasises centralised, top-down decision-making by the cultural heritage experts of the Directorate for Cultural Heritage and the national non-governmental organisations.

On the other hand, there is a typically late phase policy discourse that focuses on the preservation of a representative sample of Norwegian heritage, including coastal heritage, Sami heritage and larger, integrated cultural environments, reflecting 'everyday life' of all Norwegians. Current preservation practices in Norway are considered to be elitist and inaccessible for the public. Active and viable (re)use of the Norwegian heritage is considered crucial for its preservation and civil society should play a key role in developing and using its historic environment. Accordingly, this policy discourse calls for more decentralised, bottom-up decision-making processes in which all parties, including the Norwegian public, feel represented. Finally, the idea is emphasised that cultural heritage preservation should be incorporated in all relevant policy sectors.

One could argue that the contemporary Norwegian policy arrangement of cultural heritage preservation is mainly the institutionalisation of the early phase discourse. At the same time, there are several indications that the late phase discourse is becoming institutionalised as well. For example, since its amendment of 1992, the Cultural Heritage Act offers the possibility to protect larger cultural environments. Although several projects have been initiated to increase the number of protected monuments and sites from the coastal and Sami regions, the cultural heritage authorities are facing difficulties with the implementation. Most decision-making processes in Norwegian cultural heritage preservation continue to be rather centralistic and hierarchical in character. Many local governments still lack sufficient knowledge, budget and staff to fulfil a substantial responsibility in cultural heritage preservation and the involvement of non-governmental organisations and historic property owners in decision-making processes remains relatively marginal. Apparently, the Directorate for Cultural Heritage is rather reluctant to give up its leading position in Norwegian cultural heritage preservation.

'HISTORIC PRESERVATION' IN ARIZONA, US

The historic preservation movement in the United States developed mainly locally and in an unorganised, fragmented way. Its early development in the late 19th and early 20th century involved a large number of typically private and elitist efforts to save individual structures or sites. Occasional actions of the federal government were mainly restricted to the acquisition and establishment of national parks (Cullingworth, 1997; Tyler, 2000). This changed in 1935, when the federal Historic Sites, Buildings and Antiquities Act was established that aimed at the development of a national policy to preserve historic sites, buildings and objects of national significance. It called upon federal agencies to take account of preservation needs in their programmes and plans, and promoted the surveying and identification of historic sites, which became the base for the National Register of Historic Places some 30 years later (Cullingworth, 1997; Fowler, 1987; Stipe, 1987).

However, the Depression years, the Second World War and the early post-war period were a bad period for historic preservation in the United States. Due to poverty and urban decay on the one hand, and to urban renewal and highway construction on the other, many historic properties were destroyed. This caused a burst of historic preservation activity in the mid-1950s, which ultimately led to the establishment of the National Historic Preservation Act (NHPA) and the National Register of Historic Places in 1966. The NHPA requires federal agencies to take into account the effects of federally regulated or funded activities on historic properties that are listed in the National Register (Brown Morton, 1987; Cullingworth, 1997; Stipe, 1987; Tyler, 2000). Pursuant to the NHPA, the State of Arizona established a State Historic Preservation Office and a State Register of Historic Places in the late 1960s. Furthermore, in analogy with the NHPA, the Arizona Historic Preservation Act requires state agencies to consider the effects of their activities on historic properties listed in the Arizona Register (Bostwick, 2001; Miller, 2000).

The State of Arizona is situated in the Southwest, which is featured by a predominant individualist mentality, a widespread distrust in governmental authorities and highly valued private property rights. Consequently, Arizona, like the other states in the Southwest, has a relatively decentralised system of cultural heritage preservation in which property owners have a quite powerful position because of their well-protected property rights. Policymakers in Arizonan historic preservation typically apply economic incentives, such as grants and tax benefits, to stimulate private property owners to invest in the preservation of their historic properties. Both state and local governments must basically rely on planning and zoning instruments in order to preserve historic resources. Besides the procedural protection provided by the NHPA and the Arizona Historic Preservation Act, the state authorities have no legal instruments to protect listed historic properties. Nevertheless, the local authorities in Arizona can draw up historic preservation ordinances and zoning plans through which they can protect both individual properties and historic districts against unwanted alterations or demolition (Cox, 2002; Miller, 2000). In this respect, it is important to note that, so far, it has hardly ever occurred that historic properties were designated against the will of the property owners. Finally, there are only a small number of non-governmental organisations involved in Arizonan historic preservation. They aim to increase the public interest in historic preservation and watch over the state budget for historic preservation. They however play no role of significance in decision-making processes.

Two competing policy discourses can be distinguished in the Arizonan arrangement of cultural heritage preservation. First, there is a typically early phase policy discourse in which the individualist mentality of Arizonans and their strong belief in private property rights are perceived as the main problems for historic preservation in Arizona. According to this discourse, there is a lack of public and political support for historic preservation in Arizona mainly because most Arizonans do not want the government to interfere with their private property rights. An additional factor is that a growing majority of 'new' Arizonans does not have any connection with the state's history and that consequently, historic preservation is not regarded as significant. As the urban areas of Phoenix and Tucson experience a high development pressure, preservationists face the difficult challenge of protecting historic properties and sites against the threat of demolition and re-development. In order to create more public and political support for historic preservation, the discourse suggests that preservationists should emphasise the array of economic benefits and the relatively voluntary character of historic preservation in Arizona.

In contrast, there is a typically late phase discourse that has the significance of historic properties for the quality of life in Arizona as starting point and in which the main problem is perceived to be the reactive and obscure character of historic preservation. According to this discourse, historic preservation programmes in Arizona spend too much time reacting to emerging problems and threats instead of preventing them. In addition, many of the programs are considered to be unappealing and inaccessible for the general public. The discourse wishes for a more proactive and transparent approach, in which comprehensive and appealing historic preservation programs are developed that focus on the opportunities that historic properties offer and that stimulate individual historic preservation efforts. The necessary public and political support for historic preservation should be created through an open debate with historic property owners and the community at large. Finally, the discourse emphasises that a proactive approach is needed to deal with the huge numbers of post-war properties that will soon become eligible for the National Register.

When relating the two discourses to the organisation of Arizona's historic preservation arrangement, one could come to the conclusion that the policy arrangement mainly parallels the institutionalisation of the early phase discourse. Especially the state historic preservation programs in Arizona reflect a reactive, voluntary and incentive-based approach towards historic preservation. However, some recent developments suggest a careful shift in the organisation of historic preservation towards a more proactive, appealing and communicative approach in line with the late phase discourse. For example, several local authorities are in the process of proactively surveying and assessing the historic values of their post-war districts, while explicitly involving the concerning neighbourhood associations when applying for designation in the National Register. Furthermore, a number of local authorities have initiated cooperative projects with private property owners in which long-term maintenance plans are made stimulating the owners to carefully maintain their historic property in exchange for a maintenance grant and less comprehensive permit procedures.

'MONUMENTENZORG' IN THE NETHERLANDS

In the Netherlands, systematic care of cultural heritage started in the second half of the 19th century (Nelissen, 1993; 1996). As the Industrial Revolution progressed, many historic structures had been demolished, because they no longer served a purpose, while simultaneously the demand for new housing, factories and railways had grown enormously. In response to this, a growing number of people, typically belonging to the social-economic and intellectual elite, supported the idea of preserving the built remains of Dutch history (Richel-Bottinga, 2001; Van der Doe and Spijkerman, 1996). The preservation of historic buildings became an official task of the national government in 1874, when an item was added to the national budget for the 'preservation and superintendence of memorials of Dutch History and Art' (Ministry of Education, Culture and Science, 2003, p. 95). Government involvement initially consisted in providing grants towards the cost of restoring historic buildings. The then Dutch government had no means of forcing an uncooperative owner to maintain his property. It was not until 1961 that the Monuments and Historic Buildings Act paved the way for the legal protection by the state of exceptional historic buildings and valuable historic town- and villagescapes (Nelissen, 2001; Richel-Bottinga, 2001). With the amended Monuments and Historic Buildings Act of 1988, several tasks and responsibilities have been decentralised to the local governments, the most important of which is the authority to issue permits for the alteration or demolition of national monuments (Nelissen, 1996; 2001; Nelissen and Bogie, 2000).

In the Dutch policy arrangement of '*monumentenzorg*' (literally: monument care), many different actors have a certain amount of power and responsibility. The main responsibility for preserving national monuments is shared by the national and local governments. A number of tasks and responsibilities have been decentralised to the local level, but the national government (i.e. the National Department for Conservation) still has a rather directive role in the selection and preservation of historic properties and sites. It is responsible for selecting historic buildings and sites for national protection, advising municipalities on permit applications for the alteration or demolition of national monuments, and – with the introduction of the new BRIM grant scheme for the preservation of national monuments in 2006 – issuing grants for the restoration and maintenance of national monuments (Ministry of Education, Culture and Science, 2003; Nelissen, 2001; Richel-Bottinga, 2001). The regional governments or provinces merely have an advisory task in Dutch cultural heritage preservation, yet all of them have developed an autonomous preservation policy. An increasing number of local governments have established an autonomous policy as well, including a register of local monuments and a local grant scheme. Additionally, local governments play an important role in land use planning as they are responsible for drawing up zoning plans (Nationaal Contact Monumenten, 2004; Nelissen, 2001). In the Dutch arrangement, private property owners have an opportunity to object to the listing of their historic properties in the National Register. Once their property is designated, they are eligible for grants, low-interest loans and tax benefits for the restoration or maintenance of their property (Elbers, 2003). As a final point, a large number of non-governmental organisations are involved in Dutch cultural heritage preservation at all governmental levels. They play a substantial role as watchdogs and as partners of the Dutch government in developing and implementing cultural heritage policies.

Essentially, two competing policy discourses can be reconstructed in Dutch *monumentenzorg*. First of all, a typically early phase discourse emphasises the idea that monuments and historic buildings represent an intrinsic value that cannot be compensated for in any way when altered, damaged or demolished. Therefore, historic buildings and monuments should be protected against any unwanted development. The policy discourse sees a definite role for the national government in controlling land use developments and in supplying sufficient funding for the restoration and maintenance of at least the most vulnerable historic buildings and monuments in the Netherlands. Regional and local governments are considered to have an additional responsibility in monitoring and enforcing the implementation of national cultural heritage policies and in selecting and preserving regional and local heritage sites. Finally, the broad variety of non-governmental organisations should continue to play their role as watchdogs over the Dutch cultural heritage.

Another, typically late phase policy discourse in Dutch cultural heritage preservation, focuses on preserving the cultural-historic values of the Dutch cultural landscape as a whole. According to this discourse, cultural heritage values should be integrated in all land use planning processes and should be a source of inspiration for new land use developments. Because the Netherlands is densely populated and has a high development pressure, the emphasis lies on a combination of preserving historic properties and redeveloping them in a sensible way to accommodate new uses. The aim should be to develop an integrated spatial quality management that strives for a physical environment in which old and new qualities go hand in hand. In this discourse, many parties are considered to be responsible for the preservation of the Dutch cultural heritage: national, provincial and local governments, non-governmental organisations, property developers and historic property owners. Through public-private partnership, a system of 'smart' financing should be established.

Although the actual organisation of the Dutch policy arrangement mainly reflects the early phase policy discourse, there are several indications of an institutional shift towards a late phase of cultural heritage preservation. At provincial level, for instance, regional support centres have been developed in which both governmental and non-governmental organisations participate to support local authorities in the implementation of their preservation tasks. However, as this is a rather new and controversial development, no general statements can be made regarding the success or failure of the support centres. Another indication is the increasing number of cultural heritage projects in which private actors, such as property developers, actively participate. Although these projects typically involve highly profitable re-developments of historic sites, they also represent a trend towards more public-private partnership in cultural heritage preservation. Another indication of an institutional shift is that all provinces and a growing number of local authorities have developed a so-called cultural heritage value map, involving an inventory of all cultural-historic values within their territories, which are used as starting point for new land use plans. Although there is a great variety in the extent to and the way in which cultural heritage values are integrated in national, regional and local decision-making processes concerning land use plans and land use developments, the cultural heritage value maps are considered to be an important first step in the direction of an integrated spatial quality management in the Netherlands.

DIVERSITY

Clearly, there is great diversity in the way the three preservation arrangements are organised; hence they can be typified accordingly (Liefferink, this volume). First of all, the Norwegian *kulturminne-forvaltning* arrangement can be characterised as an etatist arrangement. Crucial resources are controlled by the national government, i.e. the Directorate for Cultural Heritage. It has the authority to select national heritage sites and establish protection orders. Other actors such as regional and local governments, non-governmental organisations and private property owners have only limited access to decision making processes regarding the selection and preservation of heritage sites in Norway. In contrast, the historic preservation arrangement in Arizona resembles a liberal-pluralist policy arrangement. No single actor dominates and resources are spread over a broad variety of national and local, public and private parties, including local governments, private property owners and developers. The state government, i.e. the State Historic Preservation Office, depends on local governments and private property owners when it comes to the establishment of historic preservation ordinances and the designation of historic properties in the National Register. Finally, the Dutch *monumentenzorg* arrangement can be typified as a neo-corporatist policy arrangement. Policies are jointly developed and implemented by state and civil actors at national, regional and local level, in relatively institutionalised settings. For example, the National Restoration Fund, an NGO, is responsible for implementing the subsidy schemes for restorations and maintenance work.

It could be argued that the three policy arrangements are basically contingent responses to their specific historical background, geographical situation and political context. The Norwegian arrangement has been strongly influenced by the fact that from the very beginning, cultural heritage preservation was closely related with 'nation building', which was a project of the social-political elite that had its base in Oslo. One of the results is that cultural heritage sites from central, inland Norway have long dominated the national register. Another consequence is that the Norwegian *kulturminneforvaltning* arrangement has long reflected the idea that the 'experts in Oslo' should have the authority to protect and preserve the Norwegian national heritage against unwanted developments. As Norway is an extremely sparsely populated country with many small communities, until today, preservation tasks have never been decentralised. Most of the local governments are still considered to lack the budget, staff and know-how to establish adequate cultural heritage preservation programs. Finally, due to the fact that there has never been broad public support for cultural heritage preservation in Norway, there are only a small number of non-governmental actors involved in the Norwegian policy arrangement. The oldest organisation in the field, *Fortidsminneforeningen*, plays a substantial role at the national level. Other non-governmental organisations in Norwegian *kulturminneforvaltning* mainly act locally.

In Arizona, the historic preservation arrangement has been strongly influenced by the ever-prevailing individualist and conservative mentality that is typical for the Southwest. It rejects governmental interference with private property rights. Consequently, the Arizonan historic preservation arrangement is based on the principle that the government cannot and should not tell private property owners what to do with their historic properties. Furthermore, as Arizona is a relatively young and fast-growing state, a majority of the people is not aware of the state's history. As a result, cultural heritage preservation has never had a high political priority in Arizona. In response, the Arizonan preservationists have developed an approach that is based on economic arguments and incentives.

Finally, the Dutch *monumentenzorg* arrangement has been determined by a widespread corporatist mentality and the prevalent practice of consensus democracy. This has led to an active involvement of a large amount of non-governmental organisations in the field of cultural heritage preservation. Furthermore, the 'major operations' of the Dutch government in the 1980s, involving the decentralization and privatisation of public tasks, have led to a relatively broad division of responsibilities between the different actors involved in cultural heritage preservation. Basically, the Dutch arrangement reveals the notion that cultural heritage preservation is a shared responsibility of state, market and civil society. This is also reflected by the relatively comprehensive system of grants and low-interest loans, which has been established with public funds in order to assist private property owners in the maintenance or restoration of their historic properties and is administrated by a private foundation.

DIFFUSION

Besides the conclusion that the three different policy arrangements could be seen as the contingent outcomes of their specific historical background, geographical situation and political context, this chapter also shows that in all three policy arrangements, competing preservation discourses have developed and various shifts in the organisation of culture heritage preservation have emerged (see Table 8.2). Moreover, the alternative discourses and organisational shifts in the three different policy arrangements show a considerable degree of similarity. They involve: (a) a shift in focus from individual objects to the cultural landscape as a whole; (b) a shift in focus from the intrinsic historical value of cultural heritage to the extrinsic, social, spatial and economic values of cultural heritage; (c) a shift in approach from protecting cultural heritage sites against unwanted developments to (re)using and (re)developing cultural heritage to accommodate new functions; and (d) a shift from a single-actor to a multi-actor approach and public-private partnerships.

For example, in Norway, a number of projects have been initiated in which the Norwegian government tries, through processes of public-private partnerships and decentralised, bottom-up decision-making, to establish widely accepted and supported preservation plans for large-scale cultural environments. In Arizona, several local authorities have introduced a more proactive and transparent preservation policy in which they explicitly involve private property owners, in exchange for a maintenance grant and less comprehensive permit procedures, in 'improving the quality of life' in their historic neighbourhoods. Some Dutch examples are: the widespread use of cultural heritage value maps in which the cultural-historic values of the Dutch landscape are presented as a source of inspiration for new land use developments; the creation of regional support centres in which both governmental and non-governmental agencies participate in order to support local preservation efforts; and the increasing share of public-private partnerships in restoration and re-development projects.

Consequently, it could be concluded that a process of policy diffusion has taken place, which causes similar discursive and organisational developments in the three policy arrangements, basically, from the early to the late phase of cultural heritage preservation. It is plausible that international organisations in the field of cultural heritage preservation such as UNESCO, ICOMOS, or the Council of Europe and international media such as the Internet, international preservation conferences and international publications on cultural heritage preservation play an important role in stimulating a process of policy diffusion. Another possible explanation is that the three policy arrangements are increasingly

Table 8.2. Gradual shifts in the three policy arrangements

Arrangement Characteristic	Norway	Arizona	the Netherlands
Definition of cultural heritage	'Real Norwegian' heritage → Historic environments representing 'everyday life'	Historic buildings and sites → Historic (post-war) neighbourhoods	Historic buildings and sites → Historic landscape as a whole
Value of cultural heritage	Source of national pride and unity → Source of local and regional identity	Source of economic prosperity → Source of local and regional identity	Intrinsic value → Source of identity and inspiration for new land use developments
Focus of preservation	Protection against threats → Preservation through viable re-use	Voluntary and incentive-based preservation → Proactive preservation of significant (post-war) areas	Protection against unwanted developments → Preservation through sensible re-development and re-use
Actors involved	Cultural heritage experts → Experts and laymen	All interested parties	State, market and civil society in relatively institutionalised setting
Control over major resources	State actors → State and civil society	State actors and private property owners	State, market and civil society
Prevailing rule of interaction	Hierarchy → Deliberation	Laissez faire → Cooperation	Consensus → Integration and cooperation

confronted with similar policy problems, which leads them in the direction of similar policy solutions. At present, preservationists in Norway, Arizona and the Netherlands deal with (a) a high demand for economic and spatial development; (b) an increasing cultural and spatial uniformity of landscapes, which is considered to be the result of the ongoing globalisation process; (c) low public and political priority for preservation efforts; and (d) a lack of budget for cultural heritage preservation. This leads preservationists in Norway, Arizona and the Netherlands to solutions in which (a) the preservation and (re)development of cultural heritage sites go hand in hand; (b) the focus is on the local and regional distinctiveness of cultural heritage; (c) a broad variety of policy actors, including citizens and property owners, are asked to participate in policy making processes; and (d) public-private partnerships are established in order to obtain private funds.

At the same time, however, discursive and institutional barriers can be distinguished in the three policy arrangements that interfere with the diffusion of new ideas and that hinder the definite institutionalisation of alternative policy practices. In the Norwegian arrangement, the traditionally powerful position of the 'elitist' national government and its reluctance to hand over certain authority to local policy actors is an important barrier against the implementation of bottom-up decision-making processes and the realization of a representative national register that includes the 'laypeople's heritage'. In the Dutch arrangement, the relatively powerful position of the national government and a number of non-governmental organisations that are convinced that cultural heritage preservation is primarily a public affair, plays an important role as a barrier against processes of privatisation and public-private partnerships. Finally, in Arizona, the belief in private property rights, which is widespread among both governmental and non-governmental actors, plays an important role as a barrier against pro-active governmental action in the field of cultural heritage preservation.

REFERENCES

Aasland, T., T. Desserud et al. (2002), *Fortid former framtid, Utfordringer i en ny kulturminnepolitikk, Utredning fra kulturminneutvalget oppnevnt ved kongelig resolusjon 9. april 1999, Avgitt til Miljøverndepartementet 21. desember 2001*, NOU 2002, 1, Statens forvaltningstjeneste, Oslo.

Allardt, E.A., N. Andrén and G.P. Gíslason (1981), *Nordic democracy: ideas, issues, and institutions in politics, economy, education, social and cultural affairs of Denmark, Finland, Iceland, Norway, and Sweden*, Det Danske Selskab, Copenhagen.

Bostwick, T.W. (2001), *City of Phoenix guidelines for archaeology*, City of Phoenix, Archaeology section, Parks, Recreation and library department, Phoenix.

Brown Morton, W. (1987), What do we preserve and why?, in: R.E. Stipe and A.J. Lee, *The American mosaic: preserving a nation's heritage*, US/ICOMOS, Washington.

Burgess, J.P. (2001), *Culture and rationality: European frameworks of Norwegian identity*, Høyskoleforlaget, Kristiansand.

Cantacuzino, S. and C. King (1999), Conservation of monuments and sites, *Conservation, the Getty Conservation Institute newsletter*, Vol. 14, no. 3, pp. 11-13.
Clark, K. (2000), From regulation to participation: cultural heritage, sustainable development and citizenship, in: P. Drury, *Forward planning: the function of cultural heritage in a changing Europe*, Council of Europe, Strasbourg.
Cox, R.S. (2002), *Design review in historic districts*, National trust for historic preservation, Washington.
Cullingworth, B. (1997), *Planning in the USA: policies, issues and processes*, Routledge, London.
De Boer, S. (forthcoming), *Dealing with diversity in cultural heritage preservation: a comparative analysis of policy arrangements in Norway, the Netherlands and Arizona*, Radboud University Nijmegen, Nijmegen.
Drezner, D.W. (2001), Reflection and reappraisal: globalization and policy convergence, *International Studies Review*, Vol. 3, no. 1, pp. 53-78.
Elbers, A. (2003), *Jaaruitgave monumenten: regelgeving, financiering en beleid*, editie 2004, Sdu Uitgevers, Den Haag.
European Heritage Network (1998), *National heritage policies: Norway*, Strasbourg, www.european-heritage.net (2003).
Fortidsminneforeningen (2002), *Fortidsminneforeningen: the society for the preservation of Norwegian ancient monuments*, Oslo.
Fowler, J.M. (1987), The federal government as standard bearer, in: R.E. Stipe and A.J. Lee, *The American mosaic: preserving a nation's heritage*, US/ICOMOS, Washington.
Goverde, H.J.M. (2000), *Global and European polity? Organizations, policies, contexts*, Ashgate, Aldershot.
Hoberg, G. (2001), Globalization and policy convergence: symposium overview, *Journal of comparative policy analysis*, Vol. 3, no. 2, pp. 127-132.
Hornby, A.S., S. Wehmeier and M. Ashby (2000), *Oxford advanced learner's dictionary of current English*, Sixth edition, Oxford University Press, Oxford.
Howard, P. (2003), *Heritage: management, interpretation, identity*, Continuum, London.
Jokilehto, J. (1999), Conservation of historic architecture, *Conservation, the Getty Conservation Institute newsletter*, Vol. 14, no. 3, pp. 22-24.
Jörgens, H. (2001), The diffusion of environmental policy innovations - findings from an international workshop, *Environmental Policies*, Vol. 10, no. 2, pp. 122-127.
Mangset, P. (2000), Norwegian cultural policy – goals and means, in: Ministry of Foreign Affairs, *Nytt fra Norge*, Oslo.
Mason, R. (2002), Assessing values in conservation planning: methodological issues and choises, in: M. De la Torre, *Assessing the values of cultural heritage: research report*, Getty Conservation Institute, Los Angeles.
Maturo, F. (2000), Ethics and policy in conservation, *Conservation, the Getty Conservation Institute newsletter*, Vol. 15, no. 1, pp. 5-9.
Miljøverndepartementet (2003), *Planning*, Oslo.
Miller, J.H. (2000), *A layperson's guide to historic preservation law: a survey of federal, state, and local laws governing historic resource protection*, National trust for historic preservation, Washington.
Ministry of Education, Culture and Science (2003), *Cultural policy in the Netherlands*, The Hague.
Nationaal Contact Monumenten (2004), *Monumenten jaarboek 2004*, Amsterdam.
Nelissen, N.J.M. (1993), De restauratie van de monumentenzorg, in: A.J.A. Godfroij and N.J.M. Nelissen, *Verschuivingen in de besturing van de samenleving*, Dick Coutinho, Bussum.

Nelissen, N.J.M. (1996), Monumentenzorg schrijft geschiedenis, in: N.J.M. Nelissen, *Monumentenzorg: dynamiek in behoud*, Sdu Uitgevers, Den Haag.

Nelissen, N.J.M. and M.J.S. Bogie (2000), The cultural historical factor in spatial planning: a new policy instrument, in: H. Goverde, *Global and European polity? Organizations, policies, contexts*, Ashgate, Aldershot.

Nelissen, N.J.M. (2001), *Monumentenzorg in de praktijk: cursusmap*, Zevende geheel herziene druk (inclusief aanvullingen 2002), Nationaal Contact Monumenten, Amsterdam.

Richel-Bottinga, S. (2001), The Netherlands, in: R. Pickard, *Policy and law in heritage conservation*, Spon Press, London.

Riksantikvaren (2003), *The cultural heritage management in Norway*, Oslo.

Stipe, R.E. (1987), Historic preservation: the process and the actors, in: R.E. Stipe and A.J. Lee, *The American mosaic: preserving a nation's heritage*, US/ICOMOS, Washington.

Tews, K., P.-O. Busch and H. Jörgens (2003), The diffusion of new environmental policy instruments, *European Journal of Political Research*, Vol. 42, no. 4, pp. 569-600.

Tschudi-Madsen, S. (2002), Nasjonalarven og Verdensarvlisten. Internasjonale perspektiver innen kulturminnevernet 1900-2000, in: J.A. Balto, *Årbok 2002, Fortidsminneforeningen, Nasjonale klenodier*, Fortidsminneforeningen, Oslo.

Tyler, N. (2000), *Historic preservation, an introduction to its history, principles, and practice*, W.W. Norton & Company, New York.

Van der Doe, F. and H. Spijkerman (1996), *Van monumentale waarde: een institutioneel onderzoek naar de rijksoverheidsbemoeienis met monumentenzorg, 1945-1990*, Rijksarchiefdienst/PIVOT, 's-Gravenhage.

Vestfold Fylkeskommune (2004), *Kulturarv i en ny tid. Utkast til Fylkesdelplan for bevaring av kulturminner i Vestfold 2004-2007*, Tønsberg.

Chapter 9

Dutch Rural Policies at a Turning Point

Froukje Boonstra

INTRODUCTION

In the 1990s we witnessed the emergence of a new trend in Dutch rural policy. Within the framework of integrated region-oriented policies, regional coalitions of state, civil society and market parties have started seeking solutions for rural problems by carrying out specific projects. Besides an emphasis on public-private partnership, joint decision-making and the regional level, a key characteristic of the new policies is the integrated approach to rural problems. Instead of dealing with one dominant sector, one single policy objective or one single point of view, the approach aims at integration, synergy and 'win-win'.

After identifying the developments causing the policy change, this chapter deals with three emerging regional policy arrangements in which the organisational reform manifests itself in the Netherlands: LEADER II in Northwest Friesland, 'Waardevol Cultuur Landschap' in a region called the Graafschap and 'Landstad Deventer' in a region called Southwest Salland. As these projects do not come about in isolation, attention is focused on the relationship between decision-making at the regional level and the complex policy context. Certain tensions may arise between the regional policy innovation and more traditional approaches to deal with rural problems. A related issue to be dealt with is the long-term effects of these regional projects. As these face different and sometimes conflicting expectations, institutional fragmentation, a multitude of overlapping policy categories and traditional 'command-and-control' policies, the following question has to be asked: To what extent can the innovative approach be fully worked out and to what extent will it have lasting effects? At the conceptual level, this question implies a focus on the process of and conditions for institutionalisation. In other words: Do the emerging arrangements institutionalise, how can they be typified and what are the explanations for (a lack of) institutionalisation?

B. Arts and P. Leroy (eds.), Institutional Dynamics in Environmental Governance, 183–201.

Methodologically, the research questions call for a case study design. Only a thorough analysis and reconstruction of the decision-making processes in conjunction with the wider institutional context, allows discernment of the characteristics of the three emerging policy arrangements. The primary focus is therefore on actors, their intentions, strategies, interactions and interpretations. Secondly these happenings and interpretations are confronted with a broader frame of meaning, in this case the policy arrangement framework and the concept of congruence.

The chapter concludes with a reflection on several aspects of the analysis. I particularly discuss the meaning of the new arrangements for the shift from government to governance and reflect on recent developments in the Dutch rural policy field and their consequences for region-oriented arrangements.

RISE OF INTEGRATED REGION-ORIENTED POLICIES

Several developments lay at the root of the rise of the integrated region-oriented policy approach (IROP) from the beginning of the 1990s onwards in the Dutch rural policy domain. First of all, there was a shift from a policy domain dominated by agrarian modernisation and neo-corporatist relationships towards fragmented domains for agriculture, environment, nature and spatial planning. In this context, IROP was meant to tackle policy failure caused by fragmentation and lack of adjustment to regional problems.

The main feature of the governance discourse underlying IROP is that the state no longer imposes general policies unilaterally but negotiates with regional and local authorities, interest groups, market parties and citizens about policies that are adjusted to specific regional needs. In this way, so called win-win solutions are stimulated and sectoral policy initiatives become integrated and adjusted to regional contexts. This is expected to enhance the support amongst parties involved and to improve the chances for successful implementation (Driessen et al., 1995; Leroy, 2000).

Besides an instrumental answer to policy failure, IROP also turned out to be an attempt from different authorities to consolidate or strengthen their position in the rural policy domain. For example, the Ministry of Housing, Spatial Planning and Environment (MHSPE) tried to gain influence in the traditional domain of the Ministry of Agriculture Nature and Fisheries (MANF) by introducing one of the first regional-oriented policy concepts (Van Tatenhove, 1993). Also, provinces embraced the new approach, to profile themselves as an important actor in the rural policy field (Driessen, 2000).

Finally, the emergence of IROP can be related to more general political and societal developments. For example, the shift from government to governance implies that the state cannot solve societal problems alone or within relatively closed neo-corporative structures. Increasingly, public authorities act as negotiators in or facilitators of multi-actor policy processes, together with representatives from market parties and civil society (Arts et al., 2001, pp. 6-7; Leroy et al., 2001, p. 221). Besides a horizontal character, the interweaving of state, civil society and market also has a vertical character. This means that administrative levels increasingly work together in making and implementing policies (Van der Zouwen and Van Tatenhove, 2002, p. 24). For example, the EU has proven to bc an important financer of region oriented projects in the Netherlands and provinces and NGOs play an important role in implementing national nature goals.

The implied retreat of the nation state is met by a growing number of initiatives in the public sphere taken by private actors (Beck, 1994). A rural example is the approximately one hundred so-called environmental co-operatives, initiated by farmers, claiming a role in, among other things, nature conservation and development (Van der Ploeg et al., 2002, p. 142). This domain was formerly claimed by the state and connected to professional nature conservation organisations. The central feature of this process of bottom up regionalisation is that citizens try to get hold of their direct surroundings – "the most immediate source of self-recognition and autonomous organization" (Castells, 1997, p. 61). Countering global uniformity trends, they cherish cultural identity and regional diversity.

Related to the previous trends, there is a growing discursive diversity on rural issues (Boonstra, 2001; Frouws, 1998). No longer does one discourse on rurality dominate the public debate and rural policies, as during the heyday of agrarian modernisation. Criticism on the effects of modern agriculture on the environment, landscape and animal welfare has induced adjustments to the modernisation discourse and the introduction of new ones. This development was reinforced by the decreasing importance of agriculture for the rural economy and the appearance of new societal demands for rural living, nature and recreation. In other words, rural areas have become contested. They no longer represent one single space, but a multiplicity of social spaces for one and the same geographical area (Mormont, 1990, p. 34).

MANIFESTATIONS OF THE POLICY SHIFT

Though triggering many new rural policy practices, the IROP has not put an end to more traditional, top-down and sectoral policy practices in the rural domain. Therefore this section focuses on the interaction between concrete manifestations of the IROP in the regions of Northwest Friesland, the Graafschap and Southwest Salland and the complex institutional context.

LEADER II Noordwest Friesland

LEADER II Noordwest Friesland originates from the interplay between the European Commission and the Province of Friesland. In 1993 the European Commission announced the succession of LEADER I by LEADER II, the community's initiative for the promotion of local social-economic development. As LEADER II objectives and provincial policies were running parallel, the Province, anticipating opportunities, moved actively to utilise the European co-funding opportunities for the economic development of the North-western part of its territory. Provincial officials played a major role, as they set the criteria and organisational conditions for regional decision-making. As they built upon an existing regional policy arrangement for rural development, improving living conditions remained a key issue, while the participating provincial bodies and municipalities consolidated their powerful position. However, in accordance with the participative LEADER discourse, organisational innovations were suggested as well, such as the extension of the regional coalition with private stakeholders.

At first a major bottleneck emerged at national level. The Ministry of Agriculture, Nature and Fisheries (MANF) refused to confer the 5b status, a category of the EU structural funds and a condition for being considered for the LEADER-programme, on a part of the area preferred by the provincial authorities. The region did not hold any major MANF policy priorities, such as nature development and landscape protection. Finally, however, a compromise was reached about the borders of the 5b area between the province and the MANF. The Ministry adapted its application for 5b funding slightly in order to enable the Province to implement a comprehensive rural development programme in the whole region.

Although many of the later coalition partners were not involved during the preparation phase, the decision-making within this group about process design and proposed actions ran smoothly. As municipalities, representatives of agriculture, small and medium enterprises, villages, and recreation and tourism managed to give a positive meaning to most of the proposals, agreement developed. Nor did concrete implementation projects inflame any controversies. This was also due to the fact that a positive attitude was rewarded financially, through supra-regional co-funding. The Province in its leading role enjoyed confidence of others, and built upon current projects and policies.

A major exception was the 'Vaarwegen project', a canal project between Bolsward and Harlingen that aimed to improve the possibilities for recreation on and near the canal by making it better accessible for small motor boats. The lack of agreement on this biggest implementation project even threatened the continuation of the entire regional policy arrangement. The Province, the in-between rural community of Wûnseradiel and a local business lobby group strongly favoured improvement of the most costly connection between the two towns. Bolsward and Harlingen were less interested, the former actively promoting a cheaper solution containing fewer bridges to be heightened. Surprisingly, the innovations in the regional arrangement did not get a hold on the decision making on this project. The interaction is best characterised as a traditional game of power between the Province and the three communities concerned, without any input from the new coalition partners. Only due to external resources made available by the Province did the process get afloat again.

Influencing policy or making new ones was not a rule in the Northwest Friesland policy arrangement. For a long time existing regulatory and redistributive policies were considered as given. The situation changed, however, towards the end of LEADER II. Due to an expected reform of the LEADER policy the regional coalition wanted to safeguard the developed collaborative relationships, the established political room to manoeuvre, the financial resources and its focus on socio-economic development. Together with other LEADER regions it addressed the MANF with specific wishes on the organisation and substance of the LEADER policy. This was because ministry officials were involved in the formulation of a new European rural policy document and responsible for the national implementation.

Waardevol Cultuur Landschap de Graafschap

In the Graafschap, the MANF initiated the major region-oriented policy project of the nineties. In 1993 the Ministry allocated the area as a 'Waardevol Cultuur Landschap' or Valuable Man-Made Landscape (VMML). With this regional policy category, the MANF aimed to decrease the tension between agriculture, nature, landscape and recreation. At first the allocation was not welcomed in the region. The Province of Gelderland, the intended leading actor in the development of the project, had difficulties with the top-down character of the imposed policy and the boundaries set for the region by the central government. As they could not ascribe a positive meaning to the policy initiative, other intended partners such as the agricultural sector and rural estate owners became major critics. The controversy focused on the relationship of the VMML-policy and other policy categories that also affected the region, dealing for example with nature development and intensive livestock breeding. In the background, the declining power of the farmers unions was also at stake. Due to their formerly privileged position in the neo corporatist arrangement, farmers' representatives were used to having a large impact on rural policy making. However, in the IROP they were forced to operate in a broader setting where also other interests were represented and a more equal distribution of power was developing. The fear of losing influence made farmers' representatives reluctant to cooperate with other interest groups. As a result the intended regional collaboration stalled. Covering for the hesitating provincial authorities, the regional MANF-representatives played a leading role in the process design. They produced a document with the practical implications of the VMML-policy for the Graafschap and supported the provincial officials in involving the intended partners. Still, the development of the obligatory regional plan was seriously delayed.

Unlike in Northwest Friesland, the regional coalition partners in the Graafschap delivered the materials for the regional document through sectoral vision papers. The method served to improve the cohesion within the represented interest groups, but also stimulated them to overclaim and take positions against one another. Another disrupting factor was the draft provincial spatial plan, which was being developed at the provincial level. But finally every partner approved a text after intensive and protracted negotiations. The policy discourse 'interweaving of spatial functions where possible, separation where necessary' expressed the common interpretation of the region. When put in practice, however, problems occurred, since the elaboration of the motto was restricted to 'green' spatial functions, such as agriculture and nature, and consequently did not address 'red' issues such as housing and infrastructure. Real choices were evaded as much as possible.

Nevertheless, the mutual relations improved after the regional plan had been realised. The distribution of seats in the steering committee, the restrictive supra-regional policies for farming and other rules of the game were no longer contested, in spite of the fact that the farmers union remained annoyed about the lack of political room to manoeuvre. Partners then focused on the development, assessment and implementation of projects. Because of its position of main financier, the Ministry kept playing an important role and remained powerful next to the Province of Gelderland. Nevertheless, overt conflicts with regional partners were avoided. The active participation of the MANF in different regional decision making arenas proved helpful for the other coalition partners to learn to make sense of the MANF-criteria for selecting projects considered for financing. The MANF also became more flexible and took a more distantiated role. The regional partners managed to get along better among themselves. The interaction on concrete subjects fostered agreement and on some items even consensus was reached.

During the implementation phase in which projects such as the renovation of cultural heritage and stimulating environmental friendly farming were carried out, the idea of interweaving functions got more attention, and integrative solutions gained ground, at the expense of the traditional separation strategy. The developments as regards the Groote Veld provide a good example. This project aimed to establish a big enclosed nature reserve in the centre of the Graafschap. Once started as a project based on the separation of functions, attention for combinations of agriculture and nature grew as a coalition of farmers and rural dwellers, who did not want to leave their farms or become restricted in their activities, took the initiative.

Landstad Deventer

In the last region studied, Southwest Salland, the idea for a region-oriented initiative on urban-rural relations was put forward by three professionals working with the Province of Overijssel, the 'Dienst Landelijk Gebied' (the land use authority) and the Keuning Institute (a process facilitator). They gained support both within and outside their organisations. The Province of Overijssel adopted the initiative in 1998 and financed the planning phase.

The regional coalition agreed quite quickly on the process design and substance, despite tensions caused by a municipal re-allocation between the intended partners Deventer on the one hand and the rural communities Olst en Bathmen on the other. Provincial funding and a rather open problem definition at the start also fostered the process of 'sense making'. For example, the most important policy theme 'improving the urban-rural relationship' was hardly operationalised at the beginning.

Unlike in Northwest Friesland and the Graafschap, emphasis was put on conceptual innovation. The coalition invited residents to develop spatial concepts for the town of Deventer and its surroundings together with designers, civil servants, policy makers and politicians. These concepts should attribute innovation of policy-making at different levels or lead to concrete implementation projects. Influencing policy thus became a major rule from the very start in the Landstad policy arrangement.

After an energetic start, the Landstad policy arrangement began to face difficulties. A gap developed between the regional coalition on the one hand and the politicians and citizens on the other. This was caused by ideas put forward by designers that opposed the prevailing spatial planning policy concepts and did not match the wishes of the rural dwellers. Furthermore, there was no shared sense of urgency. Appealing implementation results that might contribute to a greater general support were lacking as well. In its policy document, which related vision development with a possible implementation trajectory, the regional coalition tried to keep a balance between carrying through innovative policy themes, like 'new villages in rural areas', and a need to acquire more support. The coalition scored a partial success, as every constituency except one rural municipality approved with the document as such and agreed with continuation of the process.

The next step included influencing policy-making on the one hand and implementing a number of projects on the other. However, in the course of time influencing policy proved a tedious job and emphasis shifted to the latter. It was thought that appealing results might strengthen the basis for a policy arrangement which was still rather unstable. However, the number of projects that were being carried out was rather small, due to the short implementation phase and the lack of structural funding. Nevertheless, the link between the regional coalition partners and their constituencies got stronger, through some successes such as the granting of European subsidies. Yet, the distance between the regional coalition and inhabitants remained big.

COMPARING THE REGIONAL ARRANGEMENTS

Main Characteristics

Though originating from the same governance discourse, the emerging regional arrangements show at least as many differences as similarities. Table 9.1 summarizes the main features of the three arrangements. Most striking are the differences in rural discourses and in rules on access, process design and relations to existing formal policies. The discursive differences can be explained by the preferences and experiences of the most powerful actors in the policy arrangements.

Table 9.1. Main characteristics of the three regional arrangements

	Northwest Friesland	The Graafschap	Southwest Salland
regional coalition	province, municipalities, farmers, small firms, recreation & tourism companies, village councils	province, municipalities, MANF, polder- and recreation boards, farmers union, environmental groups, tourism, estate owners	province, municipalities, MANF, land use authority, large land owner
control over resources/ power	province, municipalities	MANF, province, farmers union	province, municipality of Deventer
rules of the game:			
access	relatively closed	in turn open and closed	relatively open
representation	indirect	mostly indirect	in turn indirect and direct
allocation of tasks	EC initiates; province leads; MEA and province fund; 'coordination group' coordinates implementation	MANF initiates; MANF and province lead and fund; 'steering group' steers planning and implementation	province initiates, leads and funds; 'steering committee' steers planning and implementation
process design	pragmatic	accommodating	participatory and innovative
interaction within coalition	cooperation on most issues, conflict on some	conflict followed by cooperation	cooperation
interaction with formal policies	LEADER initiative mobilised to operate independently from national rural policies	ambivalent: environmental and spatial policies are contested by some partners and mobilised as resources by others	restrictive spatial policies are contested
policy discourse	improving living conditions trough structural economic development	balancing spatial separation and interweaving of nature and agriculture	improving relationship town – countryside

The focus on economic development and employment in Northwest Friesland, for example, is based on the conviction of provincial policy makers that solutions such as direct investments in social and cultural facilities of the villages, do not structurally improve living conditions. This denounced 'soft' approach was central in former provincial rural policies and proved only partly successful. Furthermore, the choice of rural discourse is influenced by more or less objective physical, socio-economic and cultural conditions of the region as well as by the prevailing degree of policy accumulation. These conditions do however not determine policy discourses, but they demonstrably limit the scope of discursive selection. For example, the relatively peripheral location, the low population density, the extensive land use and the low policy intensity make a rural discourse problematising a clash between spatial functions in Northwest Friesland unlikely to get support, while the characteristics of the Graafschap and Southwest Salland imply the opposite. Preferences of dominating actors involved in these last regions determine what spatial and cultural clashes are problematised: urban–rural relations or the tension between agriculture and environment.

Also, rules of access differ among the regions: Southwest Salland having the highest number of actors involved in the decision making process and Northwest Friesland the least. Rules of access changed during the decision making process in the three regions though. In Northwest Friesland the planning effort is concentrated with provincial professionals, while in the implementation phase a limited number of interest groups and so-called implementing agencies gain a more influential position. In the Graafschap the regional plan is based on plans of the main interests in the region (agriculture, nature, recreation/tourism, and cultural heritage and estate owners) and framed by policy priorities of the MANF. Submitting projects is however open to an unlimited group of inhabitants, NGOs and local authorities, as long as they meet project requirements. In Southwest Salland the planning process is most open. Inhabitants and designers are actively invited to have their say on the development of the region, though they do not directly take part in the decision-making regional coalition. These differences in rules of access can be explained by preferences of initiators or leading actors of the regional processes and by former rules of the game. In the Northwest Friesland and the Graafschap former region-oriented practices are more or less reproduced, while in Southwest Salland the provincial spatial planning practice structures decision-making. It is the dominating frame of reference of the initiators, but instead of reproducing it, the Landstad project is designed as an alternative to this well institutionalized practice. It should be noted finally, that having access does not automatically bring about power and influence. Though rules of access differ, the power positions show much more similarity throughout the three regions.

Besides rules on access, other aspects of the process design also vary between the three regions: the Northwest Friesland process design being most pragmatic, the one in the Graafschap can best be typified as accommodating, while the Southwest Salland design rules aim at participation and substantial innovation. The process design rules are strongly related to the degree of conflict in the regions involved and to the ambitions of the initiators and other powerful participants in the arrangements. The degree of conflict in Northwest Friesland being low, the professionals initiating the project get away with a pragmatic approach directed at allocating the available European structural funds as smoothly and efficiently as possible. In the Graafschap the fundamentally opposing agricultural and environmental interest groups have to be pacified at first by means of making a regional plan together. In Southwest Salland the initiators have the highest participatory ambitions. Not only inhabitants get a central role, bypassing formal interest groups, also designers of good standing contribute in the regional planning effort.

Finally, the relationship with formal policies, either at supra- and sub-regional level, differs between the regions. Initially, in Northwest Friesland, the provincial authorities actively mobilise the European LEADER-initiative to act more or less independently from national rural policies and discourses. This was possible, because LEADER was considered less restrictive and more open to specific regional needs than similar national programmes. Furthermore, Northwest Friesland was no priority region in MANF-policies. The rule however changes towards the end of the project period, when the semi-autonomous course of action loses its attraction through a changing position of the MANF. In the Graafschap a MANF policy initiative lays at the root of the developing arrangement and a related MANF-subsidy is the main factor in sustaining it at first. This does not prevent regional parties from strongly opposing other, more sectoral policies of the state. Sharpened environmental regulations for example threaten intensive farming practices and oppose the common discourse of the participating farmers union that high-productive farming should be possible ‘everywhere’ (also near forests, on former marshlands etc.). However, the environmental and nature representatives in the regional coalition mobilise the environmental regulations as a resource in their struggle to get more favourable conditions for nature development and for a better environment. An ambivalent attitude towards the policy context results and potentially undermines the developing policy arrangement. In

Southwest Salland the critique on traditional provincial spatial planning practices is the main *raison d'être* of the regional arrangement. Opposition to formal spatial policies and policy-making is therefore an important discourse and rule structuring the arrangement. The conflict is played out on several occasions, but most overtly around the issue of the development of new villages in rural areas. This idea, proposed by one of the designers, fundamentally opposes the main dogma of spatial planning policies in the Netherlands aiming at concentrating new housing development in existing towns in an attempt to keep rural areas as open as possible.

Despite these differences in rural discourses and rules of the game, remarkable similarities exist between the regional arrangements also. For example, in every region a central role is reserved for a regional coalition of government bodies and NGOs, while formal decision making power firmly stays in the hands of public authorities involved. This even holds true for the most participatory arrangement of Landstad Deventer. Although actively invited to have their say, consultation is the highest degree of participation reached for inhabitants (Pröpper and Steenbeek, 2001). Within every regional coalition, provinces have a powerful position and play a leading role in setting the rules of the game, notwithstanding formally different initiators. Furthermore, every regional arrangement is influenced by supra-regional rules and resources, even the more autonomous arrangements of Northwest Friesland and Southwest Salland. Finally, though leading discourses differ between the regions, some sub-themes mobilised by the regional actors are remarkably similar implying overlap between discourses involved. For example, stimulating recreation and tourism in rural areas is a sub-theme in every region. The same holds true for diversifying agriculture.

Institutionalisation

The development of regional policy arrangements can be aptly described as a process of institutionalisation (Van Tatenhove, 1993, p. 10; Van Tatenhove et al., 2000, pp. 19-20). This process can be divided in two sub processes: the structuration of decision-making in emerging arrangements and the stabilisation of these arrangements. Striking in the forgoing examples is that though developing under sometimes unfavourable conditions and raising struggle and opposition, every decision-making process institutionalises to a certain degree. Regional coalitions, relations of power, rules of the game and leading discourses are (re)produced in every region. This process of structuration can be explained by the degree of strategic congruency developing between the regional coalition partners in

Northwest Friesland, the Graafschap and Southwest Salland. Strategic congruency refers to the ability of actors involved to give a sensible meaning to a range of central issues that are being addressed in decision-making. It is not necessary for actors to arrive at similar interpretations based on shared discourses, as long as they agree on the issues at stake. The concept of 'strategic congruency' is based on Grin and Van de Graaf (1994; 1996a; 1996b) and is further developed in Boonstra (2004). In contrast to Grin and Van de Graaf however, I consider strategic congruency not only as a 'product' of overlapping (substantial) discourses of actors involved, but also as a result of their interpretations of the strategic and structural conditions under which they operate. For example: a farmers' representative may, on the basis of his personal convictions and the rural discourse he supports, not be able to give a positive meaning to nature development in the Graafschap, but may still agree considering his future position in regional decision making. The cases show that strategic congruency is fostered by recognising interdependency by the partners involved, learning experiences and the acceptance of the existing division of power. Furthermore, externally induced changes in rural discourses, changes within the represented constituencies, and the availability of new resources such as funding and political room to manoeuvre further strategic congruency.

Still, it takes more than good intentions for the regional policy arrangements to stabilise and further institutionalise. It can be hypothesized that arrangements should be *structurally* congruent to have lasting effects as well. Structural congruency occurs when the dimensions of the arrangement have been mutually attuned (internal structural congruency), and when the arrangement matches the institutional context (external structural congruency) (Boonstra, 2004). Contrary to this rather static definition, it should be emphasized that developing structural congruency is a dynamic process of mutual adjustment between the internal dimensions of the regional arrangement on the one hand, and between the emerging arrangement and external rules, resources and discourses on the other. Learning and the presence of intermediaries who are able to link up administrative levels, arrangements and actors play an important role in this process. In developing the concept of structural congruency, I was inspired by various contingency approaches (Mayntz, 1983; O' Toole, 1990; Smits, 1995). In contrast to those more normative applications, however, my use of the concept is purely analytical. There is no pre-given hierarchical or functional relation between dimensions or between the regional arrangement and the institutional context (Arts and Goverde, this volume). Empirical questions have to be answered like: In what way do the arrangements and the institutional context influence each other? Which dimensions induce change in other dimensions during a certain phase? How does the degree of structural congruency affect the process of institutionalisation?

In the cases described above, adjustment of the arrangement to external policies is common, though there are examples of specific regional practices affecting policy making at higher levels. This proved especially successful, when external policies were not yet fixed nor firmly institutionalised. Also, the provincial level was in general more easily influenced by regional practices than other levels of policy-making. Furthermore, it should be kept in mind that effects may materialise later or in other regions. An example is the idea of creating new villages that was developed in Landstad Deventer. This idea was dropped from the regional agenda due to external incongruence, but popped up in other parts of the Netherlands several years later.

Answering the second question raised above, on which dimensions are likely to induce change in others, the cases show no dominant mechanisms. There are examples of new actors, extra resources, changing rules of the game and new ideas causing effects in other dimensions. Contrary to expectations, however, changes in one dimension do not always induce change in others. The most striking example is the Northwest Frisian arrangement, where opening up access to the regional coalition did not affect the prevailing power relations and discourse.

Addressing the third question about the relation between structural congruency and institutionalisation, especially *external* structural congruency turns out to be an important condition and explains for a great part the relatively strong institutionalisation of the policy arrangements in Northwest Friesland and the Graafschap versus Southwest Salland. Due to sufficient overlap with institutional conditions, the LEADER II arrangement in Northwest Friesland was succeeded by LEADER+ and in the Graafschap the regional coalition was integrated in the regional commission for a new IROP-scheme, called *Reconstruction*. Also, the region Southwest Salland has been merged into the reconstruction scheme, but the overlap in actors, rules and discourses turned out to be much smaller and only single aspects of the arrangement have survived.

The effect of *internal* structural congruency on institutionalisation is less clear cut. The Northwest Frisian arrangement is internally and externally congruent and shows a high level of institutionalisation. However, the Graafschap arrangement has also institutionalised, though internal congruency is low. There are at least two possible explanations for this phenomenon. The period studied is relatively short (five years). In the longer term, internal congruency may play a more important role. Furthermore, in both regions the amount and diversity of funds for rural development grew considerably at the end of the project period. Because it was relatively easy to divide this larger pie and satisfy everyone, the need to make fundamental choices on a leading discourse and to organise rules, actors and resources accordingly decreased.

However, external structural congruency is not a guarantee for stabilisation either, since the attitude of the province also plays an important role. The cases show that the provinces are powerful at the regional level. In their role of leading actor they not only design the organisation and content of actual decision-making, but they also make decisive decisions about whether and how the policy arrangements are to be continued.

Having found sufficient indications that congruence is a prerequisite for the institutionalisation of policy arrangements, the following intriguing question remains: So what? Is institutionalisation of arrangements and congruence important to solve social and policy problems? Postmodernists argue that cultural coherence is decreasing and they even announce the emergence of the post-institutional society (Albrow, 1996; Kumar, 1995). Furthermore, institutionalisation of arrangements may cause social and cognitive fixation, stagnation and lack of innovation (Termeer, 2004). The former neo-corporatist arrangement that structured agricultural and rural policy making is a striking example of this phenomenon. The so-called 'Green Front' succeeded in keeping off the agenda the manure problem caused by intensive livestock farming for years, resulting in serious environmental damage (Frouws, 1994; Termeer, 1993). With Arts and Goverde (this volume) I agree, however, that without some institutionalisation, arrangements will not exhibit governance capacity, especially in the case of potential innovative arrangements developing in a highly dynamic, policy intensive context. Though not explicitly analysed in the case studies above, the IROP experience until now underpins this proposition. It is a common understanding among IROP-professionals that older regional arrangements perform better than younger ones considering aspects such as: cooperation within the leading coalition, creating support amongst various constituencies, mobilisation of bottom-up initiatives, developing integrative solutions and making effective links to other policy levels.

DISCUSSION

In this chapter I compared the emergence and institutionalisation of three regional arrangements on rural issues in a highly dynamic and policy intensive context. To this end, an extra 'tool' was added to the policy arrangement framework. The concept of congruence was presented as a condition for institutionalisation to occur: strategic congruence being at the root of the structuration of decision-making in emerging policy arrangements and structural congruence furthering the stabilisation of these arrangements.

Remarkable similarities exist between the arrangements of Northwest Friesland, the Graafschap and Southwest Salland, despite the differences in initiators, participating parties, rules of the game and discourses. In every region a central role is reserved for a regional coalition of government bodies and NGOs in which provincial actors play a leading role. Furthermore, sub-themes overlap between the three arrangements and in all cases initiatives depend on supra-regional funding.

In accordance with theoretical expectations, sufficient coherence between the policy views of actors involved in the regional coalitions (strategic congruence) proves to be a major condition for the arrangements in Northwest Friesland, the Graafschap and Southwest Salland to emerge. A high degree of overlap with the wider institutional context (external structural congruence) turns out to be especially important for the stabilisation and further institutionalisation of arrangements. In Northwest Friesland and the Graafschap, congruency with new IROP-schemes enables the arrangements to survive, while in Southwest Salland a lack of congruency means the end of the regional arrangement as such, though single parts get embedded in other policy practices.

Taking some distance from regional experiences it is interesting to discuss the meaning of these new arrangements for processes of wider, policy change, summarized by the shift from government to governance (Arts and Van Tatenhove, this volume). On the face of it, the IROP, intended as a break with previous neo-corporatist and etatist practices dominating the rural policy domain, is a typical example of governance. New actors and coalitions are invited to enter the policy arena, multi-level policy cooperation is called for and finding new regional solutions for persistent policy problems is promoted. However, practices in Northwest Friesland, the Graafschap and Southwest Salland tell a different story. Though the new arrangements certainly display some governance features, the influence of traditional ways of making policies and doing politics is still large. For example, while access to the rural decision-making is larger than before, new actors often lack power to really have an impact, because state actors and traditional 'green' partners control major resources. Though some parties further challenging discourses, institutionalisation is rather weak because of lack of coherence with existing policy goals. Furthermore, national or provincial authorities are often not willing to re-negotiate current rules of the game and the political room for manoeuvre. This is reflected in the special position they foster in the various steering committees of the regional projects: they are not real members, but formally have an advisory status, thus keeping their distance. Therefore, the arrangements studied show a mix of government and governance features at the most.

Remarkably, the coalitions of the Graafschap and Northwest Friesland seem to be able to cope with this mix, at least in the midterm their arrangements have survived. The question remains however if stability is also guaranteed in the long term. The IROP gains popularity and gets embedded in front stage policy practices in recent years (Ministerie van LNV, 2004; Ministerie van VROM, 2004). In this process of routinisation and standardisation, though, the new arrangements are being transformed into policy instruments of the state. Policy goals are set and legitimised by classical-modernist political mechanisms of the state, while regional and local actors, both public and private, are invited to 'take their responsibility' in implementing them. Being aware of the inherent transformation of policy goals during this implementation process (Hill and Hupe, 2002), the state tries to limit deviations from formal policy objectives with mechanisms derived from the new public management discourse. Relations with 'implementing actors' like provinces are thus regulated by means of performance criteria set by the state, implementation contracts and monitoring and evaluation requirements (Van Ark and Van den Brink, 2002). This lack of real policy space risks frustrating the political ambitions of regional actors, may cause internal tensions and threatens the continuity or strengthening of the governance features of the arrangements. Of course, this development may in turn open new institutional spaces to be filled by sub-political initiatives, but successful examples are few until now.

REFERENCES

Albrow, M. (1996), *The global age: state and society beyond modernity*, Polity Press, Oxford.

Arts, B., M. Bruns, P. Leroy, D. Liefferink and J.P.M. van Tatenhove (2001), *Biologisch groeien?! Een multi-actor analyse van het beleidsarrangement biologische landbouw (2000-2020)*, Katholieke Universiteit Nijmegen, Nijmegen.

Beck, U. (1994), The reinvention of politics: towards a theory of reflexive modernization, in: U. Beck, A. Giddens and S. Lash (eds.), *Reflexive modernization: politics, tradition and aesthetics in the modern social order*, Polity Press, Cambridge, pp. 1-55.

Boonstra, F. (2001), Leren van plattelandsdiscoursen: omgaan met verscheidenheid in de regionale beleidsarena, *Tijdschrift voor sociaal-wetenschappelijk onderzoek van de landbouw*, Vol. 16, nr. 4, pp. 242-257.

Boonstra, F. (2004), *Laveren tussen regio's en regels: verankering van beleidsarrangementen rond plattelandsontwikkeling in Noordwest Friesland, de Graafschap en Zuidwest Salland*, Koninklijke Van Gorcum, Assen.

Castells, M. (1997), *The information age: economy, society and culture*, Volume II, the power of identity,Blackwell Publishers, Malden/Oxford.

Driessen, P.P.J., P. Glasbergen, P.P.P. Huigen and F.H. van der Berg (1995), *Vernieuwing van het landelijk gebied: een verkenning van strategieën voor een gebiedsgerichte aanpak*, VUGA, 's-Gravenhage.

Driessen, P.P.J. (2000), Provincies als regionaal regisseur, in: P.P.J. Driessen and P. Glasbergen (eds.), *Milieu, samenleving en beleid*, Elseviers bedrijfsinformatie, Den Haag.

Frouws, J. (1994), *Mest en macht: een politiek-sociologische studie naar belangenbehartiging en beleidsvorming inzake de mestproblematiek in Nederland vanaf 1970*, Landbouwuniversiteit Wageningen, Wageningen.

Frouws, J. (1998), The contested redefinition of the countryside: an analysis of rural discourses in the Netherlands, *Sociologia Ruralis*, Vol. 38, no. 1, pp. 54-68.

Grin, J. and H. van de Graaf (1994), Handelingstheorieën en beïnvloeding in netwerken: ongelijksoortige rationaliteiten en congruente betekenissen, *Beleidswetenschap*, Vol. 8, no. 4, pp. 349-366.

Grin, J. and H. van de Graaf (1996a), Implementation as communicative action: an interpretative understanding of interactions between policy actors and target groups, *Policy Sciences*, Vol. 29, no. 4, pp. 291-319.

Grin, J. and H. van de Graaf (1996b), Technology assessment as learning, *Science, Technology, & Human Values*, Vol. 21, no. 1, pp. 72-99.

Hill, M. and P. Hupe (2002), *Implementing public policy: governance in theory and practice*, Sage, London.

Kumar, K. (1995), *From post-industrial to post-modern society: new theories of the contempory world*, Blackwell Publishers, Malden/Oxford.

Leroy, P. (2000), Milieubeleid en beleidswetenschappen, in: P.P.J. Driessen and P. Glasbergen (eds.), *Milieu, samenleving en beleid,* Elseviers bedrijfsinformatie, Den Haag.

Leroy, P., J.P.M. van Tatenhove and B. Arts (2001), Politieke modernisering en beleidsarrangementen: een interpretatiekader voor vernieuwing in het milieubeleid, *Beleidswetenschap*, Vol. 15, nr. 3, pp. 209-228.

Mayntz, R. (1983), Zur Einleitung: Probleme der Theoriebildung in der Implementationsforschung, in: R. Mayntz (eds.), *Implementation politischer Programme II*, Westdeutscher Verlag, Opladen.

Ministerie van LNV (2004), *Agenda vitaal platteland en meerjarenprogramma vitaal platteland*, 's Gravenhage.

Ministerie van VROM (2004), *Nota Ruimte,* 's Gravenhage.

Mormont, M. (1990), Who is rural? Or, how to be rural: towards a sociology of the rural, in: T.K. Marsden, P. Lowe and S. Whatmore (eds.), *Rural restructuring: global processes and their responses,* David Fulton, London, pp. 21-45.

O'Toole, L.J. (1990), Contingentie van beleid en organisatorische arrangementen, in: J.A.M. Hufen and A.B. Ringeling (eds.), *Beleidsnetwerken: overheids-, semi-overheids- en particuliere organisaties in wisselwerking,* VUGA, 's Gravenhage, pp. 121-135.

Pröpper, I. and D. Steenbeek (2001), *De aanpak van interactief beleid: elke situatie is anders,* Uitgeverij Coutinho, Bussum.

Smits, J. (1995), *Milieubeleid gestuurd? Een onderzoek naar de invloed van het BUGM op het gemeentelijk milieubeleid in Noord-Brabant*, Dissertatie Katholieke Universiteit Brabant, Thesis Publishers, Amsterdam.

Termeer, C.J.A.M. (1993), *Dynamiek en inertie rondom het mestbeleid: een studie naar veranderingsprocessen in het varkenshouderijnetwerk*, VUGA, 's Gravenhage.

Termeer, C.J.A.M. (2004), Duurzame transities: een beknopte methodologie voor trajectmanagement, in: P. van der Knaap, C.J.A.M. Termeer and M.J.W. van Twist (eds.), *Trajectmanagement, beschouwingen over beleidsdynamiek en organisatieverandering,* Lemma, Utrecht.

Van Ark, R. and A. van den Brink (2002), Minder rijksinvloed, hardere resultaten bij gebiedsgericht beleid, *Landwerk,* nr. 1, pp. 33-38.

Van der Ploeg, J.D., J. Frouws, and H. Renting (2002), Self-regulation as new response to over-regulation, in: J.D. van der Ploeg, A. Long and J. Banks (eds.), *Living countrysides: rural development processes in Europe, the state of the art*, Elsevier bedrijfsinformatie, Den Haag.

Van der Zouwen, M. and J.P.M. van Tatenhove (2002), *Implementatie van Europees natuurbeleid in Nederland*, Natuurplanbureau, Wageningen.

Van Tatenhove, J.P.M. (1993), *Milieubeleid onder dak? Beleidsvoeringprocessen in het Nederlandse milieubeleid in de periode 1970-1990, nader uitgewerkt voor de Gelderse Vallei*, Pudoc, Wageningen.

Van Tatenhove, J.P.M. (1996), De regio als beleidsarena, *De Sociologische Gids*, Vol. XLIII, nr. 1, pp. 46-59.

Van Tatenhove, J.P.M., B. Arts, and P. Leroy (eds.) (2000), *Political modernisation and the environment: the renewal of environmental policy arrangements*, Kluwer Academic Publishers, Dordrecht.

Chapter 10

Regional Environmental Planning in the Netherlands: An Unstable Settlement of Policy Arrangements

Frans J.G. Padt

INTRODUCTION

It is generally accepted that the first Dutch national environmental policy plan published in 1989 (VROM, 1989) symbolised a major turning point in the history of environmental planning in the Netherlands (De Roo, 2001; Van Tatenhove, 1993). The plan is considered to mark the closing of a period of structuring of environmental politics and the beginning of a period of stabilisation (Van Tatenhove, 1993). In this latter period, the Ministry of Housing, Spatial Planning and Environment (VROM) aimed at integrating environmental policy with the policies on water, on nature, and on economic policies that other ministries were competent for. It considered integrated regional environmental planning very helpful and effective for this 'external integration', as it was called (VROM, 1990). Around the same time, the Ministry of Agriculture, Nature and Fisheries (LNV) was also getting more involved in regional policy (LNV, 1992). It promoted a reorientation of agriculture in the so-called Valuable Man-made Landscapes (WCL). Finally, an increasing importance of 'integrated water management' could be observed, a regional strategy of the Ministry of Transport, Public Works and Water Management (VW). All these regional and integrated planning strategies emerged and evolved during the 1990s simultaneously, but in relative isolation from each other. Despite their differences, they all contributed to the institutionalisation of regional environmental planning, as can be concluded from the increasing importance thereof in national policy plans since 1990 and from policy evaluation studies (Pleijte, 2000; VROM, 1998a, 1998b). Nowadays, a regional approach has become mainstream in environmental planning (VROM, 2004).

In the 1980s and 1990s, major reforms in public administration took place, not only in the Netherlands, but also in many other OECD countries.

B. Arts and P. Leroy (eds.), Institutional Dynamics in Environmental Governance, 203–223.

The New Public Management (NPM) movement is generally considered the driving force behind these reforms (Bovaird and Löffler, 2003; OECD, 1995; Pollit and Bouckaert, 2004). One could think of the Reagan-administration (1981-1989), the era of Prime Minister Mrs. Thatcher (1979-1990) and, in the Netherlands, the first two Lubbers cabinets (1982-1989) to recall a period of budgetary pressures, a revaluation of economic interests, a wave of privatisation, and other efficiency-oriented operations. In the 1990s, practices that are more responsive to societal demands were included in NPM, such as client and community orientation. At national level, this 'inclusive' NPM was a leading concept for the Dutch liberal/social-democratic cabinets during 1994-1998 and 1998-2002 (De Vries, 2002), and it still is for the current liberal/Christian-democratic cabinet that took office in 2002. At local level during the 1990s experiments started, such as 'social renewal', 'urban community policies' and 'interactive policy making' (Hendriks and Tops, 2003; Kickert, 1997; Van Helden and Jansen, 2003). The experiments aimed to stop the alleged 'gap' between government and citizens. The current cabinet has launched an ambitious program *Another Government* to the same end. The program's slogans are: better services, less bureaucracy, effective organisation, and responsive procedures.

NPM represents shifts in governance and hence, as one may expect, may affect policy arrangements for regional environmental planning. In this chapter, I will elaborate on this proposition. To do so, I will treat NPM as a grand political discourse and analyse it at the level of political modernisation (Arts and Van Tatenhove, this volume). Regional environmental planning will be treated at the level of policy arrangements, and the structuring and stabilisation thereof. The research questions are the following:

1. What policy practices emerge from the political discourse of NPM?
2. What policy arrangements could be observed in regional environmental planning at national level during the 1990s?
3. How do these policy arrangements manifest themselves and evolve at regional level?
4. How do actors at the regional level appropriate NPM in their regional practices, and, as a result, can we witness the structuring of a new policy arrangement at regional level?

Question 1 will be answered by unravelling the political discourse of NPM into a set of practices. Moreover, a critical discourse and counter-practices are described. For these purposes international NPM-literature was examined. To answer question 2, a typology of policy arrangements was developed first. This was done after consideration of different conceptual approaches. This typology is used to reconstruct policy arrangements at national level, using policy documents and evaluations. In order to answer question 3, the typology is applied to a case study on agricultural reconstruction in de Brabant Peel (Southern Netherlands). The methods applied here include an intensive search in the records, interviews, content analyses, and media research. The case study results are reported in a narrative style. For an answer to question 4, finally, the practices of NPM and the critical discourses are assessed against the practices and the policy arrangement in the Brabant case. This assessment is based on interview results.

THE GRAND DISCOURSE OF NEW PUBLIC MANAGEMENT UNRAVELED

The discourse of New Public Management (NPM) was articulated in the 1980s in order to handle the financial crises in most OECD-countries (Bovaird and Löffler, 2003) and the replacement of Keynesian economic politics by monetarism (Saint-Martin, 2000). The reformers initially accentuated the need for cost reduction in public policy. Practitioners and scholars gradually articulated this discourse and made it appear as a more or less coherent, necessary, and only possible way of modernising public administration (Pollit and Bouckaert, 2004; Saint-Martin, 2000). The re-formers had a taste for rhetoric, Orwellian language, for myths and symbols, demonising administration and bureaucrat bashing (Clarke and Newman, 1997; Fox, 1996; Frederickson and Smith, 2003). No serving! No bureaucracy! Value for money! Change was articulated in symbols and dichotomous couplets. Steering, not rowing! Results, not process! Production, not politics! Empowerment, not power! Collaboration, not conflict! As for content, the NPM-discourse is a "conflated aggregation of different political motivations and totally incompatible theories" (Fox, 1996). For example, in many NPM-publications it is often not clear whether contracts are treated within the framework of principal-agent theory (control by incentives), transaction-costs theory (contracting-out public services) or a hierarchic conception of government (control culture) (Barzeley, 2000).

From a constructivist viewpoint, the diction, the symbolic manipulation, the emphasis on change, contradictions and ideology serve as perfect illustrations for political discourse building. Harvey (1996) states: "Discourses are [..] embedded within material practices and modes of social relating within institutionalized frames, and operate as forms of political economic power.[..] They act to constitute the world by virtue of the multiple translations and transformations which link them to these other domains of action understood as a whole." He adds: "Only in such terms can we unpack the composite problem of how it is that things become imbued with social relations and operate with such full force as to appear to govern us (as, for example, money typically does) more ruthlessly than any political dictator could ever hope to do so." (Harvey, 1996, pp. 221-221).

Below I will describe four practices through which NPM 'does its work': transparency, businesslike practices, local empowerment, and public entrepreneurship. These practices encompass the classic and well-known aspects defined by Hood (1991) and Osborne and Gaebler (1993), as is shown in Table 10.1 and represent the common denominator in NPM-literature.

1: Transparency. By defining the tasks and responsibilities of public organisations, their mutual relationships will become transparent. Transparent relationships provide the organisations with more flexibility in decision-making and policy implementation. According to NPM, transparency should go along with devolution of authority, and disaggregation of units, thus enabling and constraining others to provide governmental services. Examples of these practices include: defining core-business, separation of policy planning and delivery of services ('steering, not rowing'), formation of quasi-autonomous non-governmental organisations (quango's), performance contracts, outsourcing and so on. Transparency has political consequences as well: it legitimises politicians for interventions within their field of responsibilities or for doing nothing outside that field.

2: Businesslike practices. In order to handle flexibility, business-like management techniques and styles are introduced within public organisations. Public managers are empowered to make decisions based on clearly defined organisational targets. They have a 'freedom to manage' or even a 'right to manage'. According to NPM, the management style should change as well: from hierarchical towards teamwork, from protective towards productive, and from activities towards results. NPM assumes that the redistribution of tasks and the introduction of businesslike practices will lead to a better performance of the organisations involved. Accordingly, NPM puts much emphasis on output controls and explicit standards and measures of performance. Performance management enhances both accountability and organisational learning.

Table 10.1. The doctrinal components of Hood (1991) and the ten principles of Osborne and Gaebler (1993) as a basis for discerning practices of NPM

Practices	Hood (1991)	Osborne and Gaebler (1993)
Transparency	Shift to disaggregation of units	
Businesslike practices	Hands-on professional management Stress on private-sector styles of management practice Explicit standards and measures of performance Greater emphasis on output controls	Decentralized government: from hierarchy to participation and teamwork Results-oriented government: funding outcomes, not inputs
Local empowerment	Shift to greater competition in public sector	Community-owned government: empowering rather than serving Competitive government: injecting competition into service delivery Costumer-driven government: meeting the need of the costumer, not the bureaucracy Market-driven government: levering change through the market
Public entrepreneurship	Stress on greater discipline and parsimony in resource use	Anticipatory government: prevention rather than cure Catalytic government: steering rather than rowing Mission-driven government: transforming rule-driven organizations Enterprising government: earning rather than spending

3: Local empowerment. Public organisations should be sensible and responsive to their citizens ('costumers' in NPM-jargon). Service delivery should become more competitive in order to provide the best services. Communities are empowered to realise their own goals in market-like arenas of choice, provided by public organisations.

4: Public entrepreneurship. Public managers have an active role in resolving difficulties with politics and public administration, such as misty decision-making, failing politicians and bad communication. They are empowered public servants arranging public choices. Because of their 'constitutive' role, public managers should be liberated from the 'bad system' and become public entrepreneurs (instead of being administrators). Public entrepreneurship is a core-value of NPM, not only in this broad sense, but also in a narrow sense of resourcefulness, i.e. greater discipline and parsimony in resource use. Rules and procedures are considered too restrictive. Instead, the mission of an organisation and the desired outcome should give direction to investments.

Overall, it seems appropriate to consider NPM as a political discourse and as a set of policy practices referring to the level of political modernisation (Arts and Van Tatenhove, this volume). More particularly, NPM can be conceived as an aggregate of operating practices and operating instructions that indicate or reflect how to organise these 'shifts in governance' and how to behave in their midst. As a particular way of operating, NPM thus results from 'shifts in governance' and reinforces them in turn. Yet, critical observers of NPM seriously criticise its public impact (Christensen and Lægreid, 2002; Clarke and Newman, 1997; Denhardt, 2004; Denhardt and Denhardt, 2003; De Vries, 2002; Tonkens, 2003). According to the 'critical discourse', NPM has a 'dark side' regarding democratic and public values. The first point of critique is that NPM brings along a democratic deficit. It is said that the control of the political process becomes of greater importance than a public political debate. Consensus becomes an end in itself, rather than a mean to achieve political ends. The near-term emphasis on efficiency takes a toll on social equity. Wicked problems are put aside when they do not fit into the prevailing management views and organisational structures. The animosity of public managers towards democratic institutions and the trias politica implies a depoliticisation of policy making. Public managers are opportunistic and just want to make good deals. They commit power politics and take too many social risks. Their arrogance and flashy style attracts hostility and suspicion in the public sector and undermine the public's confidence in government.

The second point of critique is the lack of 'publicness' that is involved with NPM. It is said that there is no such thing as a public interest for public managers. "Underlying the market model of government is an article of faith, a belief that the free play of market forces will bring the self-interested participants – individuals, social groups, agencies, firms – into an equilibrium that represents in some way the maximum achievable social good." (Denhardt, 2004, p. 141). As a result, the public interest is equated with superficial public opinion and democracy becomes synonymous for freedom of choice. Consumers are regarded as citizens only when they can reduce costs. The model of the welfare state as a market-based delivery system for passive and discriminating customers involves the dismantling of society as a collective entity responsible for complex problems. People learn to distrust each other and democratic institutions by the contract-based accountability. NPM encourages 'exit' and discourages 'voice'.

Within this critical discourse new counter-practices have been developed that include public leadership, citizen engagement, dialogue, and community building. This chapter will explore for the Brabant case to what extent such practices are actually present in regional environmental planning and counterbalance the influence of NPM.

A TYPOLOGY FOR POLICY ARRANGEMENTS

The word typology literally means the study of types. The main typological term in sociology is 'ideal type'; a term coined by the sociologist Max Weber as an accentuation of certain elements common to most cases of a social phenomenon. It is not meant to correspond to all of the characteristics of any particular case. Nor does an ideal type refer to perfect things, moral ideals or statistical averages. Ideal types are an abstraction for the understanding and the explaining of social phenomena. For the purpose of this study, a framework for ideal types can be found in the literature on the organisation of the state. A common distinction is that between etatism, liberal-pluralism and neo-corporatism. This distinction has been proposed for PAA too (Liefferink, this volume). Etatism and liberal-pluralism can also be grounded by other frameworks such as social order theory or governance models (called hierarchical coercion and market exchange here). Yet, neo-corporatism does not fit into these frameworks unambiguously. In social order theory, a third type (next to hierarchy and market) is called 'community' (based on collaboration) and in the governance model it is called 'networks' (based on state-society partnerships), but these three types do not necessarily point to the same type of policy arrangement. So we still need a somewhat more precise framework.

Harvey (1996) has presented such a framework, when he provides a comprehensive overview of ideal types that can be found in the environmental-ecological debate. Following Harvey, I propose three basic types of policy arrangements: authoritarian, pluralistic-liberal and decentralised-communitarian. According to the first type, authoritarian solutions are regarded as the only possible political solution to the 'tragedy of the commons'. Although this style of argument was at its height in the 1970s, it still seems to accompany hierarchical, coercive, state-led environmental politics. I prefer to use the label 'authoritative' instead of 'authoritarian' to prevent any totalitarian and dictatorial connotation. The pluralistic-liberal policy arrangement opens up for negotiation, power plays and consensus building between interests groups on environmental issues. It provides an opportunity to keep the environmental issue on the agenda. Finally, the decentralised-communitarian policy arrangement derives inspiration from a participatory form of society. Egalitarianism, non-hierarchical organisation, local empowerment, and participation in decision-making are usually depicted as the political norm. Although communitarism knows different and sometimes extreme versions on the left and right side of the political spectrum, communitarism basically fits into the mainstream politics in Western-European countries (Pierre and Peters, 2000; Van der Meer, 2003). The basic tenet of communitarism is about scale and not about the government system itself. In fact, communards argue that the large-scale society and government need to be replaced by smaller units of governing, whereas individuals need to have their self-interest modulated by less selfish commitments to community (Pierre and Peters, 2000). This view is also obvious from the modest applications of the communitarian logic in governance practices as expressed by, for example, interactive policy making and self-governance.

Summing up, the ideal types labelled 'authoritative', 'pluralistic-liberal' and 'decentralised-communitarian' will be used as ideal types for policy arrangements in regional environmental planning. In order to draw up a typology, I have interpreted the general description of these ideal types in terms of discourse, coalitions, resource allocation, and rules (Table 10.2). A short explanation of the three basic types of policy arrangements runs as follows. The authoritative policy arrangement is based on an intervention discourse and governmental coalitions that aim at solving problems in the region. Legitimised regulatory state power (or 'political capital') is used as the main resource for strategic planning. The rules are supported by legislation and legal procedures. The pluralistic-liberal policy arrangement is based on an integrated approach (including negotiations) and partnership coalitions between governmental bodies and stakeholders that aim at integrating different interests in the region. A state budget allocated to stakeholders (or 'economic capital) is used as the main resource for coordinated policy implementation. The rules are laid down in covenants that take current legislation for granted. The decentralised-communitarian policy arrangement is based on promoting local initiatives and building semi-autonomous authorities of governmental bodies, stakeholders, and local people that aim at realising specific goals in the region. Social capital is used as the main resource for grassroots projects. The rules apply to experiments that anticipate or go beyond legislation.

Table 10.2. The typology for regional environmental policy arrangements used in this study

Ideal types Dimensions	Authoritative	Pluralistic-liberal	Decentralised-communitarian
Discourse	State interventions	Stakeholder involvement and negotiations	Local initiatives
Coalitions	Governmental bodies solving problems	Partnership between governmental bodies and stakeholders integrating policies	Semi autonomous authorities of governmental bodies, stakeholders and local people realising area specific goals
Resource distribution	Legitimised regulatory state power for strategic planning	State budget allocated to stakeholders for coordinated policy implementation	Social capital for grassroots projects
Rules	Legislation	Covenants	Experiments

POLICY ARRANGEMENTS AT NATIONAL LEVEL

Around 1990, the Ministry of VROM increasingly interfered in rural affairs. The carriage for this was the Spatial Planning and Environmental Experiment (ROM) in ten large areas throughout the Netherlands. The ROM-experiment applied for both the countryside and urban areas and essentially aimed at solving persistent environmental problems. The basic tenet of the ROM-projects was that specific areas need specific goals and 'tailor made' solutions, an integrated approach and societal negotiations (De Roo, 2001; Van Tatenhove, 1993; VROM, 1990). Provinces had a leading role in the ROM-projects. Evaluations have shown that governmental representatives, professionals and stakeholders highly appreciated ROM from the beginning. In most ROM-projects (eight out of ten) ROM forced a breakthrough in the integration of spatial and environmental policies. Moreover, the ROM-projects accelerated the implementation of prevailing policies (VROM, 1998a, 1998b).

The discourse of ROM held that the generic goals and strategies should be adapted to the problems and circumstances in specific areas. Furthermore, stakeholders should be involved with vigour in negotiations on regional planning. Coalitions of governmental bodies with stakeholders (interest groups, societal parties, private parties) were considered of crucial importance to make a success out of ROM. Moreover, the Ministries of VROM and LNV allocated substantial resources for the ROM-projects. Covenants were applied as a pragmatic rule to deal with the various stakeholders and their interests, and with the allocation or resources. These characteristics of ROM largely point at a pluralistic-liberal policy arrangement (Table 10.2). It should be noted that the Ministry of VROM persisted in a dominant role for itself in the ROM-projects, especially regarding the resources and the rules. Funding of projects was only possible when based on detailed integrated implementation plans. Measures had to be supplementary to generic policy and had to lead to a 'specific environmental quality'. Provinces had to give a detailed account on performance and expenditures of individual measures on a yearly basis. As for rules, regional actors hardly had any room in the ROM-projects to deviate from the environmental standards. Because of these constraints in rules and resources, the ROM-projects have always experienced strained relations between central government and regional actors (VROM, 1998a, 1998b).

Around 1990, the Ministry of LNV was also getting more involved in regional planning. This involvement can be explained from the breakdown of the traditional neo-corporatist model in agricultural policy. Neo-corporatism can be defined as "the extra-parliamentary political practice of ongoing negotiations between the formal representatives of the organized interests of capital and labour, facilitated by the state and conditioned upon substantive outcomes, over issues of social and economic policy-making under the primacy of the democratic constitutional state." (Visser and Hemerijck, 1997, p. 66). The *Landbouwschap* represented the 'organised interests of capital and labour' in Dutch agricultural policy and was assigned a formal role in agricultural policy making since the early 1950s. The neo-corporatist model was highly contested during the 1980s due to some major social changes (Frouws, 1994; Hees, 2000). Citizens increasingly moved from urban areas to the countryside that considered their new environment not the exclusive domain of farmers any longer. In addition, the public concern about the environmental damage of (intensive) livestock farming rapidly increased. The Ministry of LNV was increasingly criticised for being a 'closed bastion' out of reach of parliamentary control and unable to respond to societal change. In reaction to that, the ministry decided to embark on a new course that placed the agricultural interest in a broader rural and societal context. The new approach was applied to eleven so-called Valuable Man-made Landscapes (WCL). The basic tenet of WCL was to decrease the tension between agriculture, nature and landscape thus offering a new impulse to agriculture. The practical implication of this was that farmers were supposed to look for new derived incomes such as agro-tourism, agricultural nature management, and landscape protection. The ministry emphatically intended the reorientation to be established through local initiatives and local participation rather than from the narrow agricultural interest (Baerselman and Kusiak, 1994).

The discourse of WCL was 'rural development by local initiatives'. With this discourse the Ministry of LNV distanced itself from unilateral steering in the WCL-projects. It endeavoured to establish autonomous coalitions under provincial control and with participation of local people. These coalitions were assigned to translate abstract policy goals into area-specific operational goals and programs. The Ministry of LNV encouraged regional actors to cooperate and to develop new initiatives. Hence it used the local social capital as a resource. Informal rules dominated the game in WCL. Examples included the establishment of temporary project agencies and advisory agencies, the appointment of regional brokers, and the support of agricultural corporations and rural entrepreneurs. As for policy arrangements, WCL policies largely reflect the decentralised-communitarian ideal type (Table 10.2). Yet, in practise the bottom-up approach in WCL was only partly realised due to a lack of trust between central government and local actors, the noncommittal attitude of farmers and the inexperience of local organisations with the bottom-up process (Pleijte, 2000). Moreover the Ministry of LNV frustrated its own policy since it disapproved many local initiatives that would be 'good' for the region, because they did not fit into legal frameworks. This has led to many disappointments and frustration in the region (RLG, 1999).

A third strategy in regional environmental planning was applied by the Ministry of VW and was called 'integrated water management' (Wiering and Crabbé, this volume). 'Integrated water management' was born in practice. Its roots trace back to the 1970s as a working practice of RWS (Directorate-General of Public Works and Water Management, the implementing organisation of the Ministry of VW). One of the core-business of RWS is the protection of the Netherlands against flooding. Until the mid-1970s, public safety ('dry feet') was determinative for the water management but gradually a societal discussion took place about the effects of water management on nature, wildlife, and the fishing industry. RWS anticipated that discussion by deploying a 'water system approach'. The water system approach stresses the internal cohesion within a water system and its relation with the environment. This approach took root during the 1980s and was elaborated on in the subsequent national water management plans (Grijns and Wisserhof, 1992; VW, 1989). The water system approach also led to more cooperation between organisations within and outside the water sector and to a pursuit for 'integrated water management'. The current definition of integrated water management runs as follows: "Having and keeping a safe and inhabitable land and to maintain and to strengthen healthy and resilient water systems, with which a sustainable use remains guaranteed." (VW, 1998, p. 11). With this definition, the Ministry of VW clearly took integrated water management beyond the water domain and 'upgraded' it as a strategic integration frame that was relevant for other ministries (the Ministries of VROM and LNV in particular) too.

The water system approach and integrated water management that developed during the 1980s and 1990s served as a discourse for water management. The coalitions of agencies involved in integrated water management were limited to governmental bodies. Private parties were usually kept out of the coalitions using the argument that they only should trigger conflicts of interests without taking responsibility (Van der Veen et al., 1991). This rather spiteful argument reflected the highly technical approach of integrated water management at that time. Scientific and technical expertise was an important resource for making long-term 'integrated water management plans'. These plans overruled diverse interests to carry through major constructions developing the infrastructure in territorial and coastal waters. Also, these plans were to be considered the main rule for integrated water management, yet an informal rule next to formal legal rules (Van der Veen et al., 1991). All in all, the integrated water management largely reflected the authoritative policy arrangement until recent times (Table 10.2). Nowadays the coalitions are more open to private and societal stakeholders. Moreover, integrated water management encompasses a wide range of issues: from short-term local technical problem solving to long-term ecological and safety problems at national and international scale and includes more 'liberal' and 'communitarian' characteristics to deal with this. Its major challenge is to mobilise organisations and citizens to take collective action to tackle shared experienced problems (Van Leussen, 2002).

In sum, regional environmental planning practices gradually institutionalised into three distinctive policy arrangements at the national level during the 1990s. In spatial and environmental planning the ideal type of a pluralistic-liberal policy arrangement could be recognised; rural development policy displays a decentralised-communitarian type of policy arrangement; the integrated water management comes close to an authoritative ideal type of policy arrangement. These distinct policy arrangements developed at the same time and can be regarded as rather stable around the millennium change. In a word: regional environmental policy in the late 1990s showed a high degree of compartmentalisation.

POLICY ARRANGEMENTS IN THE BRABANT PEEL

The municipality Gemert-Bakel is situated in De Peel, the densest livestock farming area in the Netherlands. The area faces huge pollution of ground water, surface water, and air by agricultural nutrient sources for more than two decades. Moreover, expansion in agriculture has affected the traditional rural landscape and the resilience of the livestock. This section goes into state interventions to solve these problems, the way the Province of Brabant reacted to that and the way local authorities moulded their own policy arrangement. The period under scrutiny encompasses the period 1992 through 2002. The policy events at national level, in the Province of Brabant and in Gemert-Bakel are described chronologically.

State Interventions for Agricultural Reconstruction

In 1992, the Ministry of LNV intervened in the region to solve the persistent environmental problems caused by the intensive livestock farming. To this end, a governmental committee proposed an ambitious vision for the region. This vision, however, evoked many protests among local stakeholders. It was then decided to invite stakeholders to join the committee, and to focus on implementation of current policies rather than on creating ambitious visions. Moreover, it was decided to follow an integrated approach and to agree on a covenant. Yet, when this approach began to pay off in the region, central government frustrated it. The reason for this was a severe veterinary crisis.

On February 4th 1997, swine fever broke out on a pig farm in the municipality of Venray in the Brabant Peel. The swine fever rapidly spread all over the area, partly because the pig farmers anticipated the prohibitive order on the transportation of animals by doing the reverse. Moreover, the General Inspection Service of the Ministry of LNV (AID, *Algemene Inspectiedienst*) failed to control the situation. Ten million pigs had to be slaughtered, most of them because it was not allowed to transport them from the overcrowded stables. The large-scale killing mobilised the public opinion against 'factory farming'. On World Animal Day in 1997, thousands of people made an appeal to the national government in four national newspapers to "end the awful circumstances under which pigs are being fattened." The same year, the well-known writer J.J. Voskuil raised the *Stichting Varkens in Nood* (Foundation 'Pigs in Trouble') that started several campaigns against factory farming with the help of well-known Dutchmen. The public opposition against factory farming quickly opened a window of opportunity, which the veterinary crisis had created, for central government to announce a drastic 'reconstruction' of the intensive livestock sector in the sandy vulnerable areas in the Southern and Eastern part of the Netherlands.

The core of this reconstruction was a generic cut of 10% of the livestock herd, without compensation (Pig Farmers Act). This intervention evoked strong protests among Dutch farming organisations that engaged in a bitter juridical fight with the Ministry of LNV for many years. The reconstruction also included precautionary veterinary measures: the realisation of pig-free zones and regional pig-clusters. Pig clusters had to include pig farms, veterinarians, animal-feed companies, slaughterhouses, and destruction companies. Pig-free zones had to separate these respective clusters spatially. The pig clusters and pig-free zones were supposed to prevent large scale spreading of veterinary diseases and thus to make the pig chain less vulnerable. The Ministry of LNV also decided to lower the density of livestock in 500-meter zones around vulnerable nature areas through the realisation of 'ammonia zones'. The rationale of this measure was that acidification through ammonia is a local problem: the greatest part of the ammonia emitted by pig farms falls down within 500 meters. Both the veterinary and ammonia measures were elaborated in the Reconstruction Bill (1998). The Reconstruction Bill assigned provinces to draw up reconstruction plans and proposed to establish reconstruction committees with stakeholders that should advise the province on the reconstruction plans. It comes as no surprise that the provinces reacted enthusiastically about this new legal instrument and perceived it as support for their regional environmental planning.

Start of the Reconstruction in Brabant

The Province of Brabant anticipated the reconstruction during 1999. It invited stakeholders to join a Reconstruction Platform. This platform soon agreed on the starting points for the reconstruction in Brabant. These starting points, however, deviated from the Reconstruction Bill. The platform wanted to follow an integrated approach rather than to intervene in the livestock herd. The platform also argued that implementation and not planning should have priority. The strongest deviation from the Reconstruction Bill concerned the zoning, as the platform proposed not to establish fixed ammonia zones of 500 meters around vulnerable nature areas with a low livestock density according to the Reconstruction Bill. They argued that these zones would lead to the loss of many livestock farms and a loss of jobs in agriculture. In order to find an alternative for the zoning rules, the platform proposed to set up an experiment to determine the most appropriate way of zoning.

The area of Gemert-Bakel (henceforth GB) offered an exquisite opportunity for experimenting with the zoning and was given a pilot status. In fact, GB had developed and applied the concept of 'integrated zoning' in the local reconstruction plan for GB. This concept was based on the relocation of intensive livestock farming from 'extensification zones' of 250 meters around vulnerable nature areas towards 'developmental zones' elsewhere in the province. This proposal clearly deviated from the Reconstruction Bill that had proposed ammonia zones of 500 meters, without any obligation for making them free from livestock. There were three reasons for this deviation. Firstly, livestock free zones of 250 meters were supposed to be more effective than low-density livestock zones of 500 meters. Secondly, the small-scale landscape in Brabant did not allow delineation of zones of 500 meters. Thirdly (and most important), the province and its reconstruction partners did not accept the loss of jobs in the agribusiness that would result from 500-meter zones. After all, pig farms were not allowed to develop in these zones and farmers thus would have to give up their income. The province and its reconstruction partners, on the contrary, wanted to offer them new prospects in development zones.

A Local Reconstruction Committee prepared the reconstruction in GB with representatives of the local community, the province, and national government. The local reconstruction promoted local initiatives. These initiatives had a bias towards agriculture, although other themes were included as well (water management, liveability, and cultural-history). This indicates that GB aimed at new economic prospects for the livestock sector. The Province of Brabant supported GB in this. This interpretation of the reconstruction, however, largely challenged the government's intentions for the reconstruction, i.e. reduction of the livestock herd. As we are still in the start-up phase of the reconstruction here, we cannot yet speak of a 'policy arrangement'. Yet, it is clear that GB moved provisionally towards a communitarian-like policy arrangement that both substantially and organisationally challenged the more authoritative intentions of central government. The Province of Brabant acted as a go-between: on the one hand it was committed to the reconstruction 'intervention', while on the other it respected and endorsed locally institutionalised practices. This position logically follows from the middle position of a province in the Dutch unitary state. Yet, the special thing in the Brabant case was that the province aggressively acted as a policy broker or agent purposively 'hybridising' two conflicting policy practices. The province was even prepared to endeavour a change in The Hague rules and it was powerful enough to do so as we will see in the next section.

An Urge for Integration of Policies

In 2000, a political struggle broke out on the Reconstruction Bill. The agricultural sector and the provinces had mobilised resistance towards the 500-meter zones. They convinced the Lower House to reduce the zones to 250-meters and to make them free of livestock. When the Lower House discussed the Reconstruction Bill at the end of 2000 (two years after it had been published!), it decided to include the 250- meter zones in the Reconstruction Bill. In January 2002, the Upper House agreed on this amendment in the Reconstruction Act.

In the meantime, the Province of Brabant anticipated the reconstruction with a lot of enthusiasm. It established eight regional Reconstruction Committees with stakeholders in Brabant and assigned them to make integrated implementation-based reconstruction plans. The assignments were laid down in an Umbrella Plan (2001), a framework of 'obligations' of different rigour. This plan encompassed a wide range of themes (from soil management to social-economic policy) and hence stimulated an integrated approach for the reconstruction. At the same time the province laid down additional zoning rules in the draft version of the Town and Country Plan for the provincial territory. The province also endeavoured to generate financial resources for the reconstruction through public-private partnerships: local authorities were allowed to distribute extra building plots and the revenues were partly pumped back in the reconstruction. It should be noted that the province used the phrase 'revitalisation' rather than 'reconstruction' to emphasise that it aimed at an integrated developmental approach. It obviously considered this the most feasible way to carry through the more narrow reconstruction and the accompanying limitations for agriculture. Again the province played its role as policy broker with vigour.

GB endeavoured to make a success out of the pilot. The emerging communitarian policy arrangement from 1999 (see above) was consolidated during 2000 by the establishment of a special project office for GB. This office established new alliances between local people, stakeholders and provincial and local representatives. It promoted a wide range of local, yet mostly agricultural, initiatives and allocated resources accordingly. The zoning, however, caused many conflicts since the zoning had to meet the legal rules of the Reconstruction Bill, the provincial Town and Country Plan and the local reconstruction plan. These conflicts were pacified when the Minister of LNV (financially) met the wishes of the local agricultural community to relocate some farms from extensification zones.

In 2001, the project office decided to follow an integrated approach in line with the provincial Umbrella Plan. To fulfil this new task, it was up-scaled to a 'Developmental Office'. This Developmental Office had to make special programmes, next to the local reconstruction plan, for 'social-economic policy' and 'quality of life' through a bottom-up approach. This integrated approach in GB mirrored the integrated approach that the province applied to the revitalisation (see above). Both GB and the province obviously aimed at a trade-off of more substantial integration with more regulatory compliance. Whereas the province acted as a policy broker towards central government, GB acted as a policy broker towards the local community.

To conclude: at the end of 2001, a 'hybrid' policy arrangement could be observed in GB consisting of a pluralistic-liberal discourse, decentralised-communitarian coalitions and resource distribution and authoritative rules. In 2002, the Province of Brabant established the Developmental Office in GB (see above) formally. The Developmental Office can be considered as the material evidence and institutionalisation of the hybrid policy arrangement described above.

NPM IN THE BRABANT PEEL

In this section I explore to what extent NPM can explain the hybrid policy arrangement in GB. First, I will assess two sets of NPM-practices (transparency & businesslike practices and public empowerment & local entrepreneurship) against the practices in GB. Next, I will elaborate on the way the actors dealt with the alleged democratic and public shortcomings of NPM and how we can understand the role of NPM in the reconstruction.

The Developmental Office in GB played a crucial role in the reconstruction in GB as became clear in the previous section. The Province of Brabant created this office to facilitate the reconstruction in GB. This indicated a purposeful 'transparent' separation of policy (steering) and implementation (rowing). The Developmental Office had the freedom to manage (because of its pilot status) and it considered teamwork and the production of projects to be very important. There was, however, no indication that the Developmental Office applied performance management explicitly. In short, transparency and businesslike practices could be recognised in GB, although in a diffuse version. There was a separation of policy and implementation, but this was not based on a formal devolution of authority or an area-based contract. There was also freedom to manage, but this was not based on clearly defined targets or performance management. In short, one could speak of an informal and softened approach of NPM in these respects.

The entrepreneurial spirit in GB was paramount. This spirit arose from the impatience with institutions and the desire to set up nice outcomes (or projects) that somehow contributed to the reconstruction mission. This entrepreneurial spirit had a constitutive effect. The support of a powerful public manager turned out to be a prerequisite.

> The assignment was to set to work, get experience and to show what issues we run into. What attempts fail and why? Showing the bottlenecks clearly, providing examples, getting a dialogue going with the authorities and trying to find solutions together: that is what our work is all about. [...] Our alderman steers the implementation strongly. He sketches the outlines with us when a project gets stuck and he points the desired direction. He constantly supports us and is a powerful manager in that respect. He knows his colleague-alderman, knows what is going on and knows how far he can go (interview with a local official).

Indeed, the institutions did slowly change and the community was getting more involved in resource allocation. One could not speak, however, of 'market-like arenas of choice' that empowered local people to realise their own goals (that would reflect the influence of NPM more directly).

In conclusion, the practices of NPM could be observed in GB although in a modified and 'softened' version. Therefore one could expect that GB is also less vulnerable to the alleged shortcomings of NPM. This seemed to be the case indeed. GB spent much time in bringing the projects in accordance with political conditions (long-term goals, priorities, availability of money). This democratic way of acting included a lot of checks and balances. Yet, it should be noted that democracy not only referred to formal governmental (decision-making) procedures, but rather to informal governance practices. These governance practices went along with a continuous search for the public interest. Area-based projects had a strong preference since they could meet the public interest better than single projects. Moreover, GB invested a lot in the public support for these projects. In short, the Developmental Office seemed to apply a democratic governance model, rather than a traditional government model in the local reconstruction.

Now that we have observed a 'softened' version of NPM in GB, we can discuss the question to what extent this NPM mirrors the hybrid policy arrangement. As was shown above, the hybrid evolved from an urge to compensate for the compliance with state rulings on the reconstruction. The Province of Brabant and GB were 'partners in policy broking' for implementing the reconstruction with endorsement of locally institutionalised practices. In doing so, they in fact produced a liberal discourse as well as communitarian coalitions and resource distribution under the flag of 'revitalisation'. The same argument applies to the role of NPM in GB. Also this discourse produced hybrid practices, namely of public entrepreneurship, the involvement of the community and democratic governance, with the aim of serving the implementation of the reconstruction.

DISCUSSION

During the 1990s, regional policy arrangements gradually institutionalised at a national level into three distinct policy arrangements that can be regarded as stable around the millennium change. After this period of stabilisation a new period of structuring seems to have arrived, in which the stable policy arrangements at the national level 'tumble down' and mix up into hybrids in regional practices. The GB case showed that a hybrid policy arrangement could be observed consisting of a liberal discourse, communitarian coalitions and resource distribution and authoritative rules. At the same time, this hybrid has to be defined in new terms. On the one hand, GB appropriated NPM considering the 'mission driven' entrepreneurial and constitutive spirit and community involvement. Hence, the communitarian coalitions and resource distribution of the hybrid tie up to 'local empowerment and public entrepreneurship' On the other hand, GB counterbalanced the alleged democratic and social shortcomings of NPM considering the democratic governance model. Hence, the liberal discourse ties up to 'democratic governance'. This might be a comforting thought for critical observers of NPM. Obviously, GB follows a balanced approach and succeeds in meeting the alleged shortcomings of NPM.

How about the authoritative legal rules of the hybrid? Do they have to be defined in NPM-terms of contracts and performance rather than in legal terms? The answer seems to be no, considering the dominance of legal rules and the virtual absence of contracts and performance in GB. This leads to the conclusion that the hybrid of GB is an unstable settlement of three different logics, derived from distinct policy arrangements: a 'governmental logic' (authoritative rules), a 'governance logic' (liberal discourse) and an 'NPM logic' (communitarian coalitions and resources). From this Brabant case we can learn that this is not necessarily a problem, considering the positive role of the Developmental Office in keeping the hybrid going.

REFERENCES

Baerselman, F. and L. Kusiak (1994), *Sturing op maat: een andere benadering van milieuproblemen in de land- en tuinbouw*, Ministerie van LNV, 's-Gravenhage.

Barzeley, M. (2000), How to argue about the new public management, *International Public Management Journal*, Vol. 2, no. 2(A), pp. 183-216.

Bovaird, T. and E. Löffler (2003), *Public management and governance*, Routledge, London.

Christensen, T. and P. Lægreid (2002), New public management: puzzles of democracy and and the influence of citizens, *The Journal of Political Philosophy*, Vol. 10, no. 3, pp. 267-295.

Clarke, J. and J. Newman (1997), *The managerial state*, Sage Publications, London.

Denhardt, J.V. and R.B. Denhardt (2003), *The new public service, serving, not steering*, M.E. Sharpe, New York.

Denhardt, R.B. (2004), *Theories of public organization*, Thomson Wadsworth, California.

De Roo, G. (2001), *Planning per se, planning per saldo; over conflicten, complexiteit en besluitvorming in de milieuplanning*, Sdu Uitgevers, 's-Gravenhage.

De Vries, J. (2002), *Paars en de managementstaat,* Garant, Leuven.

Fox, C.J. (1996), Reinventing government as postmodern symbolic politics, *Public Administration Review*, Vol. 56, no. 3, pp. 256-261.

Frederickson, H.G. and K.B. Smith (2003), *The public administration theory primer*, Westview Press, Boulder, Colorado.

Frouws, J. (1994), *Mest en macht: een politiek-sociologische studie naar belangenbehartiging en beleidsvorming inzake de mestproblematiek in Nederland vanaf 1970*, Landbouwuniversiteit Wageningen, Wageningen.

Grijns, L.C. and J. Wisserhof (1992), *Ontwikkelingen in integraal waterbeheer, verkenning van beleid, beheer en onderzoek*, Delft University Press, Delft.

Harvey, D. (1996), *Justice, nature and the geography of difference*, Blackwell Publishers, Malden/Oxford.

Hees, E. (2000), *Trekkers naast de trap: een zoektocht naar de dynamiek in de relatie tussen boer en overheid*, Grafisch Service Centrum van Geels.

Hendriks, F. and P. Tops (2003), Local public management reforms in the Netherlands: fads, fashions and winds of change, *Public Administration*, Vol. 81, no. 2, pp. 301-323.

Hood, C. (1991), A public management for all seasons?, *Public Administration*, Vol. 69, Spring, pp. 3-19.
Kickert, W.J.M. (1997), Public management in the United States and Europe, in: W.J.M. Kickert (eds.), *Public Management and Administrative Reform in Western Europe*, Edward Elgar, Cheltenham, pp. 15-38.
Ministerie van LNV (1992), *Structuurschema groene ruimte*, 's-Gravenhage.
Ministerie van VROM (1989), *Nationaal Milieubeleidsplan: kiezen of verliezen*, Tweede Kamer, vergaderjaar 1988-1989, 21137, nrs. 1-2.
Ministerie van VROM (1990), *Gebiedsgericht milieubeleid, Actieplan*, Tweede Kamer, vergaderjaar 1990-1991, 21896, nrs. 1-2.
Ministerie van VROM (1998a), *Evaluatie ROM-aanpak*, 's-Gravenhage.
Ministerie van VROM (1998b), *De proef op de ROM, ervaringen met gebiedsgericht beleid in 10 ROM-gebieden*, 's-Gravenhage.
Ministerie van VROM (2004), *Nota ruimte, ruimte voor ontwikkeling*, 's-Gravenhage.
Ministerie van VW (1989), *Derde nota waterhuishouding: water voor nu en later*, Sdu Uitgevers, 's-Gravenhage.
Ministerie van VW (1998), *Vierde Nota waterhuishouding: regeringsbeslissing*, Sdu Uitgevers, 's-Gravenhage.
OECD (1995), *Governance in transition: public management reforms in OECD countries*, Organization for Economic Co-operation and Development, Paris.
Osborne, D. and T. Gaebler (1993), *Reinventing government: how the entrepreneurial spirit is transforming the public sector*, Plume, New York.
Pierre, J. and B.G. Peters (2000), *Governance, politics and the state*, Macmillan, Basingtoke.
Pleijte, M. (2000), *WCL's ingekleurd: monitoring en evaluatie van het beleid voor Waardevolle Cultuurlandschappen*, Alterra, Wageningen.
Pollit, C. and G. Bouckaert (2004), *Public management reform, a comperative analysis*, Oxford University Press, Oxford.
RLG (1999), *LNV tussen Europa en de regio; tweede interimadvies; randvoorwaarden en uitvoering rurale ontwikkelingsplannen*, Raad voor het Landelijk Gebied, Den Haag.
Saint-Martin, D. (2000), *Building the new managerialist state, consultants and the politics of public sector reform in comparative perspective*, Oxford University Press, Oxford.
Tonkens, E. (2003), *Mondige burgers, getemde professionals; marktwerking, vraagsturing en professionaliteit in de publieke sector*, Nederlands Instituut voor Zorg en Welzijn, Utrecht.
Van der Meer, J. (2003), *Communitarisme en vertrouwen in politieke instellingen; verslag van een empirisch onderzoek*, Erasmus Universiteit Rotterdam, Rotterdam.
Van der Veen, J., M.C. Groenenberg and P. Glasbergen (1991), Bestuurskundige invalshoek: methodische aspecten van integrale beleidsplanning, in: P. Glasbergen, M.C. Groenenveld, J. van der Veen, I. van Zanten, P.J.J. van Buuren and A.A.J. de Gier, *Integrale beleidsplanning voor grote wateren*, Sdu Uitgevers, Den Haag, pp. 121-135.
Van Helden, G.J. and E.P. Jansen (2003), New public management in Dutch local government, *Local Government Studies*, Vol. 29, no. 2, pp. 68-88.
Van Leussen, W. (2002), *Leven met water; vermaatschappelijking van het waterbeheer – consequenties voor de civiel ingenieur en voor waterbeheerorganisaties*, Inaugural lecture University of Twente, Enschede.
Van Tatenhove, J.P.M. (1993), *Milieubeleid onder dak? Beleidsvoeringprocessen in het Nederlandse milieubeleid in de periode 1970-1990, nader uitgewerkt voor de Gelderse Vallei*, Pudoc, Wageningen.
Visser, J. and A. Hemerijck (1997), *A Dutch miracle; job growth, welfare reform and corporatism in the Netherlands*, Amsterdam University Press, Amsterdam.

Chapter 11

Corporate Environmental Management in the Netherlands and in the Czech Republic

Jacques Klaver and Emiel Ypma

INTRODUCTION

Giving environmental considerations a place in strategic and operational decision making in companies has gained more and more support from governments and from a lot of companies themselves. This development is partially reflected in the growing number of companies that have a certified environmental management system in place.

To analyse how this development has taken place in different political and social contexts, a comparative research project was started in the Netherlands and in the Czech Republic. These countries have been chosen because of their comparable size and their pioneering roles in introducing policies of corporate environmental management (CEM). The Netherlands was one of the first countries to have such a policy and was, together with other larger European countries, an important instigator of a European regulation for CEM, namely the Eco-management and Audit Scheme or EMAS. In turn, the Czech Republic was the first accession country to have fully implemented this EMAS regulation in 2000, indicating a pioneering role regarding CEM in Eastern Europe. An underlying motive for the choice of these countries was the wish to make an estimation of the effects of the unification of Europe on policy arrangements around CEM.

Another reason for choosing pioneering countries was the need for comparable data that covered a larger period of time. In the Netherlands, the early elaboration of policies regarding CEM and the presence of policy-oriented research guaranteed that sufficient data were available and accessible. Similar circumstances were necessary in the accession country of our choice. After a short analysis focusing on ISO 14001 certification and EMAS implementation, the Czech Republic proved to be the best country to investigate, as it had a relatively large number of ISO 14001

B. Arts and P. Leroy (eds.), Institutional Dynamics in Environmental Governance, 225–243.

certified companies and, as was mentioned before, it was the first newly accessing country to have fully implemented the EMAS regulation.

The central question of this chapter is how differences and similarities in the development of CEM in both countries can be understood in terms of the policy arrangement approach. As an indicator of CEM development we use the number of certified environmental management systems from 1995 till now. This indicator, of course, only partially reflects what is going on. Therefore, we also use information from interviews with persons who are familiar with the issue and who know more about the reality behind the quantitative data. Persons from several key organizations in the Netherlands and Czech republic were interviewed: civil servants at the Dutch ministry of the environment, a representative of the Dutch chemical business organization, a manager of a big chemical multinational, a person involved in the writing and revision of ISO 14001, the director of the Czech Environmental Management Centre, and a person with wide experience in the Czech Ministry of the Environment, also involved in writing and revising ISO 14001 and who is now a project manager in a consultancy firm.

The first section of this chapter introduces our key concepts. Then we describe some of the differences and similarities in the political, administrative and legal contexts in the Netherlands and the Czech Republic. The next section analyses the developments of CEM in these two countries. Subsequently, we reconstruct the CEM policy arrangements concerned. The final section draws some conclusions and answers the central question of this chapter.

KEY CONCEPTS

The first central concept of this chapter is 'corporate environmental management', henceforth CEM. CEM is a general term for all activities and facilities by and in companies that may contribute to control and improve their environmental performance. When these activities and facilities are systematized, we use the term 'environmental management system' (EMS).

In the recent past, several standards for EMSs have been developed. The most recent one is the ISO 14001 that was introduced by the International Organization of Standardization in 1995. A related standard that we have to mention here is the Eco-management and Audit Scheme (EMAS). This scheme was introduced by the European Union in 1993. Since then, member countries are obliged to create institutions within their jurisdictions, which facilitate firms to adopt and implement an EMAS scheme. The intention was to enhance the environmental performance of companies by promoting the use of (certified) EMSs, by having the companies and their EMSs audited and by promoting environmental reports being published by the companies. Participation in EMAS, however, has not been obligatory for companies.

A company can have its EMS certified according to the EMS-standard concerned, which gives a certain guarantee that the company has the (management) capacity to control and improve its environmental performance. Of course, the degree to which this capacity can be guaranteed depends on several variables (Klaver and Jonker, 1998). One of these is the capability of the certifying body to assess the quality of an EMS. Another is the fact that the actual level of environmental performance of a company is *not* subject to the certification procedure. This only attests to whether a system is in place. So having a certified EMS is not a guarantee that a company performs well. A comparison can be made with a driving permit: it is not a guarantee for good driving.

CEM has its roots in the 1980s (Gunningham et al., 1998; Gunningham and Sinclair, 2002). During this decade, it became clear that many Western European states, including the Netherlands, could not cope with their environmental problems by means of their traditional physical regulations and regulatory strategies. This 'state failure' paved the way for the rise of alternative forms of regulation. Economic and communicative instruments and self-regulation were supposed to replace or supplement traditional regulations. One of these instruments was CEM. Gunningham and others (1998, 2002) have investigated and described these shifts in the field of environmental regulation in general and for specific countries and industrial sectors in particular. The research described in this article can be considered a specification and elaboration of their work, albeit from a different theoretical perspective.

The other key concepts that we use in this chapter are those related to the policy arrangement approach. These concepts have been explained in the introductory chapters of this volume. The central concept is 'environmental policy arrangement', which offers an analytical framework, consisting of several dimensions: actors and coalitions, resources and power relations, rules of the game and policy discourses (Liefferink, this volume).

THE DUTCH AND CZECH CONTEXTS COMPARED

Policy arrangements do not emerge out of the blue, nor do they evolve or change autonomously. For a good understanding of the structure and development of policy arrangements, it is necessary to take their contexts into consideration. Therefore, this section describes and compares the social, political, administrative, legal and economic contexts of CEM policy arrangements in the Netherlands and the Czech Republic. Although these Dutch and Czech systems have quite different histories, both countries display numerous similarities nowadays.

The Netherlands as a state has its roots in the 17th century, during which the Republic of the seven united provinces was founded, after a long war against Spanish rule. The republic evolved into a constitutional monarchy. Its current political system can be characterised as a decentralized state with a parliamentary democracy. Decentralisation is displayed in the division of power between the central government, the 12 provincial and the 467 municipal administrations. Special power is also given to the *Waterboards*.

We distinguish two complementary lines of renewal in the history of environmental policy in the Netherlands (Van Loosbroek and Klaver, 2001). The first line is that of direct regulation. In 1952, the environment permit was introduced as a legal instrument to control the environmental performance of companies and other organisations. Since that introduction, a lot of experience has been gained with this kind of direct regulation. However, the practices of this command and control strategy have been the subject of much evaluative and critical research (Aalders, 1980; Berenschot, 1982; Evaluatiecommissie Wabm, 1988, 1992, 1994; Evaluatiecommissie Wet milieubeheer, 1998; Gilhuis, 1999; Kooij and Tonnaer, 1984; Raad voor het Milieubeheer, 1993; Ringeling, 1993; Smits, 1995; Twijnstra and Gudde, 1979). Many shortcomings were recognized and formed the impetus for improvements, especially for efforts to improve the effectiveness of environmental permits.

A second and parallel line of development is the introduction of new ways and modes of environmental governance. Market instruments, communication strategies and various ways of facilitation are more and more used to influence the behaviour of companies. The quest for an optimal mix of policy instruments is characteristic for this development (Gunningham et al., 1998). From around 1985, governments attempted to gradually transfer environmental responsibility to companies themselves. The discussion evolved around concepts such as remote steering, self-regulation, deregulation, etcetera (CRMH, 1988; Drupsteen et al., 1998).

Corporate environmental management, standardization and certification, eco-labelling, covenants and environmental reporting all neatly fit into this development towards new practices of environmental governance vis-à-vis industry. We also see hybridization of traditional and new governance practices coming up. For instance, more flexible environmental permits are granted by governmental authorities in case companies have a certified EMS in place and regularly publish environmental reports.

The Czech Republic as a nation has its roots in 1918, when it emerged as a united state with Slovakia. After the Second World War, it came under communist rule. However, Czechoslovakia freed itself from communism in 1989 and the political system drastically changed thereafter. The parliamentary democracy with a house of representatives was restored and a senate with more political parties involved regained its real significance. The administrative system – with a central government, regional and municipal administrations nowadays – also changed, although devolution is not a dominant feature in the Czech administrative system. On the contrary, this administration has a strong tradition of centralisation (Kamstra, 2003).

The legal system of the Czech Republic is quite comparable to that of the Netherlands nowadays, although the Czech experience with an independent legal power is still limited. In 1993, the new Czech constitution came into force, when the Republic separated from Slovakia. A constitutional state, democracy and sovereignty of people, a parliamentary system, human rights and division of powers became the basic principles of the new Czech Republic. In this constitution, the country has adopted a Charter of Fundamental Rights and Freedoms. These principles are basically the same principles as those in the Netherlands: freedom of expression, freedom of choosing representatives, freedom of self organization, etcetera.

The new Czech environmental legislation has evolved from 1990 onwards. In 1993, the General Law on the Environment came into force. Other more sectoral environmental laws also date from the beginning of the nineties. In The Czech Republic, the development of environmental governance had quite a different starting point than in the Netherlands. Recently, however, it has been heavily influenced by the accession to the EU. As to the starting point: the environment has never had the political priority it had in the Netherlands. As a result, the need for and the effectiveness of environmental policy were not societal and political topics of discussion and effort. Nor has the 'new modes of governance' debate been a political issue. Besides, the accession to the EU almost automatically placed priority on the legal system: the Czech Republic had to meet the requirements of the European environmental *aquis*. Adapting the legal system had top priority. Related to that, the adaptation of the administrative system was seen as necessary. Nowadays, the administrative capacity of the Czech Republic is recognized as one of the main problems that has to be dealt with (Kružíková, 2004). The discourse about environmental governance in a wider sense never had much attention from government, business or civil society. The fact that for example business self-regulation reached the political agenda was mainly due to the influence of EU accession, especially the implementation of the EMAS regulation. This urged the Czech government to create the institutions necessary to meet the requirements of this regulation.

The economic context in both countries is quite similar in a lot of respects during the period studied. Both countries have an open economy. The level of import and export compared to the gross national product is quite high. The main trade partner for both countries was and is still Germany. The economy of both countries has shown growth since 1990. Yet a striking difference between the Dutch and Czech economic context has been the ownership of production capital. In the Czech republic, many (big) companies were state-owned, a heritage from the communist regime. This state ownership was and is much more limited in the Netherlands. After 1990, the number of state-owned companies in the Czech republic has however sharply decreased (from 3505 in 1990 to 126 in 2003, according to the Czech Statistical Office 2005).

The Dutch and Czech social context is quite different as far as civil society is concerned. Dutch civil society is quite well developed and the environmental movement is diverse and rather influential. Dutch government acknowledges environmental organisations as a partner in decision making and often supports them financially as well. Nowadays, these government subsidies are not that dominant anymore. Today, environmental groups get a lot of their financial resources from the National Lottery system (which is private in nature).

In contrast, the Czech civil society had to adapt itself to the new situation after 1989. It got more freedom to organize and express itself. It also could communicate much easier across borders. On the other hand, it could no longer gain advantage from its (silent) oppositional role against communism, now the latter system had disappeared. Moreover, civil society was faced with the fact that most people did not have much to spend and that it did not get much financial and human support from the Czech population. Also, national government does not give much support to the groups (Fagan and Jehlicka, 2003). As a consequence, the Czech environmental movement has become much more dependent on external funding nowadays. External funding obviously has the advantage of extending the resource base, but also has the disadvantage of 'short-termism' due to project funding (Jansen, 2005).

In sum, we obviously see differences and similarities in the contexts of CEM policy arrangements in the Netherlands and the Czech Republic. The differences in political, administrative, legal, economic and social contexts have gradually decreased in the past 15 years. The main factors in this convergence process are, in our view, the collapse of communism, the economic transition of the Czech Republic thereafter, the accession of this country to the EU and – as a consequence of all this – the fact that market conditions have grown quite similar from 1989 till now. However, there remain several dissimilarities: the role of state ownership in the means of production, which is still higher in the Czech Republic, and the role and diversity of environmental movements, which are still less prominent in the Czech Republic. Other dissimilarities concern the steering model used. There is a long tradition of what is called *poldering* in the Netherlands: trying to reach agreements between government and social partners (companies, trade unions, environmental NGOs) with a minimum of state regulations. In the Czech Republic, the government still largely adheres to the command and control model and to making and enforcing regulations. However, although there are apparent differences in the context of CEM arrangements in both countries, these do not seem to have strongly influenced the development of EMSs, as we shall see in the following sections.

CORPORATE ENVIRONMENTAL MANAGEMENT IN THE NETHERLANDS AND IN THE CZECH REPUBLIC: A REVIEW

In this section we give an overview of the development of CEM policies in the Netherlands and in the Czech Republic respectively. In the former country the initiative for a policy on corporate environmental management, incorporating EMSs as its main tool, originated from the employers' organisation VNO-NCW. The first public report about this subject was published in 1986 (VNO-NCW, 1986). The ideas were elaborated by representatives of employers and public authorities in the Commission Environmental Management Systems (in Dutch: *Commissie Bedrijfsinterne Milieuzorgsystemen*, 1988). The fact that this emerging policy strategy is dealt with by a mixed committee – consisting of both public and private actors – reflects the Dutch *poldermodel*.

The government presented a policy to stimulate the implementation of EMSs in 1989 (Tweede Kamer der Staten-Generaal, 1989). An elaborate network of public-private corporations and facilitating organisations was created to implement this policy in the years that followed. One of the important parts of the institutional framework was the creation of an organization for coordinating the certification of EMSs in the Netherlands (SCCM). Next to that, it was denoted as a competent body for the coordination of EMAS as well. In parallel, the self-regulation-model in environmental policies was shaped by the Dutch Minister of the Environment at that time, Winsemius. He formulated a new philosophy of environmental management in his book "Guest in ones own house" (*Gast in eigen huis*). This philosophy was based on three basic concepts: the quality of the environment, the internalisation of environmental responsibilities and sustainability. In his own words: "To behave as if we were guests in our own house and to reach a quality of the environment that we together experience as good" (Winsemius, 1987). These principles are still central to Dutch environmental policy.

The concept of internalisation (*verinnerlijking*: integration of environmental concerns in all human activities, including corporate processes) is considered to be necessary to reach a better quality of the environment as well as to achieve sustainability. According to the view of the government, producers and consumers both cause environmental pressure and thus affect environmental quality. Therefore they have the obligation to take the environment into account in their day-to-day activities. For companies, this means that they should "acknowledge the necessity of changing their behaviour and from this acknowledgement of their own responsibility seek for possibilities to make environmental care part of their day-to-day behaviour" (IMP-M 1986-1990, 1985; in: Van Tatenhove, 1993). Environmental management systems (EMSs) became the main policy instruments for this internalisation process in companies. Until 1995, corporate environmental management was the most important elaboration of this concept (Van Tatenhove, 1993). Later on, other instruments of this kind were developed as well, as for instance CO_2-emissions trading (next section).

The number of (certified) EMSs in companies has grown steadily from 1990 till now. In the beginning, there was only one standard for certification available, BS 7750, which originated from the UK, but also gained significance outside this country. Soon thereafter, the ISO 14001 standard entered the scene and captured its dominant position from 1995 onwards. It was quite easy for companies with BS 7750-certified EMSs to get an ISO 14001 certification. This explains why 75 ISO certificates already existed in the Netherlands in December 1995. This was about one third of the total number in Europe and 0,27% of the world's total. The Dutch number of ISO 14000 certificates increased to 1073 in December 2002, which was 4,6% of Europe's and 2,2% of the world's total amount (ISO 2005). However, the EMAS numbers have always been quite low. The number of registered organizations was 25 in April 2004. The main reason for this low Dutch enthusiasm for EMAS – compared to ISO – is that EMAS has a limited validity (only in the EU) and that EMAS registration is more demanding for companies: a public and verified environmental report is obligatory. Therefore the costs are also higher than for ISO certification. Apart from the companies with a certified EMS, there are also companies with an uncertified system. Data from the chemical industry in the Netherlands show that this number is quite high (Table 11.1). The main 'missing item' in these uncertified EMSs is the external audit.

Table 11.1. Percentage of Dutch chemical companies with a certified EMS or having (parts of) a non-certified EMS

Percentage of companies*:	1998	1999	2000**
With a certified EMS (BS 7750, ISO 14001, EMAS)	28	36	43
Without a certified EMS, but with:			
- environmental policy statement	96	96	96
- environmental program	94	94	96
- division of tasks, responsibilities and competences	86	86	90
- integration of tasks in procedures and instructions	85	87	87
- systematic monitoring and registration	91	92	94
- environmental reporting	100	100	99
- internal instructions and training	92	94	93
- internal audit	64	70	71
- external audit	33	31	28

source: FO Industrie, 2000a, 2000b, 2001.

*The total number of companies was 118, 121 and 122 in 1998, 1999 and 2000 respectively.

**2000 was the last year with the progress of EMSs recorded. In the year 2002, about 50% of the companies had adopted a certified EMS. There was a fall back to 46 % in 2003.

CEM policy has developed quite differently in the Czech Republic. With the breakdown of the Berlin Wall in November 1989, Czechoslovakia at that time, together with the other countries of the former Warsaw Pact, disposed itself of the communist rule. The new independent Czech Republic was formed in 1993, after the peaceful separation of the Czech and Slovak parts of Czechoslovakia. The Europe Agreement between the EU and Czechoslovakia was replaced by a similar agreement with the Czech Republic. In this agreement, the co-operation between this country and the EU was arranged in the fields of economics, culture and politics. The final goal was free trade between the Czech Republic and the EU. One of course also anticipated the end goal: accession to the EU.

Free trade meant new opportunities and new demands for Czech trade and industry. One of those demands was the need for implementing EMSs. At that time, EMSs were mainly being standardised according to the international standard ISO 14001. From 1995 onwards, Czech companies picked up this international development and started implementing EMSs according to this standard. Additionally, in March 1998, the EU decided to start accession negotiations with the Czech Republic and, with that, it became a candidate member of the EU. As a consequence, it had to adopt the laws and regulations applying to all other EU member states, also in the environmental field. Hence, the Czech Republic was confronted with policies on corporate environmental management as well, in particular the European Regulation 'concerning the voluntary participation of organisations in an EC environmental management and auditing system (EMAS)', dating from 1993 (EEC, 1993). This regulation urged the Czech government to create an institutional framework for the application of EMAS in the Czech Republic. One of the main parts of this framework had to be a 'competent body', which became the 'EMAS Agency' in the Czech Republic (Ypma, 2003, p. 83). The EMAS regulation also demanded to establish a national program to promote the knowledge and use of the system. During the implementation of this program, intermediate organizations like consultancy firms played an important role (Ypma, 2003, p. 84). Financial support came from the EU (Phare project). Contrary to what might be expected from the title of the program, EMSs in general were stimulated, including ISO 14001.

The number of ISO 14001 certificates in the Czech Republic grew from 4 in December 1997 to 318 in December 2002 (ISO 2005). EMAS registration stayed low in this country too: from 0 in 2000 to a poor 19 in April 2005. There are several reasons for the lagging behind of EMAS. The economic benefits of EMAS and ISO 14001 are comparable, whereas the demands of EMAS are higher (verified and public environmental report) while its validity is lower (EU countries only).

COMPARATIVE ANALYSES OF DUTCH AND CZECH CEM POLICY ARRANGEMENTS

In this section we present a comparative analysis of the development of CEM in the Netherlands and in the Czech Republic. This comparative analysis is based on a more elaborate study of the CEM policy arrangements in both countries (Ypma, 2003). This analysis is twofold: it has a temporal component and a geographical element. On the one hand, we distinguish between the period from 1989 until 1995 (referred to as 'national policy making') and the one since 1996 (referred to as 'internationalisation'). The other part of the comparison, on the other hand, is that between the arrangements in the Netherlands and those in the Czech Republic. We consider 1995 to be a pivotal year because of the official introduction of the ISO 14001 standard in that year.

The First Period: National Policy Making (1989-1995)

The *actor constellations* around corporate environmental management policy in the Netherlands and the Czech Republic generally comprised the following group of players: governmental actors, NGOs and trade and industry. However, trade and industry were differently represented in the Netherlands and the Czech Republic: by traditional representative organisations in the former country, particularly VNO-NCW, and by newly established organizations, especially promoting corporate environmental management, in the latter. These latter organizations were the Czech Environmental Management Centre (CEMC), established in 1992, the Czech Business Council for Sustainable Development (CzBCSD), established in 1993, and several sectoral trade and industry organisations.

Another difference is the position and attitude of environmental NGOs. At first, these were rather indifferent towards CEM in the Netherlands. However, when they observed the growing popularity of EMSs, they started to play a more active role and tried to make the best of it by demanding legislation on obligatory environmental reporting and auditing. They also stressed the importance of transparency. In contrast, Czech environmental NGOs hardly showed any interest in CEM at that time. They were more oriented towards nature protection, management of natural resources, energy saving and nuclear energy (Ypma, 2003, p. 64).

The *resources* available to the members of the policy coalitions were – overall – similarly divided in the Netherlands and the Czech Republic. Trade and industry had most resources, because of their knowledge about managing company processes and the financial means to put this knowledge into practice. The Dutch government made also some resources available for stimulating EMSs: personnel and financial resources for stimulating programs and monitoring implementation. This was not done so in the Czech Republic at that time. Also, in both countries, we observed differences in resource availability between the larger enterprises and the small and medium sized ones. This was also reflected in the relatively higher number of large enterprises with certified EMSs.

The *rules of the game* applying to the policy making process on corporate environmental management considerably differed between the Netherlands and the Czech Republic. Whereas in the Netherlands legally obligatory rules and mutually agreed covenants were combined, Czech public authorities depended more upon the traditional command-and-control steering model. Self-regulation did not fit within this model. In the Netherlands, the emergence of the policy on corporate environmental management was exemplary for the rise of the communicative or interactive steering model (with the command and control at the background and only used when necessary). There was another difference in the rules of the game. The Dutch government retained the right to impose a legal arrangement on corporate environmental management, if trade and industry did not show enough progress in implementing EMSs and temporarily used this threat to put trade and industry under pressure. The implementation of EMSs was often part of the covenants that were agreed upon by national government and businesses as well. The government of the Czech Republic, on the other hand, only used its legal means to enhance the environmental performance of companies. EMSs did not get a special place in environmental policy. As to EMSs themselves: they were already used by leading companies. A real international standard was not present at that time, although the regional EMS standard of the British Standardization Organization – the BS 7750 – was accepted by internationally operating firms as a general one. Besides, it also formed the basis for developing the ISO 14001 standard later on.

In the Netherlands, at that time, the *discourse* on corporate environmental management could be typified as an all-embracing discourse, in which sustainable development is central. This term was also used in the Rainbow Programme, launched by the Czech Ministry of the Environment in 1991. The programme was aimed at the recovery of the environment in the Czech Republic. The content of the discourse in both countries was mainly about reconciling economic and environmental goals. The presence of this discourse was also demonstrated by the founding of the Czech Business Council for Sustainable Development in 1993. Another discourse, which became apparent in the Netherlands, was that of internalization and corporate responsibility. EMSs were discussed as a means for companies to display their own environmental responsibility and to increase their capacity to improve environmental performance. This discourse had no prominent place in the Czech Republic.

When we try to characterise and compare the policy arrangements on corporate environmental management in this first phase, the one in the Netherlands is best typified as a neo-corporatist arrangement, in which state and business actors co-operate, share resources and try to create a solution with which both parties are satisfied. In contrast, we do not see much of a 'real' CEM arrangement in the Czech Republic at all in this first phase.

The Second Period: Internationalisation (Since 1996)

In the second period, changes in CEM policy are apparent in both countries. First of all, CEM *actor constellations* significantly changed. For example, the EU began to play a more prominent role. This new role was primarily based on the EMAS Regulation dating from 1993. This regulation obliged all member states to create the necessary conditions and institutions for the EMAS registration, including the auditing, validation and verification of the standard as well as the accreditation of certifying bodies. Another actor that gained access to the constellation was the *International Organisation of Standardisation* (in short: ISO). ISO is a hybrid NGO of public and private actors and consists of a network of national standard institutes of 150 countries nowadays. This organization promotes and develops standards, which are useful to industrial and business organizations of all types. The ones most widely known are the management system standards of the ISO 9000 and ISO 14000 families for quality management and environmental management respectively.

Taking the *resource* constellation of both CEM arrangements into account, it is striking that the role of the Dutch national government in supporting and promoting EMSs has diminished in this second phase. This was mainly due to the fact that this government was of the opinion that enough had been done to stimulate EMSs and that most companies had been making sufficient progress (Tweede Kamer, 1998). The Czech government, next, only acted as an intermediary between EU and businesses by creating the necessary institutions to make the implementation of EMSs possible. However, it was the EU that made the necessary resources available, for instance by means of the PHARE- project funding, to implement the Czech EMAS Programme.

The *rules of the game* regarding the CEM policy arrangement changed in the Netherlands in this second phase. The Dutch government used its legal means to promote EMSs by making environmental reporting obligatory for about 320 (big) companies (Tweede Kamer, 1996). Another way in which the Dutch government has exerted influence was by offering regulatory relief under certain conditions. One of those conditions has been the presence of a certified EMS in a company. Under such conditions, an environmental permit can be given that only contains the environmental performance goals for a company, but that does not prescribe how companies should reach these goals in detail (a so-called *Vergunning op Hoofdzaken* or Framework License). Environmental NGOs and law enforcing organisations have however been reluctant to give their support to this type of regulatory relief. The highest Dutch administrative court – the Council of State – did not even approve of these permits in some cases. Therefore, it is not yet clear how this way of dealing with environmental permits will develop in the near future.

Contrary to the Netherlands, in the Czech Republic the system of environmental permits does not take into account the presence of EMSs. EMS is a supplementary tool there, not interchangeable with aspects of a permit, such as in the Netherlands Whereas in the latter country several steps in developing voluntary instruments have been made, the emphasis in environmental policy is still on a command and control approach in the Czech Republic. Whether this will continue in the future remains to be seen. It also depends on the emphasis that the EU will put on the use of voluntary instruments.

Regarding other rules of the game, namely the EMS rule systems themselves, the following developments have taken place. The ISO 14001 standard was introduced in 1995 and has conquered the world since, with nearly 50,000 certificates in 118 countries (end 2002). This number is still growing (ISO 2005). Stimulated by the EU and by the issuing of the EMAS regulation and the ISO 14001 standard in both countries, conditions and institutions were created for 'building trust' in both standards. This process was accelerated by the decision of the Czech Republic to join the EU and the beginning of the accession procedure in 1998. In that year, the Council of the EMAS Program, the Agency for the EMAS Program and the Institute for Accreditation were created. (Ypma, 2003, p. 65). These Czech institutions were also used as an infrastructure for ISO 14001. In the Netherlands, though, more effort was put in institution-building for ISO 14001. It soon became clear that ISO 14001 would become more popular amongst companies than EMAS. One of the issues which needed to be solved with ISO 14001 was a uniform interpretation by the certifying companies (Klaver and Jonker, 1998). This was done by the Foundation for Coordination and Certification of EMSs (SCCM in Dutch), that was initiated by Dutch government and in which business, environmental NGOs and national government co-operate.

The above makes clear that the Dutch government conceived its policies as a kind of trade-off between state regulatory strategies (permits) on the one hand and self-responsibility (EMS) on the other. The word "relief" reflects the relative interchangeability of the two strategies, as does the threatening with regulatory strategies, if an EMS would not deliver. As to the Czech Republic, it seems that EMS has been a welcome supplementary instrument for a state that had to cope with new EU obligations. However, there is no element of regulatory relief in Czech environmental policy.

In both countries, a central element in *the discourse* about CEM and EMSs is the voluntary character of CEM. A legal obligation for companies to implement an EMS was subject of discussion in the Netherlands for years, but has vanished in this second period. CEM is regarded as the responsibility of companies themselves. A new element in the CEM discourse in both countries is related to product stewardship, or product-oriented environmental management (POEM). This discourse is linked to the one on integrated chain management and on a producer's responsibility. Government and some branch organisations in the Netherlands were convinced of the necessity of the introduction of product stewardship. The VNCI for instance – the Union of Dutch chemical industrial companies – puts effort into convincing and informing its members of product stewardship as an important element of Responsible Care. Apart from some leading companies, product stewardship is still not common practice in Dutch trade and industry, however (Ypma, 2003, pp. 50-59). The same goes for Czech companies, with this difference that less effort has been put into stimulating this development in the Czech Republic. Here, more attention has been paid to product eco-labelling, which is another way of stimulating product-oriented environmental management. This instrument is also promoted by the European Union. It is however more directed towards the consumer and less so to the producer.

Summarizing the second period, we observe quite some changes in the CEM policy arrangements. Especially the actor constellations and the rules of the game have considerably changed in both countries. EU and ISO appeared on the stage and have had a clearly distinguishable impact on the policy arrangements and on the development of environmental management systems. In the Czech republic, EU support by means of PHARE-project funding has been an important element in this second period. Given these developments, the policy arrangements can be best typified as arrangements in transition in both countries in the second period. At first, governmental actors (especially EU and the national governments) have played a significant role in the accommodation and stimulation of EMSs in both countries. The EMAS regulation in particular is an important impetus in this respect. Later on, the role of governments diminished and market actors have gradually taken over. The introduction of the worldwide standards of the ISO 14000 series marks the beginning of this process that gradually has taken more momentum. Nowadays, we can typify the CEM policy arrangements as liberal-pluralist in both countries. There still exists a role for governments to play, but this concerns maintaining pressure on companies by enforcing (stricter) demands concerning environmental performance. As to how companies improve or maintain their environmental performance, that is their own business. It is particularly up to themselves and their market stakeholders whether they use (certified) EMSs or not.

CONCLUSIONS

Since the early 1990s we observe a continuous growth of (standardized) environmental management systems around the world, particularly ISO 14001. This development is however quite uneven. For example, about half of the total number of ISO 14001 certified companies can be found in Europe. This continuous increase in numbers of certified companies can also be observed in the Netherlands and in the Czech Republic. The start of this increase manifested itself in the Netherlands about a decade earlier. This earlier start of EMS growth can be related to the establishment of a CEM policy arrangement in the Netherlands already from 1986 onwards. In the Czech Republic, the CEM policy arrangement as we know it today only emerged after the year 2000.

These differences in growth and phases of CEM policy arrangements in both countries can be explained by differences in their contexts. Especially the disappearance of communist rule in 1989 and the accession to the EU in 2000 paved the way for and stimulated the growth of CEM policy in Czech Republic. These political changes were paralleled by economic changes that were beneficial for the development of EMSs. The most apparent change in this sphere was the privatization of formerly state-owned companies and the increase of competition and market opportunities. In general, we can say that economic development creates favourable conditions for companies with (certified) EMS systems. In turn, the introduction of an internationally recognized environmental management system standard in 1995, the ISO 14001, has opened up new economic opportunities for both countries (a competitive edge, a means of building trust and levelling of the economic playing field).

In terms of structural change of the CEM policy arrangements in both countries, we can conclude the following. In the Netherlands, the CEM policy arrangement before 1995 can be typified as a neo-corporatist one with government and business jointly facilitating EMSs in several ways. The introduction of new rule systems – EMAS in 1993, but especially ISO 14001 in 1995 – marked the beginning of a period in which market agencies and market factors gradually gained influence, while the Dutch government stepped back. In contrast, a CEM policy arrangement was non-existent in the Czech Republic before 1995. Here the introduction of EMAS and ISO 14001 and the accession to the EU created some government involvement at first, but soon market forces became dominant and a liberal-pluralist CEM policy arrangement emerged in this country as well.

REFERENCES

Aalders, M.V.C. (1980), *Handhaving van de Hinderwet, verslag van een onderzoek handhavingsproblemen bij de Hinderwet,* Staatsuitgeverij, 's-Gravenhage.

Berenschot (1982), *Landelijk onderzoek naar de organisatie en uitvoering van de Hinderwet en aanverwante milieutaken,* Utrecht.

Centraal Bureau voor de Statistiek (2005), *Statistisch Jaarboek 2004,* Den Haag.

Centrale Raad voor de Milieuhygiene (1988), *Het milieu: besturen op afstand?* Verslag van studiedag in samenwerking met de Natuurbeschermingsraad op 8 juni 1988, Sdu/DOP, Den Haag.

Commissie Bedrijfsinterne Milieuzorgsystemen (1988), *Milieuzorg in samenspel,* Den Haag.

Czech Statistical Office (2005), http://www2.czso.cz/eng/redakse.nsf/i/cr:_key_macroeconomic_indicators.

Drupsteen, T.G., P.C. Gilhuis, C.J. Kleijs-Wijnnobel, S.D.M. de Leeuw and J.M. Verschuuren (1998), *De toekomst van de Wet milieubeheer,* W.E.J. Tjeenk Willink, Deventer.

Europese Unie (1993), *Council Regulation nr. 1836/93 van de het Europees Parlement en de Raad van de Europese Unie van 29 juni 1993 inzake de vrijwillige deelneming van bedrijven uit de industriële sector aan een communautair milieubeheer- en milieuauditsysteem,* Publicatieblad Nr. L 168 van 10/07/1993 p. 0001 – 0018, Brussel.

Evaluatiecommissie Wet Milieubeheer (1988), *Om de kwaliteit van de vergunning,* Sdu, Den Haag.

Evaluatiecommissie Wet Milieubeheer (1992), *De milieuvergunning in bedrijf: fase 1,* Sdu, Den Haag.

Evaluatiecommissie Wet Milieubeheer (1994), *De milieuvergunning in bedrijf: fase 2,* Sdu, Den Haag.

Evaluatiecommissie Wet Milieubeheer (1998), *Evalueren met beleid: de Evaluatiecommissie Wet milieubeheer in bedrijf,* Sdu, Den Haag.

Facilitaire Organisatie Industrie (FO Industrie) (2000a), *Uitvoering intentieverklaring chemische industrie*, Jaarrapportage 1998, Den Haag.

Facilitaire Organisatie Industrie (FO Industrie) (2000b), *Uitvoering intentieverklaring chemische industrie*, Jaarrapportage 1999, Den Haag.

Facilitaire Organisatie Industrie (FO Industrie) (2001), *Uitvoering intentieverklaring chemische industrie*, Jaarrapportage 2000, Den Haag.

Fagan, A. and P. Jehlicka (2003), Contours of the Czech environmental movement: a comparative analysis of Hnuti Duha (Rainbow Movement) and Jihoceske matky (South Bohemian Mothers), *Environmental Politics,* Vol. 12, no. 2, pp. 49-70.

Gilhuis, P.C. (1999), Het milieurecht na 2000: een blik vooruit (slotbeschouwing), *Milieu & recht*, Vol. 26, nr. 3, pag. 86-90.

Gunningham, N., P. Grabosky and D. Sinclair (1998), *Smart regulation,* Clarendon Press, Oxford.

Gunningham, N. and D. Sinclair (2002), *Leaders and laggards, next-generation environmental regulation*, Greenleaf Publishers, Sheffield.

International Organisation of Standardisation (2005), *The ISO Survey of ISO 9000 and ISO 14000 Certificates*, Twelfth cycle: up to and including 31 December 2002, http://www.iso.ch/iso/en/.pdf.

Jansen, N. (2005), *Strike a blance, a comparative case study of environmental NGOs in Hungary and Romania as nations in transition*, Master thesis of Social and Political Sciences of the Environment, Radboud University Nijmegen, Nijmegen (not published).

Kamstra, J. (2003), *Patronen van bestuurlijke verandering in Tsjechië onder invloed van Europese druk*, Master thesis Opleiding Bestuurs- en Organisatiewetenschap, Radboud University Nijmegen, Nijmegen (not published).

Klaver, J. and J. Jonker (1998), The significance of recent EMS standards as an Impetus for Improvement. *Eco-Management and Auditing*, Vol. 5, no. 1, pp. 1-5.

Kooij, Chr. and F.P.C.L. Tonnaer (1984), *Vergunningverlening in stroomversnelling*, Pre-advies van de Vereniging voor Administratief Recht, 's-Gravenhage.

Kružíková, E. (2004), EU accession and legal change, accomplishments and challenges in the Czech Case, *Environmental Politics*, Vol. 13, no. 1, pp. 99-113.

Raad voor het Milieubeheer (1993), *Milieu van jaar tot jaar 1992-1993; twintig jaar Nederlands milieubeleid,* Delwel, Den Haag.

Ringeling, A. (1993), *Stappen verder*, Eindrapport van de Adviescommissie Evaluatie Ontwikkeling Gemeentelijk Milieubeleid, Rotterdam-Den Haag.

Smits, J. (1995), *Milieubeleid gestuurd? Een onderzoek naar de invloed van het BUGM op het gemeentelijk milieubeleid in Noord-Brabant*, Dissertatie Katholieke Universiteit Brabant, Thesis Publishers, Amsterdam.

Stichting Coördinatie Certificatie Milieu- en abomanagementsystemen (SCCM) (2005), www.sccm.nl.

Tweede Kamer der Staten-Generaal (1989), *Notitie Bedrijfsinterne Milieuzorg*, vergaderjaar 1988-1989, 20633 nr. 3, Den Haag.

Tweede Kamer der Staten-Generaal (1996), *Uitbreiding van de Wet milieubeheer (milieuverslaglegging)*, vergaderjaar 1995-1996, 24572, nr. 3, Den Haag.

Tweede Kamer der Staten-Generaal (1998), *Beleidsstandpunt naar aanleiding van de evaluatie bedrijfsmilieuzorgsystemen van oktober 1996*, vergaderjaar 1997-1998, 20633, nr. 10. Den Haag.

Twijnstra and Gudde (1979), *Uitvoering Hinderwet*, Deventer.

Van Loosbroek, R.G.M. and J.C.M. Klaver (2001), Vergunningverlening op hoofdzaken: van regulering naar zelfregulering? Gevolgen voor derden, *Milieu,* nr. 4-5, pp. 209-222.

Van Tatenhove, J.P.M. (1993), *Milieubeleid onder dak? Beleidsvoeringprocessen in het Nederlandse milieubeleid in de periode 1970-1990, nader uitgewerkt voor de Gelderse Vallei*, Pudoc, Wageningen.

Verbond van Nederlandse Ondernemingen & Nederlands Christelijk Werkgeversverbond (VNO-NCW) (1986), *Milieuzorg in bedrijven*, Den Haag.

Winsemius, P. (1987), *Gast in eigen huis, beschouwingen over milieumanagement*, Samson, Alphen aan den Rijn.

Ypma, E. (2003), *The development of corporate environmental management in the Netherlands and the Czech Republic; a study of the policymaking process on corporate environmental management and its implementation in the chemical industries of the Netherlands and the Czech Republic,* Master thesis Social and Political Sciences of the Environment, Radboud University Nijmegen, Nijmegen (not published).

Chapter 12

A Target Group Approach in Flemish Environmental Policy: Establishing New Government-Industry Relations?

Bruno Verbeeck and Pieter Leroy

INTRODUCTION

This chapter analyses a specific change in Flemish environmental policy: the development of a target group policy. As specific as this case might be, it is one of the many experiments we witness in recent environmental policies throughout Europe. Target group policy is paralleled indeed by a wide variety of new policy approaches aiming at more integrated and more interactive environmental policy making, as other chapters in this volume illustrate. Despite their differences, these experiments basically reflect the quest for a more effective policy on the one hand, while illustrating gradually changing relations between state, market and civil society on the other. As such they are said to represent new styles and practices of governance. The empirical question arises, however, whether and to what extent these new practices actually represent a new environmental policy and under what conditions they institutionalise as new forms of governance.

We restrict to new government-industry relations in environmental policies here. Since the late 1980s we witness the emergence of different voluntary approaches in this area: covenants, public-private partnerships and other voluntary agreements between state agencies and industrial branches' representatives, both at national and European level (Carraro and Lévêque, 1999; EEA, 1997; Glasbergen, 1998; Mol et al., 2000; OECD, 1999; OECD, 2003). These new policy approaches have been developed, often in combination with more traditional instruments, to take into account concerns of target groups.

A specific example are target group policies, as developed in many EU countries, in particular in the Netherlands and at European level from the 1990s onwards (Driessen and Glasbergen, 2002). Target group policies, firstly, imply the elaboration of environmental policies for specific target

B. Arts and P. Leroy (eds.), Institutional Dynamics in Environmental Governance, 245–266.

groups such as industry, agriculture and consumers. Governmental agencies and branches of industry negotiate on feasible goals for emission reductions or, more pro-actively, for reductions in the use of resources. The subsequent agreements often result in covenants dealing with issues on products and processes, and setting a commonly agreed timetable. At first one might consider this as yet a further step in the differentiation and specification of environmental policy. From a strategic perspective target group policies this can be regarded as the preliminary outcome of the perpetual quest for more effective environmental policies. The implementation of these target policies, however, is explicitly a common responsibility of government and industry representatives. Hence, from an institutional perspective, target group policies also represent new practices of policy making, introducing new interrelations between government and industry, anticipating new institutional patterns. As such, target group policies refer to new modes of governance.

In the 1990s the Flemish government announced a so-called 'target group policy' in environmental policy. It was said to aim at policy integration and at target groups' participation, and echoed the quest and ambitions evoked above. A project team was set up to explore the opportunities, and to launch a pilot programme in which governmental agencies and representatives from two industrial sectors are involved.

This chapter describes this approach and project, firstly in order to assess whether it indeed represents the so-called shift from government to governance and, secondly, whether it will institutionalise as such. We assess whether target group policies tend to supersede traditional policies, or whether, to the contrary, traditional policies tend to restrain target group policies.

To answer these questions we focus on the goals and ambitions of this target group policy, on its actual development and on its chances to trigger real policy change. The first section sets out our perspective and conceptual framework. Section two describes the development of Flemish target group policy. Section three then analyses target group policy as a newly emerging arrangement and looks for explanations for its (lack of) triggering a real policy change in Flemish environmental policies. In the final section some conclusions are drawn.

ENVIRONMENTAL POLICIES: CHANGES TOWARDS GOVERNANCE

As stated above, recent changes in environmental policies can be regarded as both the result of strategic deliberations among governmental bodies and other agencies involved, and as an indication of more encompassing institutional changes. The latter refer to what several scholars label new modes of governance – or *shifts in governance* – in general and to its implications in environmental policies in particular. This section, although briefly, elaborates on these shifts in governance, depicting our perspective, our conceptual framework, and our methodology.

Perspective: Shifts Towards Governance?

The renewal of environmental policies, such as the emergence of a Flemish target group policy, occurs within a context of more encompassing social, political and economic changes (Van Tatenhove et al., 2000). Some of these social and political changes are referred to as shifts from government to governance (Hajer and Wagenaar, 2003; Kooiman, 2003; Pierre, 2000; Rhodes, 1997; Rosenau and Czempiel, 1992). These shifts imply changes in both the content and the organisation of the policy making process. Restricting to environmental policies, scholars firstly notice a *discursive change*, in which environmental issues are related to a variety of side-by-side issues such as (technological) innovation, energy and consumption (Hajer, 1995). Secondly, *changes in instrumentation* are noticed. As regulatory 'command and control' strategies proved insufficient to deal with environmental problems, they were gradually complemented with economic or market-oriented and social or communicative instruments (De Clercq, 2002; Golub, 1998). Thirdly, one notices a *change in policy strategy* towards private actors, as the predominant strategy within environmental policies shifted from a hierarchical, top-down, state initiated regulatory approach towards one based on more horizontal relations between actors involved. This new approach aims at a negotiated policy making, endorsed by consensus, and characterised by co-operative relationships between government and private actors (Glasbergen, 1998). The latter implies, fourthly, *changes in the interrelations* between state, market and civil society, as environmental issues gradually become a shared responsibility of state bodies, market agencies and civil society representatives, as distinct phenomena such as deregulation, liberalisation and privatisation of environmental tasks indicate. The emergence of a target group policy, as a shift in governance with regard to market agencies, seems the example par excellence of a gradual institutionalisation of new institutional relations on the intersection of state and market (Leroy, 2002; Van Tatenhove and Leroy, 2003). The above should not be read though as a unilinear evolution. Traditional policy making still plays an important role in environmental policy, in Flanders as elsewhere.

Conceptual Framework

As the policy arrangement approach serves as the framework for our analysis, policy arrangement, institutionalisation, political modernisation and congruency are its key concepts (Liefferink, respectively Arts and Goverde, this volume). Encompassing structural changes, mentioned above as shifts in governance, are reflected by the process of political modernisation. According to the definition of a policy arrangement we look upon Flemish target group policies as a "temporary stabilisation of the organisation and substance of a policy domain". We will pay attention to its four dimensions: the actors and their coalitions, the division of power and resources, the rules of the game and the policy discourses. As institutionalisation is defined as "a process of structuration and stabilisation by which policy arrangements are produced, reproduced and transformed", this concept is helpful to describe longer term changes in Flemish environmental policies. From this, we will identify the key forces and factors that brought about the demand for a target group policy. Furthermore, we will analyse the emergence of target group policy, as an approach and as a project. The final section will raise the question whether and to what extent this target group policy indeed represents a shift from government to governance. This assessment includes the question whether we anticipate target group policy in Flanders to institutionalise, juxtaposed to traditional policy strategies and practices. In this assessment we use congruency as an indicator (Boonstra, 2004). We distinguish *strategic* and *structural* congruency. Strategic congruency refers to the ability of actors involved to give meaning to central themes addressed. Structural congruency refers to 'sufficient coherence' between the dimensions of a policy arrangement (*internal* structural congruency) on the one hand, and between the policy arrangement and its institutional context (*external* structural congruency) on the other.

Methodology

Our analysis is based on a qualitative case study (Yin, 1994). Empirical research consisted of a content analysis of policy documents and minutes of formal meetings within the Flemish environmental government. In addition, we participated in meetings of the Steering Committee on Target Group Policy. These methods were complemented by in-depth-interviews with key persons from the environmental administration (Verbeeck and Loots, 2004).

THE DEVELOPMENT OF A TARGET GROUP POLICY IN FLEMISH ENVIRONMENTAL POLICY (1996-2004)

The Political-Institutional Context of Flemish Environmental Policy

Environmental policy in Flanders gradually institutionalised from the 1980s onwards. This section depicts its most relevant institutional characteristics and changes.

As was the case elsewhere, Flemish environmental policies initially were dominated by a sectoral approach of media and areas such as water, air, soil, land and waste, as can be seen from the legislation, policy plans and other predominantly sectoral policy instruments. This approach, however, has gradually broadened, as sectors have been linked to more integrated themes and to adjacent policy fields. Yet the organisation of Flemish environmental policy still reflects a sectoral approach.

There is a second reason for the competencies for Flemish environmental policies to be divided and fragmented among a number of ministries, governmental bodies and agencies. As Belgium is a federal state, competencies in most environmental matters have been allocated to the three Regions (Flanders, Wallonia and Brussels), each of which is entitled to legislate on all environmental issues (except for three matters: product standards, the transit of waste and nuclear matters, which are still state competencies). At regional level, Flanders' environmental policy is a political responsibility of the Flemish government, in particular its Minister for Environment. This policy is designed and implemented by a number of governmental bodies and agencies: the environmental department of the Ministry of the Flemish Community i.e. the Administration for Environment, Nature, Land and Water Control (Dutch acronym: AMINAL); the Flemish Environment Agency (acronym: VMM) responsible for water and air policy and for environmental monitoring; the Flemish Public Waste

Agency (acronym: OVAM) for waste processing and waste prevention; the Flemish Land Agency (acronym: VLM) for rural development, land reclamation and manure policies, to name but the most important. As a consequence and despite some gradually established strategies and mechanisms of co-ordination, agencies from market and civil society have to deal with a diversity of governmental bodies and with their respective – and sometimes conflicting – practices and demands, e.g. in permit granting, in maintenance et cetera (Crabbé and Leroy, 2003).

Traditionally the instrumentation of Flemish environmental policies is largely based upon regulatory strategies (Deketelaere, 1998). Direct regulation, in particular by permits and maintenance, is established on an extensive, detailed and robust legislative framework (Dutch acronym: VLAREM). In addition, economic instruments, e.g. taxes, levies and subsidies have been put in place, particularly in water, waste and technology policies. More recently, social and communicative strategies are experimented, particularly in nature conservation and land reclamation policies. On top of that, a number of environmental agreements or covenants were concluded between individual environmental agencies and industrial bodies, especially on waste management since the 1990s.

Belgium and Flanders have a strong tradition of dialogue and compromise in many policy domains, particularly on sensitive societal and political divides, such as ethno-linguistic and socio-economic issues. While the first provoked a series of consecutive talks and agreements on the gradual federalisation of the state, the latter gave rise to the establishment of neo-corporatism. Neo-corporatism can be characterised as a particular strategy for conflict resolution, resulting in a typical institutionalisation of the interrelations between the state and societal interest groups. Both market and civil society take part through (a small number of) interest groups, to which a formal, representative status is granted in policy formulation, decision making and implementation (Frouws, 1994).

In states with a neo-corporatist tradition, as is the case for Belgium and Flanders, these neo-corporatist practices tend to be reproduced in recently emerged policy domains, such as welfare. Therefore one can anticipate neo-corporatism to colour environmental policy as well. Despite its recent emergence, Flemish environmental policy indeed has an already well-established tradition of formal and informal consultation, of negotiated decision-making etc. Flemish public authorities in general have an extensive network of advisory councils at their disposal, giving binding or non-binding advice, in some cases with regard to strategic headlines, in others with regard to the fine tuning of policy measures. The same applies to environmental policies, displaying a series of advisory boards and consultative committees on a variety of issues. Two main advisory bodies should be mentioned here: the Social and Economic Council of Flanders (Dutch acronym: SERV), where the socio-economic partners meet, and the Environment and Nature Council of Flanders (Dutch acronym: MiNa Raad), where representatives from the environmental movement (guaranteed majority) and from the same socio-economic groups meet. Both advisory bodies are consulted either on strategic issues or at the very end of the rule-making process, in a stage that directly precedes decision-making. As a result, discussions in both councils tend to be rather formal negotiations with only marginal effects on final decisions.

Besides this formal consultation, politics in general and environmental policy making in particular also relies on informal consultation between the state and interest groups. Hence the development of a series of informal and ad hoc consultation practices between governmental bodies and stakeholders. The ministerial cabinet, grown into a kind of parallel administration, plays a pivotal role in these ongoing negotiations, either on general standards or on specific issues and cases.

Therefore, new forms of consultative policy making, experiments with target group policies being an obvious example, can be regarded as attempts to adjust existing, but separate formal and informal consultation practices. On the one hand formal practices might be complemented by more flexible approaches that take into account specific circumstances, on the other hand informal and therefore hardly controllable negotiations might be regulated a bit. We will discuss below whether the target group approach is likely to fill in that gap.

Currently, Flemish public authorities at regional level anticipate a substantial administrative reorganisation, called Better Administrative Governance (Dutch acronym: BBB), implemented by the Flemish government since 2001. The starting points of this reorganisation are threefold: (1) the restructuring of public administration in thirteen ‘homogeneous policy domains’ (in order to overcome policy fragmentation), (2) the reorganisation of advisory boards and processes (in order to reaffirm the primacy of politics), and (3) the strengthening of the policy making function within the administration by reduction of the ministerial cabinets (in order to decrease the influence of informal and back stage negotiations). Since its launching in 2001 some progress has been made on the first, whilst hardly anything happened on the second and third point. Of course, that is a matter of political opposition, mainly from the larger opposition parties, whose members and supporters have penetrated into key positions in the administration. Part of the delay, however, is ‘institutional’, caused by the fact that the line up of formal advisory bodies and the informal network of personal contacts in and around ministerial cabinets do provide an essential structure in bringing together public and private agencies. This structure is not only essential for the very sensitive functioning of the state, it also proves nearly irreplaceable.

Though there is no formal linkage between the BBB-reorganisation and the establishment of a target group policy, they are actually interrelated in two ways. Strategically, further decision-making on the target group approach will depend upon awaited developments of BBB'S organisational implications. And institutionally, both processes, though very different in scale and scope, indicate the quest and the difficulties in bridging formal and informal politics.

In summary, despite formal and informal procedures and platforms of participation, Flemish environmental policy still reflects a largely state-initiated style of governance, with predominant state-defined discourses, rules and resources. We therefore characterise Flemish environmental policy, although it displays some neo-corporatist characteristics, as a *modern-etatist arrangement* with a strong division of competencies amongst governmental actors. Efforts have been accomplished to deal with this institutional fragmentation and to improve the coordination of procedures and working relations, among governmental agencies as well as with private actors. With regard to government-industry relations we refer to the considerable efforts (in terms of staff, procedures and resources) put into the elaboration and implementation of VLAREM since the mid 1980s, reinforcing the individual (and partly integrated) permit as the main instrument to regulate industrial activities in Flanders. In the 1990s governmental bodies developed a strategy of (also partly integrated) environmental planning, thereby again reinforcing the *modern-etatist* style and character of environmental policy-making. As a result, the target group policy initiative is, paradoxically, also state-driven, as we will see.

Driving Forces for the Introduction of Flemish Target Group Policy

The above characterisation of Flemish environmental policies may have revealed also the major driving forces behind the launching of a target group policy approach from the late 1990s. One can, schematically, distinguish between driving forces from within environmental policies and from a more general perspective.

As to the internal considerations, both governmental bodies and industries faced substantial steering and co-ordination problems, mainly resulting from the fragmentation of Flemish environmental policy. In practice, this led to the side-by-side existence of a variety of formal and informal policy processes initiated by different environmental agencies, in each of which target groups were involved. As a result, target groups were appealed upon separately and differently on waste issues, on water sanitation, on climate change and on a series of other environmental topics, all displaying their own goals, schedules and timetables. Hence, there emerged a demand for more integration and co-ordination.

In the same period Belgium and Flanders discussed the renewal of politics in general, the redefinition of the role of the state, the new citizenship, corporate's social responsibilities and other political issues that were simultaneously in debate elsewhere. With regard to environmental politics, this debate implied, even though defined only in opaque terms, a reallocation of tasks and responsibilities between state, market and civil society. These debates are discussed at full length in the opening chapters of this volume.

The combination of these internal considerations and some general issues of debate resulted in a quest for a redefinition and a restructuring of environmental policies that could increase its performance and its effectiveness, its efficiency and its legitimacy, while reflecting new conceptions of governance and new interrelations between state, market and civil society.

A target group policy seemed a promising way, all the more so since the Dutch example offered very practical inspiration. Dutch environmental target group policy was set out formally in the first National Environmental Policy Plan (1989), but experimented before and strengthened since (Liefferink, 1999). From very specific issues and narrow scoped policies (e.g. on specific pollutants, on waste reduction etc.), it gradually widened its reach and scope to whole branches of industry and to comprehensive issues such as climate change. It is built on consultation, on participation, and negotiation, and urged the self-regulation of economic branches and sectors (Glasbergen, 1998; Liefferink, 1998; Vermeulen, 2002). Target group policy thereby gradually complemented traditional 'command and control' approaches.

As to its elaboration, the general environmental policy goals established in the National Environmental Policy Plan were translated – in consultation with industry, agriculture, consumers and others involved – into specific environmental tasks for each of these target groups. These environmental objectives were then set out in agreements at branch level. These covenants specified the results that are required by a certain deadline, while allowing the sector to decide for itself about the mix of technological, economic and other ways of achieving them. Subsequently, these environmental objectives at branch level were specified into tasks for individual companies, and these tasks in turn were to be included in the company's internal environmental plan and in the permit (FO-Industrie, 2002). As we will see below, the Dutch example was a beacon to Flemish policy makers.

The Emergence of a Target Group Policy Approach (1996-2001)

The target group approach was firstly announced in the Environmental Policy and Nature Development Plan II (in Dutch: MiNa-Plan II, Ministerie van de Vlaamse Gemeenschap, 1997), covering 1997-2001. This document paid ample attention to the deficiencies of existing environmental policies discussed above, particularly the fragmentation of policies towards economic and societal target groups. As a response, the MiNa-Plan II advocated the development of innovative policy strategies. Integration (with regard to content) and participation (with regard to design and implementation) were among the key words of that plea. As a consequence, two main approaches were formulated: the integrated region-oriented policy on the one hand, the target group policy on the other. We restrict to the latter here (for the former, see Boonstra and Padt respectively, this volume).

We will now characterise this target group policy in terms of the four dimensions of a policy arrangement to make clear to what extent this newly emerging arrangement tends to juxtapose or conflict with the existing one(s).

Looking at the *discourse* dimension, the introduction of the concept 'target group policy' indicated a discursive innovation in Flemish environmental policy. Target group policy drives and elaborates upon discourses on policy integration on the one hand, on responsibilisation and participation on the other. The former refers to the fragmentation issue, the latter to the limited problem resolution capacity of government. Both have been set out above. The term 'target group policy' seemed to be sensitising and vague at the same time. Although everybody seems to support both discourses, or put more precisely, although no one dares to oppose them openly, they do represent changing styles and practices.

As to 'integration', a target group policy firstly aims at the co-ordination of the designing and implementation of environmental policies towards particular target groups, formulated separately thus far. By aiming at the co-ordination thereof, target group policies should contribute to the consistency of these strategies and practices, to their acceptance and compliance, and eventually, to their effectiveness. But that would imply co-operation and co-ordination between the environmental agencies, AMINAL, OVAM, VLM and VMM.

Target group policy, secondly, aims at the co-ordination of environmental policies with adjacent policy fields, and the tuning with the goals and demands they address towards the same target groups. We talk about spatial planning here, about agriculture and nature conservation, about traffic policies, technology, industrial development etc. The identification of target groups makes it possible to allocate environmental objectives ('targets') to specific sources, e.g. to (groups of) economic activities, and to involve the target groups concerned by means of negotiations. The challenge in terms of 'external integration' then is to develop and implement policy strategies to integrate environmental imperatives in working practices of distinct target groups, while not obstructing their own rationales and the other objectives they face.

Thirdly, the concept 'target group policy' aims at the development of more interactive forms of policy making, and therefore at a shift in the instrumentation of environmental policies. Besides traditional regulatory strategies, there is greater emphasis now on communicative strategies to get target groups involved, and on economic strategies to appeal to their own sense of responsibility.

These three aspects, however, not only represent strategic or instrumental changes, but have organisational and institutional consequences on the actor setting, the rules of the game and resources and power relations as well.

Looking at the *actor* dimension, it is clear that target group policies imply the broadening of the agencies involved, as integration appeals for the involvement of representatives from adjacent policy fields both within and outside the 'environmental domain'. In addition, responsibility and participation anticipate the active engagement of market parties (and probably also civil society) in finding solutions. It is beyond doubt that this will affect the position of those governmental agencies traditionally engaged in permit procedures.

This brings us to the *rule* dimension. A target group approach evokes a changing of the rules for the designing, the decision-making and the implementation of environmental policies, as it is based on the acknowledgement of mutual dependencies between government and target groups. Current forms of policy-making and policy implementation thus have to be complemented with more flexible and consultation-oriented policy styles and practices. In most cases this implies an intensification and a change in character of the contacts and interactions between the governmental bodies and the branches of industries' representatives.

Target group policies affect *resources and power* relations, since the acknowledgement of mutual dependency in itself changes the perception and the reality of power interrelations. It is unsure, though, whether traditional practices, rules and power relations between government and industry, either formalised in permit granting procedures or largely informal in character, and those agencies that are involved in them, will allow these changes to take place.

In short, looking at the discourse, actor, rule and power dimensions, we witness the possible juxtaposition of two conflicting policy arrangements in the government-industries relations. This juxtaposition raises the question whether it is likely for target group policy to institutionalise, a subject which we will discuss below.

So far we have discussed the launching of a target group policy as a discursively innovative approach in the MiNa-Plan II (1997) with far-reaching consequences on actor settings, rules of the game and power relations. But this 'white paper' went further than just paying lip service to it. One of the more operational initiatives, in this case the so-called Action 122, stipulated 'the establishment of an organisation structure for a target group policy' and the recruitment of target group co-ordinators. This action, however, was classified as a non-binding action – indicating in itself its relative priority – which meant that there was no administrative capacity nor a budget on the short term to actually effectuate it. Moreover, Action 122 was an interdepartmental initiative under the responsibility of the Regional Environmental Policy Co-ordinating Board (in Dutch: *Gewestelijk Milieu-Overleg*, acronymed into GMO). The GMO is a co-ordination board in which the directors-general of the environmental administration (AMINAL) and the environmental agencies (OVAM, VLM and VMM) participate. As such it is one of the already mentioned mechanisms of coordination and integration. It is therefore quite understandable that the target group initiative was allocated to the GMO, as it was supposed to be a common action, aiming at further integration. At the same time, though, the initiative now became dependent upon the willingness and the capacity to co-operate, which was aimed at by the very initiative itself. In other words: target group policies really became a test case for this willingness and capacity. To allocate the responsibility over its implementation to the GMO therefore was quite a challenge and a risky thing to do.

Despite its launching in 1997, it lasted till 1999 before any further step was taken, even though the need for a target group policy approach was repeated in the consecutive *Flemish Environmental Policy Year Programmes* (1998, 1999 and 2000). Action 122 thus was not implemented. The only step taken was the call for and the carrying out of a preparatory study (PriceWaterhouseCoopers, 1999). This study identified the opportunities for a target group policy in the Flemish context, highly inspired by the Dutch example. The study hardly mobilised any political and administrative support, and it did not clarify the way to operationalise and effectuate the concept. In retrospect one can state, though, that it did set the work programme for the project to be launched.

The project itself, however, wasn't launched until 2001-2002, since it was not politically supported, as was already indicated in the above. However, with the establishment of a new Flemish government in 2000, the target group strategy regained political momentum, as can be deduced from its emphasis in the Coalition Agreement (*Regeerakkoord*) of 1999 and, even more so, in the Environmental Policy Year Programme of 2001.

The Project and Pilot Programme 'Target Group Policy' (2001-2004)

As of the end of 2001, a project team was eventually established to carry out a pilot programme on target group policies. Staff members of the different agencies (AMINAL, OVAM, VLM and VMM) participated in the team, whereas a Steering Committee Target Group Policy (Dutch acronym: STUDOE) was appointed, grouping leading representatives from these agencies. The GMO, as said, held the overall responsibility. Interesting thing to note: all of these three groups had only governmental representatives as members.

The project on target group policy was divided into a 'general project' (again: with governmental agencies only), and a 'pilot programme' with both governmental actors and representatives of market parties. The general project aimed at exploring the possible embedding of a target group policy approach within the broader institutional context. The pilot programme would involve two industrial sectors, the steel and the food industry respectively.

As the preparation for the project was rather poor, it was clear from the beginning that the pilot would run as a 'learning by doing' experiment. Even though there might have been some vague consensus on the need for a target group policy, it remained unclear, however, what the main goals of it were, what its key concepts, strategies and measures would look like, how the process could be managed, what subjects would be negotiated and decided upon, what kind of participation and impact of the target groups one could expect, how target group policies related to existing policies etc. In other words, the pilot programme had to be considered as an experiment.

The pilot programme addressed two industrial sectors, as said. The *food industry* can be characterised as a heterogeneous sector with many sub-branches and specific firms. FEVIA Flanders and UNIZO represented the food industry. FEVIA Flanders is the Flemish wing of the Belgian Food Industry Association, the representative employers' organisation. UNIZO is the main interprofessional organisation for the self-employed, from one-man businesses to SME's (small and medium sized enterprises). The *steel industry* in Flanders, to the contrary, is a homogeneous sector with only two major steel companies, SIDMAR Ghent and Ugine & ALZ Genk. Besides those two companies, the Belgian Steel Federation was also represented.

Within the pilot programme and for each of the branches involved, an informal consultation platform (Dutch acronym: VLIMO) was established to function as the new institutional setting for consultation between governmental bodies and branch organisations. These VLIMOs met on a bimonthly basis, chaired by a process co-ordinator from the project team. As to the working process and its preliminary products, those were largely copies of the target group approach experienced in the Netherlands. The overall line concerned a stepwise differentiation and specification of the targets from the Environmental Policy Plan towards more operational targets for each sector and, eventually, for each production plant. These consecutive steps resulted in an *Integrated Environmental Analysis* (Dutch acronym: IMA), an *Integrated Environmental Task* (Dutch acronym: IMT), and an *Environmental Action Plan* (Dutch acronym: DGP). These three documents – in brief the assessment, the targets and the strategy respectively – all had to be the product of a close collaboration between governmental and target groups' representatives. To enable this co-operative work, the VLIMOs made a selection of issues (e.g. environmental reporting, waste water levies, odour standards, alluvial deposits, climate related issues, waste and scrap) and delegated these to issue managers.

While the VLIMOs were at work, the Environmental Policy and Nature Development Plan III, covering 2003-2007, was debated. Due to changing political circumstances on the one hand and to actual experiences on the other, there was growing scepticism about the section on 'participation of actors in environmental policy' in the anticipated Plan. Therefore a consultation with representatives of key players in the field (advisory councils, unions, environmental groups, interest groups, branches of industry etc.) was organised (December 2002). A series of actors echoed and multiplied the scepticism on participatory approaches in general, and on the target group pilot programme in particular. As the latter was – only a year after its actual start – still rather unclear in its ambitions and performances, there was a lot of questioning and criticism on its added value.

Despite this scepticism, the general project installed two working groups for the target groups 'industry' and 'agriculture', the latter also involving people from agricultural policy's agencies. The aim was to elaborate the institutional conditions of target group policies for industry and agriculture by broadening the circle of governmental actors involved. Following a schedule preliminary agreed upon, the conclusions of these working groups would be subject to approval of the leading representatives from the environmental policy departments, representatives of the respective target groups, and finally of the GMO itself. Besides these initiatives towards industry and agriculture, initial steps were also taken regarding target group policies for consumers. In March 2003 a workshop with (only) governmental agencies discussed distinct aspects of consumer-oriented environmental policy, making clear the complexity of the integrated and participatory consumer-oriented approach some aimed at.

Along the way, the VLIMO for the steel industry ceased its activities on a regular basis, as the consultation platform suffered from a lack of relevant discussion topics. This was partly due to the fact that the steel industry in Flanders, as mentioned above, can hardly be characterised as a target group, since it comprehends only two major companies.

Currently (summer 2005) the general project and the pilot programme are still in process. The final conclusions of the working groups for industry and agriculture, already repeatedly postponed, must be awaited, let alone their formal approval by governmental and target group representatives. At the same time, it is unclear whether the pilot programme will be continued or not, and which lessons have to be drawn from it anyway. An evaluation of the programme's implementation and performance is foreseen.

FLEMISH TARGET GROUP POLICY: (WHY NOT) TOWARDS A POLICY CHANGE?

Up till now we have analysed the emergence and development of the Flemish target group policy approach, while considering it as a policy arrangement in an early stage of institutionalisation. In this final section we first analyse this target group policy, as it is experimented within the pilot programme, in terms of the four dimensions of a policy arrangement, in order to characterise it as an emerging arrangement. This should enable us to assess its probability to institutionalise, respectively to explain its lack of success in the Flemish context.

Target Group Policy as an Emerging Arrangement

Although one could anticipate the target group policy to widen the arena of *actors* or agencies involved, in fact that hardly happened. The project remained restricted to a closed circle of government representatives and industrial stakeholders. This restriction was amply argued for by referring to the programme's pilot character, and by the complexity of the problems it already faced without multiplying the number of actors involved. Yet the absence of new actors hindered the possible emergence, let alone the institutionalisation of, new interrelations that could overrule pre-existing practices and styles of interaction between the traditional actors, representatives of the governmental bodies AMINAL, OVAM, VLM, and VMM and their counterparts, representatives of industrial sectors.

As consultation was not widened beyond traditional agencies whose practices, styles and interests are mutually well-known, the pilot programme deprived itself of the opportunity to provoke new ideas, new interrelations, new practices etc. The fact that the pilot programme did not invite other stakeholders or key institutions (advisory bodies: MiNa Council and SERV, NGOs, joint municipal authorities, provincial or local authorities, environmental and consumer groups, unions) not only made it unlikely for a policy change to occur. Also, the limited number of participants made the pilot programme unknown, unfamiliar and, as a result, unwanted for a series of agencies that were not involved. As a consequence, a project the actual implementation of which has been postponed, due to a lack of political priority, even more so suffered from decreasing support, once it was in operation. It is unsure whether this lack of support might be fatal in the future. In any case, the pilot so far has not affected, let alone renewed traditional government-industry relations and policies.

Yet the target group approach in general and the pilot programme in particular have introduced new *discourses* and concepts, such as 'shared responsibility' and 'internalisation', either of which appeal to the willingness of polluters to contribute to the solution of environmental problems by invoking their sense of social responsibility. Within the pilot programme a debate developed on the role and responsibility of the different actors involved. At first sight the debate is on scientific and technical issues, elaborations and justifications of an integrated environmental analysis (IMA), the definition of integrated environmental tasks (IMT) and the designing of environmental action plans for the sectors involved (DGP). In fact, though, one discusses new ways of governance and new policy instruments that coincide with the logic of changing responsibilities and practices. So far, however, many of those concepts and their elaborations remain unspecified, lack elaboration and debate, and have not been translated into action.

The pilot programme was set up with caution and restraint. As is made clear in the above it has not led to new *rules of the game* hitherto, except (but very restricted) with regard to rules for access and involvement: invitations have been sent to the two branches involved only, but the negotiations have not been opened to other actors from market and civil society. A public debate has not taken place, whereas access to the negotiations is privileged to the branches involved and their governmental counterparts. Until and unless these negotiations bring about new and negotiated policies that will supersede the existing regulatory framework of individual permit procedures, target group policies might not alter the rules of the game in government-industry's relations.

As to *resources and power,* government-industry relations are traditionally characterised by mutual dependencies. Government primarily has its regulatory power and its legal resources, whereas industry's position largely relies upon its technical expertise and its economic power. For obvious reasons this power balance differs from sector to sector. Yet environmental targets and goals reflect that balance, even as it is calculated in terms of emission reduction and justified by cost-benefit analyses and the like. The pilot programme so far only seems to confirm that mutual dependency and exchange of resources, without having altered or even affected them. Especially expertise is an important feature here. As has been experienced in Dutch target group policy as well, the preliminary Flemish experience indicates that target group policy leads to the co-production of even more expertise, particularly to its clustering from individual plants to the sector level, and from individual standards and permit procedures to sectoral standard setting. In other words, target group policy urges for and provides new expertise, the requirement of which appeals not only to government-industry co-operation (e.g. within VLIMO), but also urges for a new governmental organisation, i.e. for an administrative integration between the governmental bodies involved. Currently, however, it is uncertain whether and how target group policy will entail any such reorganisation of Flemish administration that would facilitate the integration of that expertise and the creation of an organisation able to draw upon the other lessons from the pilot programme. The latter seems to be of utmost importance when it comes to increase the governments' power positioning vis-à-vis the industry.

Target Group Policy as an Institutionalising Arrangement

As Flemish target group policy is still in its earlier stages, it seems premature to say whether it indeed represents a shift from government to governance, and whether it will stabilise as such. Yet we can anticipate the likeliness of its further institutionalisation by using 'congruency' as an indicator.

As said we refer to either strategic (in)congruency, the convergence or divergence of views, concerns and interests of the actors involved on the one hand, and to structural (in)congruency, the similarities and dissimilarities between target group policy and existing environmental policies on the other. These two, we presume, largely indicate whether target group policy is likely to institutionalise and to entail changes in existing policy, or is likely to face too many institutional barriers to ever develop into a mature policy arrangement. We should be clear, however, on what we mean by '(in)congruency' here: we do not refer to (functionalist) principles of 'fit', 'match' or their opposites. Strategic and structural incongruency are indicative and predictive for the further institutionalisation of emerging arrangements to the extent that it provokes differences in views and practices, or even conflicts between actors. Not incongruency in itself, e.g. the so-called incompatibility of discourses, rules etc., is decisive, but the fact that some of the actors involved do problematise the challenging arrangement, since it is challenging without contributing to more performance, more effectiveness, more legitimacy etc.

As to strategic (in)congruency, we mentioned that, from the policy documents, there seemed to be a concord on the need for a more integrated and more participatory approach in Flemish environmental policies. Yet the development of this approach over the years, more precisely, its lack of political priority, the lack of budget, the postponement of the elaboration of the famous Action 122 and others indicate that its basis, either political or administrative, was rather poor. Put negatively, one can argue that those having well-established positions in environmental policies were reserved as they anticipated a possible loss of that position. In this context of fragmented power, the GMO is only a platform and not an authority that could overrule this restraint. Put positively, one can also argue that, over the last years, governmental bodies have done their best to improve their policies and their implementation, have even accepted some initiatives for co-operation and integration, while anticipating an encompassing reorganisation with BBB. Therefore they assessed target group policy to be premature and a bridge too far.

As to structural (in)congruency, and gradually moving from *internal* structural congruency (the coherence between the dimensions of a policy arrangement) to *external* structural congruency (the coherence between a policy arrangement and its institutional context), we refer to the following:

- It is clear that, despite superficial concord, *discourses* on integration and participation are not that widely endorsed among governmental agencies. Over the years neither the minister nor the administration has made much effort to initiate the target group approach. And once the approach was elaborated into a pilot programme, questioning started: about its added value, its legitimacy, its efficiency and its effectiveness. In short, governmental bodies themselves did not propagate target group policies unequivocally.
- Though target group policy restricts to negotiations with industry branches, excluding other partners to participate, it actually competes with the existing policy practices of individual negotiations over the location, the emission standards and other aspects of industry-related environmental policies. As the latter are the privilege of well-established and highly experienced governmental bodies, it is hard to see the newly set up pilot programme gathering the expertise, the status and the power to overrule them.
- The same applies to the instrumentation: traditional 'command and control' instruments such as single permits are so predominant in Flemish environmental policy that there is hardly any room to experiment with innovative initiatives. This is all the more understandable, given the tremendous regulatory, organisational and procedural efforts that have been put in those 'traditional' instruments over the last ten years (VLAREM).
- The project team that carries out the pilot project till now lacks the resources in terms of manpower, expertise, budget, mandate etc. to indeed conquer a strong position vis-à-vis other governmental bodies as well as the target groups' representatives. This weak position of course results from the lack of endorsement and even the reluctance of those other bodies. This position, however, tends to be reproduced as the project team, under these circumstances, cannot demonstrate the added value of the project and, as a consequence, is questioned. As to the wider context, the target group policy initiative suffers from an inappropriate timing as its preparation runs more or less parallel with the announced administrative reorganisation labelled BBB-programme. As BBB is announced to be an encompassing and ambitious programme, and was therefore welcomed with great scepticism and a

bit of fatalism by a lot of civil servants and their managers, target group policy turned out to be ill-timed. Even more so, a lot of opponents of target group policy used BBB as an alibi, arguing that BBB would create the circumstances (organisational integration, new advisory bodies, participatory policy making) that would favour target group policies.

CONCLUSION

Whereas target group policy is said to renew environmental policies, both in terms of issue integration and stakeholders participation, Flemish environmental policies are still holding on to a rather traditional top-down way of governing, including this target group project. Therefore, target group policy is still an emerging policy arrangement, with an uncertain chance to stabilise and with a rather small influence on existing policies. Structural differences between government and governance styles and practices within Flemish environmental policy seem to be responsible for this rather slow institutionalisation of target group policies and its limited impact on regular environmental policies. On top of this structural incongruency, we establish divergent views, concerns and interests of the actors involved (strategic incongruency).

In conclusion, our analysis shows the difficult co-existence of new and traditional forms of governing, e.g. the persistence of traditional styles of policy making at the expense of newly emerging arrangements. Therefore, for the time being, we do not expect target group policies to survive, let alone to institutionalise in Flemish environmental policies, as existing environmental policy arrangements regarding government-industry relations seem very solid and narrow the opportunities for the newcomer. We therefore expect the pilot programme to fade away.

REFERENCES

Boonstra, F. (2004), *Laveren tussen regio's en regels: verankering van beleidsarrangementen rond plattelandsontwikkeling in Noordwest Friesland, de Graafschap en Zuidwest Salland*, Koninklijke Van Gorcum, Assen.

Carraro, C. and F. Lévêque (eds.) (1999), *Voluntary approaches in environmental policy,* Fondazione Eni Enrico Mattei (FEEM), Series on Economics, Energy and Environment, Kluwer Academic Publishers, Dordrecht.

Crabbé, A. and P. Leroy (2003), Milieuvergunningverlening in afvalwatergebonden dossiers, in: M. Van Steertegem, *Milieu- en natuurrapport Vlaanderen: beleidsevaluatie,* Vlaamse Milieumaatschappij, Brussel, pp. 53-88.

De Clercq, M. (eds.) (2002), *Negotiating environmental agreements in Europe: critical factors for success*, Edward Elgar, Cheltenham.

Deketelaere, K. (1998), New environmental policy instruments in Belgium, in: J. Golub (eds.), *New instruments for environmental policy in the EU*, EUI Environmental Policy Series, Routledge, London, pp. 107-124.

Driessen, P.P.J. and P. Glasbergen (eds.) (2002), *Greening society: the paradigm shift in Dutch environmental politics,* Environment & Policy, Kluwer Academic Publishers, Dordrecht.

European Environment Agency (1997), *Environmental Agreements – Environmental Effectiveness*, Copenhagen, p. 93.

Facilitaire Organisatie Industrie (FO Industrie) (2002), Doelgroepbeleid milieu en industrie, Jaarrapportage 2001, Den Haag, p. 28 + bijlagen.

Frouws, J. (1994), *Mest en macht: een politiek-sociologische studie naar belangenbehartiging en beleidsvorming inzake de mestproblematiek in Nederland vanaf 1970*, Landbouwuniversiteit Wageningen, Wageningen.

Glasbergen, P. (eds.) (1998), *Co-operative environmental governance: public-private agreements as a policy strategy*, Environment & Policy, Kluwer Academic Publishers, Dordrecht.

Glasbergen, P. (1998), Partnership as learning process: environmental convenants in the Netherlands, in: P. Glasbergen (eds.), *Co-operative environmental governance: public-private agreements as a policy strategy*, Environment & Policy, Kluwer Academic Publishers, Dordrecht, pp. 133-156.

Golub, J. (eds.) (1998), *New instruments for environmental policy in the EU*, EUI Environmental Policy Series, Routledge, London.

Hajer, M.A. (1995), *The politics of environmental discourse: ecological modernization and the policy process*, Oxford University Press, Oxford.

Hajer, M.A. and H. Wagenaar (eds.) (2003), *Deliberative policy analysis: understanding governance in the network society, theories of institutional design*, Cambridge University Press, Cambridge.

Kooiman, J. (2003), *Governing as governance*, Sage, London.

Leroy, P. (2002), Environmental politics, participation and political inequality, in: L. Draetta and F. Lai (eds.), Naturalia, Sciences Sociales et Environnement: entre cadres théoriques et approches empiriques, *EUROPAEA*, Vol. VIII, no. 1-2, pp. 153-167.

Liefferink, D. (1998), New environmental policy instruments in the Netherlands, in: J. Golub (eds.), *New instruments for environmental policy in the EU*, EUI Environmental Policy Series, Routledge, London, pp. 86-106.

Liefferink, D. (1999), The Dutch national plan for sustainable society, in: N.J. Vig and R.S. Axelrod, *The global environment: institutions, law and policy*, CQ Press, Washington D.C., pp. 256-278.

Ministerie van de Vlaamse Gemeenschap (1997), *Vlaams Milieubeleidsplan 1997-2001*, Brussel.

Mol, A.P.J., V. Lauber and D. Liefferink (eds.) (2000), *The voluntary approach to environmental policy: joint environmental approach to environmental policy-making in Europe*, Oxford University Press, Oxford.

OECD (1999), *Voluntary approaches for environmental policy: an assessment*, OECD, Paris, p. 143.

OECD (2003), *Voluntary approaches for environmental policy: effectiveness, efficiency and usage in policy mixes*, OECD, Paris, p. 143.

Pierre, J. (eds.) (2000), *Debating governance: authority, steering and democracy*, Oxford University Press, Oxford.

PriceWaterhouseCoopers (1999), *Finaal rapport doelgroepenbeleid*, Brussel, Price-WaterhouseCoopers.

Rhodes, R.A.W. (1997), *Understanding governance: policy networks, governance, reflexivity and accountability*, Open University Press, Buckingham.

Rosenau, J.N. and E.-O. Czempiel, (eds.) (1992), *Governance without government: order and change in world politics*, Cambridge Studies in International Relations, Cambridge University Press, Cambridge.

Van Tatenhove, J.P.M., B. Arts and P. Leroy, (eds.) (2000), *Political modernisation and the environment: the renewal of environmental policy arrangements*, Kluwer Academic Publishers, Dordrecht.

Van Tatenhove, J.P.M. and P. Leroy (2003), Environment and participation in a context of political modernisation, *Environmental Values*, Vol. 12, pp. 155-174.

Verbeeck, B. and I. Loots (2004), *Een Vlaams doelgroepenbeleid: vernieuwing van milieubeleid?*, Universiteit Antwerpen, Steunpunt Milieubeleidswetenschappen, Antwerpen, p. 83.

Vermeulen, W.J.V. (2002), Greening production as co-responsibility, in: P.P.J. Driessen and P. Glasbergen, *Greening society: the paradigm shift in Dutch environmental politics*, Environment & Policy, Kluwer Academic Publishers, Dordrecht, pp. 67-90.

Yin, R.K. (1994), *Case study research: design and methods*, Sage, Thousand Oaks.

Chapter 13

Institutional Processes in Environmental Governance: Lots of Dynamics, not Much Change?

Bas Arts and Pieter Leroy

INTRODUCTION

Environmental policy is a dynamic and expanding field, as many scholars have observed. It is also a much studied field. This book adds to the extensive literature by offering a specific theoretical perspective: the policy arrangement approach (PAA). With that, key themes of this book are: the emergence of new environmental policy arrangements at or over different administrative levels, the change or continuity of existing arrangements, the juxtaposition of traditional and innovative ones, their governance capacity, as well as the understanding of these changes, continuities and capacities. As far as understanding is concerned, a number of explanatory factors and processes were identified in the preceding chapters of this book, which will be summarised in a scheme below. Besides, we will draw some descriptive, analytical, explanatory and normative conclusions, which can be deduced from the contributions in this book. Also, we will reflect on its contents. This is done by confronting the empirical chapters of this book with the theoretical ones as well as by confronting this book *as a whole* with previous publications on the PAA. While reflecting, an agenda for further research will be identified.

NEW ENVIRONMENTAL POLICY ARRANGEMENTS

Environmental policy has been renewed during the last two decades. That observation is nothing new. However, our understanding of how this happened in specific cases, what the 'newness' exactly consists of, how to contextualise and explain these processes of environmental policy change and how to judge these developments is much more limited. Therefore, in this book, some interesting cases were analysed from the PAA perspective: integrated water management, nature policy, cultural heritage policy,

B. Arts and P. Leroy (eds.), Institutional Dynamics in Environmental Governance, 267–282.

integrated region-oriented policy, corporate environmental management and target group policy. Besides, the example of Dutch organic farming was used as an illustration of the different claims in the theoretical and methodological chapters. Although not a 'real' case compared to the others, insights with regard to organic farming will nonetheless be included in this final chapter. The cases dealt with in this book are mainly located in the Netherlands and Belgium (Flanders), some in other countries like Spain, the UK, the US (Arizona), Norway and the Czech Republic. With that, the comparative perspective is rather dominant in this book.

The illustrations regarding Dutch organic farming show a small policy arrangement, which is currently in a process of 'partial integration' with the mainstream agricultural one. In fact, mainstream organisations and retailers have become part of the organic arena. They did so, because they saw organic farming as another market opportunity, while some organic organisations hoped to increase their selling through the regular market as well. Yet large parts of the organic community remain rather hostile to 'big business'. As a consequence, the organic policy arrangement is fragmented and not very successful in expanding the sector in the Netherlands. This is strengthened by: (1) a 'double face' of the Dutch state (a market philosophy on the one hand, restricted subsidies for the sector on the other), (2) the average Dutch consumer, who does not want to pay more for organic products, (3) the 'hierarchical nesting' of the organic arrangement in the mainstream one, which constrains its further development, and (4) structural trends, like Europeanisation. Hence, we see a renewal and extension of the policy arrangement on organic farming in the Netherlands, yet it so far remains limited, incongruent and hardly successful at the same time.

We see more dynamics, so it seems, in the water sector. Due to, amongst others, shock events (floodings) and a new EU directive (Water Framework Directive), the water policy discourse has been renewed. 'Integrated water management' is the buzzword now. But one may question whether this discursive innovation is just lip-service or whether it has had or will have an impact on the old water institutions in the Netherlands and Flanders. Wiering and Crabbé come up with a nuanced conclusion. They observe 'second order' change, at the level of policy actors and policy instruments (legislation). Yet, paradigmatically, at the level of worldviews, there is not much change. Moreover, the power balance – favouring the traditional water institutions – has remained rather intact so far.

A more or less similar picture emerges in the field of nature policy. Here again, we see discursive renewal – with policy concepts such as ecological networks, nature development and biodiversity – in a field that is characterised by rather old institutions (established since the late 19th century). Still, new actors have entered the scene, such as the European Union, which has launched a rather offensive nature policy since the 1980s. Yet the impact of these innovations on traditional nature policy might differ. Bogaert and Gersie conclude that the Dutch nature policy arrangement has changed more and has been more successful – for example in realising an ecological network of protected areas – than the Flanders' one. The main reasons for these different outcomes are the resistance of adjacent policy fields – like spatial planning and agriculture – and the various claims on ground in Belgium, constraining an expansion of the nature sector. In Holland, on the contrary, the ground issue has been less delicate and there was already support being mobilised for the 'new politics of nature'.

Van der Zouwen also points to situations of different countries. She studied nature conservation policy in three European countries, while taking the role of the EU in this field into account as well. The theoretical starting points of her research were Europeanisation of nature policy on the one hand and a shift from government to governance in this field on the other. Yet she found that the effect of the EU on nature conservation policy in Spain and the UK have been (relatively) substantial, whereas she could not find such an effect in the Netherlands (at least in the protected area studied). In turn, she discovered a substantial impact of non-governmental actors in the Dutch case, where this was less so in Spain and the UK. Overall, she concludes – despite the introduction of new discourses and some governance practices – that institutional stability and governmental domination are still prominent characteristics of nature conservation policy in Europe.

In the field of cultural heritage, we again observe the emergence of a new discourse, which is much broader than the preceding one. From single site protection, based on historic-intrinsic values of objects and governmental interventions, the discourse has evolved into historic landscape development, based on people's preferences and governance practices. According to De Boer, this discourse is slowly but surely diffusing among western countries, inspired by international organisations such as UNESCO. Yet its impact should not be overstated, for two reasons. Firstly, the old discourse is far from dead. At best, we see the emerging of new ideas in a rather traditional setting. Secondly, the policy arrangements, which De Boer studied, are very much coloured by their national-institutional settings. In the US we find a liberal-pluralist policy arrangement (dominance of private site owners), in Norway an etatist one (dominance of state regulation) and in the Netherlands a neo-corporatist one (dominance of state-market-civil society negotiations). These structures seem to be rather stable and they do mediate the introduction as well as the specific national contents of the new discourse.

The situation is a bit different in the realm of Integrated Region-Oriented Policy (IROP). Here we observe the emergence of 'real' new policy arrangements at regional level, in order to decentralise, integrate and improve environmental, spatial and agricultural policy initiatives. Boonstra deals with regional projects in Friesland, Graafschap and Salland and Padt with a reconstruction project in Brabant (all in the Netherlands). Boonstra wonders whether these innovative policy initiatives had any chance of institutionalisation, or in other words, could 'survive' in an environment with many competing traditional policies. To answer this question, she assesses the strategic and structural congruency of these IROP arrangements. Particularly the latter type of congruence is essential for institutionalisation, as the weak position and performance of the Salland project shows. Yet the other two projects turned out to be rather stable and successful. At the same time, Boonstra notices that governmental actors played leading roles (like the Provinces), that success was much dependent on external funds (e.g. from the EU) and that new stakeholders had difficulty in acquiring resources. As a consequence, real governance practices have been scarce in IROP. And insofar as these were present, they were instrumentalised by the Dutch national government, in order to execute its own policies through regional networks.

Padt, however, uses a different focus and comes to additional conclusions. He, firstly, typifies the new arrangements within IROP and concludes that hybrids of – what he calls – authoritative, liberal-pluralist and decentralised-communitarian arrangements have been created. These are regional expressions of policy styles and administrative structures of different national policy domains and ministries (water, environment, agriculture respectively). Here again, traditions colour new initiatives. Secondly, Padt assesses the influence of the New Public Management (NPM) discourse on IROP, which seems definitely present, even in a local 'reconstruction project' such as Gemert-Bakel in the Province of Brabant. Nonetheless, a soft version of NPM was adopted at this local level, exhibiting both an entrepreneurial spirit and a taste of democratic governance.

Corporate environmental management (CEM) is a next policy innovation in the environmental domain. Corporations are ever more expected to show social responsibility and to manage their environmental matters beyond given legislation. The introduction of private, standardised, environmental management systems, like ISO 14001, is an expression of this development. Currently, these standards are rapidly diffusing around the world. In their contribution, Klaver and Ypma deal with the emergence and use of ISO 14001 and EMAS in the chemical industry in the Netherlands and the Czech Republic. Both countries have been pioneers in this respect, although their recent history is quite different (particularly since the Czech Republic faced a transition from communism to capitalism and from being part of the Republic of Czech-Slovakia to national sovereignty). Quite similar in both countries is the steady rise of the number of certifications in CEM, particularly in big firms. Dissimilarities can be found in the role of the government (more prominent in the Netherlands), the linking of private to public regulation (ibidem) and the discourse (production *chain* focus in the Netherlands versus a single *firm* focus in the Czech Republic).

A final environmental policy innovation dealt with in this book is target group policy (TGP). For several reasons – a need to increase efficiency, effectiveness and legitimacy in policy making, a belief in voluntary approaches and a need for more integration of adjacent policy fields – governments started to develop so-called TGP. Direct negotiations with branches of industry should lead to covenants, in which state and market agree upon specific targets and timetables, as an alternative for binding legislation (although states often use legal instruments as an option for the future, in case industry is not committed or non-compliant; this is the so-called 'shadow of hierarchy'). Verbeeck and Leroy show how a TGP is slowly developing in Flemish environmental policy. They conclude that it is an emerging and weak arrangement at best with not much chance to institutionalise in the near future. Reasons for this are a lack of sufficient consensus with regard to TGP, a troublesome interference with the traditional state-industry relationship concerning permit procedures, a lack of resources and a dominance of the Flemish federalisation and administrative reorganisation process.

THREE TYPES OF POLICY CHANGE

In the previous section, the case studies of this book are summarised, which all deal with the emergence of new policy arrangements in various environmental policy domains. The 'newness' of these arrangements however differ. Given the case studies, we can observe three types of environmental policy change or innovation: 1. the (partial) *integration* of existing, juxtaposed policy arrangements (organic farming); 2. the discursive and/or organisational *renewal* of existing policy arrangements (water, nature, cultural heritage); and 3. the *introduction* of new policy arrangements (integrated region-oriented policy, corporate environmental management, target group policy). Each type of policy change leads to the formulation of different research questions, as the previous chapters show.

A common research question related to the first type of policy change – the (partial) *integration* of existing, juxtaposed arrangements – is how the old ones relate to each other in the new setting. To theorise about this, an analytical scheme of Liefferink (this volume) is helpful. He distinguishes between nested, overlapping and clustered arrangements, the first category being hierarchical in nature, the latter two horizontal (the typology of *competing* arrangements is not dealt with here, since this type refers to autonomous arrangements, which are neither fully nor partially integrated). If we take the organic farming case, we then distinguish a nested and overlapping arrangement. It is partially and hierarchically nested within the mainstream agricultural arrangement and it is partially overlapping with it (hence, not entirely integrated in it). In the book, we also found several examples of more horizontal arrangement relations. These for example appeared with regard to water and spatial policy.

A common research question related to the second type of policy change – *renewal* of existing arrangements – is whether a discursive renewal has had institutional effects and vice versa. Discursive renewal was detected in the water, nature and cultural heritage domains, but institutional effects were different, although not much in general. A new water discourse, for example, produced second-order organisational change, whereas a new cultural heritage discourse had hardly any organisational consequences so far. In contrast, organisational renewal was seen in Dutch organic farming (entrance of new actors), but this hardly changed or integrated the competing discourses on organic farming.

A common research question related to the third type of policy change – the *introduction* of new arrangements – is whether these are able to institutionalise and to perform. The picture however is mixed. Integrated region-oriented policy and corporate environmental management seem to have become rather stable and quite successful policy arrangements, although not all individual projects succeed, whereas target group policy (at least in Flanders) seems to have failed. Besides, the question of how the new arrangements relate to the given institutional context is interesting. Here again, Liefferink's scheme might be helpful. For example, the (probable) failure of Flemish target group policy can be (partially) explained by the fact that the emerging arrangement has to compete with and to respect the rules of the (more powerful) policy arrangement of traditional environmental pollution control and government-industry relationships.

The three types of policy change – integration, renewal and introduction – puts the notion of 'hybridisation', often used in this book, into perspective, since it can mean different things. It can, firstly, refer to hybrid structures as a consequence of the (partial) integration of different, formerly independent policy arrangements (organic farming). Secondly, it can mean the hybridisation of 'old' and 'new' coalitions, discourses, rules or resources, in case one existing arrangement is being renewed (water, nature). Finally, it might refer to the emergence of a new, more or less autonomous policy arrangement, in which (parts of) more traditional institutional structures are nonetheless reproduced (integrated regional policy, corporate environmental management, target group policy).

SHIFT FROM GOVERNMENT TO GOVERNANCE?

The emergence of new environmental policy arrangements, as described and analysed in this book, begs the question whether these policy changes coincide with the much heralded shift from government to governance. In terms of the PAA, given the four dimensions of a policy arrangement, this shift would imply, amongst others: (1) new roles for civil society and market parties in policy making, (2) a diffusion of political power from the public to the private domains and from the national to the sub-national and international levels, (3) less importance of legal instruments and formal rules, and (4) new discourses on steering and governing.

To some extent, we indeed observe such changes. Both individual civilians and NGOs ,as well as firms and corporate interest groups, seem to have recently increased their say in environmental policy making (water management, cultural heritage, regional policy, corporate environmental management). Yet, as the case studies also make clear, we should not exaggerate their impact, since the traditional governmental policy actors remain rather dominant in most cases, both in renewed as well as in new arrangements. It seems that new stakeholders find difficulty in getting real access to policy arenas and in acquiring sufficient resources. And if they succeed, there is still a chance that they become instrumentalised by governmental politics, as region-oriented policy making shows. At the same time, we should be aware of the fact that public roles for private actors is not so much of a new phenomenon as it seems at first hand, given pluralist arrangements (e.g. nature policy) or neo-corporatist arrangements (e.g. industrial pollution) in earlier generations of environmental politics.

Hence, new and extended roles for private stakeholders, yes, but with limited power and impact on the one hand and being a continuation of past practices in some domains on the other.

Where we *do* see (some) diffusion of power and authority, however, is in the sphere of multi-level governance, as the entrance and impact of the EU in national environmental politics cannot be dismissed (e.g. directives in the sphere of agriculture, water management, nature policy and corporate environmental management). In addition, sub-national environmental politics has gained importance as well (region-oriented policy). But here again, we mainly talk about the empowerment of *governmental* actors at international or sub-national levels, compared to national ones, not about non-governmental stakeholders, although the latter do generally play a role in policy making at these levels as well.

A next claim of the 'shift thesis' is that formal and traditional law has lost importance, whereas informal rules and non-legal instruments have gained momentum. This claim seems valid at first hand. For example, we observe the emergence of informal coalitions and policy plans (nature policy), regional contracts (regional policy), regulatory relief (corporate environmental management) and covenants (target group policy). At the same time, however, formal EU and national law remain of the utmost importance. In some cases, formal law even 'frustrates' the further development of new and informal policy arrangements, as national agricultural reconstruction policy shows with regard to regional environmental policy making in the Netherlands and national pollution control with regard to target group policy in Flanders.

The shift from government to governance thesis is probably best verified at the level of policy discourse. Nearly in all case studies of this book, ideas – held and advocated by policy makers – on the necessity to include private, international or local actors and to use new policy instruments can be found. However, the question is whether these ideas are put into practice, remain lip-service or cannot be implemented after all. A good example is the plea for 'multi-sector' governance. As a consequence of functional differentiation patterns in (early) modern public administration, with all kind of negative externalities, such as co-ordination problems, there is a current trend towards integration of adjacent policy fields. Several cases in this book indicate this trend: for example water policy, nature policy and integrated region-oriented policy. Yet this ambition is hard to realise. It appears that adjacent policy fields often contradict each other and are hard to integrate. Even in regional policy, where integration is the key objective, compartmentalisation is still rather dominant.

All in all, given the considerations in this section, we observe the emergence of hybrids of 'new' governance and 'old' government practices, both in renewed as well as in new policy arrangements. These hybrids are partly policy innovations, partly continuations of past practices. *As a consequence, a general shift from government to governance cannot be discerned in environmental politics, despite all the 'governance talk'.*

POLITICAL MODERNISATION

The core of the PAA is to understand policy change and continuity at the crossroads of day-to-day policy making and political modernisation processes. In methodological terms, this means combining a strategic analysis with an institutional one in order to understand the role of agency vis-à-vis structures in institutionalisation processes. In this section, we concentrate on political modernisation and on the institutional analysis, whereas agency and the strategic analysis will be dealt with in the next one.

Political modernisation was defined as "the shifting relationships between the state, market and civil society in political domains of societies – *within* countries and *beyond* – as a manifestation of the 'second stage of modernity', implying new conceptions and structures of governance" (Arts and Van Tatenhove, this volume). The last dimension of this definition – governance – was dealt with in the previous section. We concluded that new *conceptions* of governance are definitely present in environmental politics, but this is less clearly the case for governance *practices*. Overall, we find hybrid structures of 'old' government and 'new' governance practices.

This brings us to the second dimension of political modernisation: the issue of 'second modernity'. It closely follows from the previous sections that 'sub-political' arrangements of only non-state actors – the existence of which is one of the manifestations of second modernity – are not dealt with nor present in this book. An exception might be corporate environmental management, but even here, the input and impact of governments is substantial. The question is whether we deal with a bias of the book or a bias of environmental politics in general. Curiously so, we think *both*. It is a bias of the book, because we could have dealt with other cases, which are more close to sub-political arrangements, as for example private partnerships in global forestry or local *Agenda 21* initiatives. At the same time, we think that these examples are not representative for environmental politics *in general*, as this book and many others overwhelmingly show the persistence and adaptation potential of governmental power and traditional institutional arrangements. In other words, a lack of sub-politics is also a characteristic of environmental politics in its broadest sense.

Another argument which might falsify the second modernity thesis is the importance of domestic institutional structures. Nearly all comparative case studies in this book indicate the importance of these. For example, water policy in the Netherlands and Flanders, although coloured by similar international discourses and legalisation processes, develop quite differently, because domestic institutions filter the effect of international processes. The same goes for cultural heritage policy, nature policy, corporate environmental management and target group policy. While policy diffusion processes over countries are traceable in these fields, making their policies looking more similar over time, a 'national flavour' to government and governance models and practices does not yet exist. Hence, processes such as globalisation should be put into perspective, since it is obviously too early to get rid of the nation state model.

Does this imply, then, that the thesis of second modernity should be dismissed, at least for the environmental domain? No, that would be a too hasty conclusion for two reasons. The first is that *traces* of second modernity are definitely present in environmental politics in general as well as in the cases of this book, such as (some) Europeanisation of domestic institutions and policies (e.g. nature conservation) and the emergence of new ecological risks (e.g. water management). A second reason for us not to immediately dismiss the second modernity thesis is that we do not believe in the two *phases* of modernity – the first and second one – but in the two *faces* of modernity. In other words, we favour *synchrony* over *diachrony*. Modernity is definitely renewing itself, however not entering a new phase, but developing different faces of so-called *early* and *late* modernity at the same time. This image can help us to understand why government and governance go hand in hand, why state and non-state actors alternately pop up in different policy arrangements, why discursive innovation and organisational stability or organisational renewal and discursive continuity go along with each other, why the effects of the EU and domestic institutions go hand in hand, etc.

A final dimension of political modernisation is the shifting relationships between state, market and civil society, implying the sharing of formal responsibilities by public and private actors. Several cases in this book witness such changes. Yet, as referred to earlier, both theoretically and empirically, this does not imply a dramatic decrease of the power of the state or a dramatic increase of the political power of the market and civil society. For sure, there has been a decrease of policy autonomy and a diffusion of (functional) authority – upwards, downwards and sidewards – but this does not mean that the power of the state has been hollowed out.

OTHER DRIVING FORCES

In the previous section, political modernisation as a 'motor of change' in policy arrangements was dealt with and, based on the case studies in this book, put into perspective of the persistence of nation state power, the continuity of early modernity, the adaptation capacity of traditional policy practices and the 'traditional governance' role of non-state actors. This 'motor of change' should however be understood properly. It is not about top-down impacting of social processes and actions by 'grand' structures and structural processes, but about the local manifestation of these through reflexive conduct by agencies. To give an example, Van der Zouwen conceptualises and studies EU rules and resources as relevant factors in sub-national nature policy, being strategically mobilised and used by local players.

Other case studies in the book nicely show the various roles of agency in policy change and political modernisation too. In water policy, the dissatisfaction of several 'inside' and 'outside' players with the lack of governance capacity of the traditional policy arrangement, both in the Netherlands and Flanders, to successfully deal with the new water challenges (safety, water quality, floodings, climate change) has been a driving force for policy change. For example, the sector has become more responsive to ecological and socio-economic arguments (besides hydrological ones) and NGOs, politicians and policy makers have campaigned – all in their own way – for new legislation. At the same time, the traditional power holders in water policy (the engineers) have successfully defended their original positions, adapting their vocabulary to the changed circumstances. Other case studies show similar dynamics in the motivation for policy change on the one hand and the search for continuity – or incremental change at the most – by the traditional power holders at the other, for example in nature policy and target group policy. Here we see an interesting interplay between 'policy entrepreneurs' and those who defend the *status quo*.

Besides 'political modernisation' (structure) and 'policy entrepreneurs' (agency) as driving forces, other factors to understand policy change have been identified in the book. Particularly the chapter of Wiering and Crabbé is instructive in order to design an overall explanatory model (Figure 13.1). They distinguish between 'endogenous' and 'exogenous' factors – although always a problematic distinction – to understand the integration of, change of or change in policy arrangements (compare the three types of policy change dealt with in the above: 'integration', 'renewal', 'introduction' respectively). Endogenous factors refer to (1) 'policy entrepreneurs' and their perceptions of the need to improve the governance capacity of arrangements, exogenous factors to (2) the influence of shock events on the policy arrangement concerned; (3) the influence of adjacent policy arrangements; and (4) the influence of political modernisation processes. The first and fourth factors have already been dealt with. Examples of shock events in this book were the (nearly) floodings in Belgium and the Netherlands in the 1990s and the mine spill in Doñana National Park in Spain in 1999, which all induced discursive and institutional change in the policy domains concerned. It should be nonetheless realised that such shock events have both a 'material' and a 'social' dimension. The first refers to what is happening at the material level, e.g. a rise of water level or a spill of substances into the water, the second to how people perceive these happenings. Particularly the latter dimension determines whether an event becomes a *shock* or not.

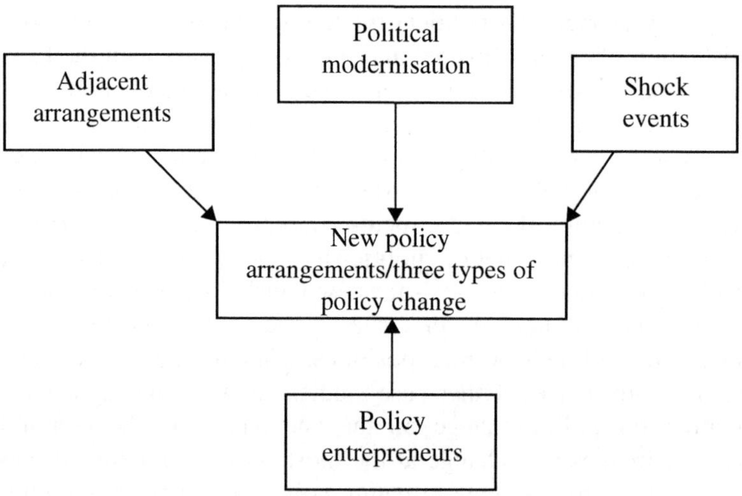

Figure 13.1. Key explanatory factors to understand policy change.

A final change factor, according to Wiering and Crabbé, is the effect of developments in adjacent policy arrangements on the one under consideration. This influence can take place both horizontally (at one administrative level) or vertically (over different administrative levels). The case studies in this book show several examples of the two phenomena.

Both regional and nature policies have been substantially influenced by agricultural policy making, both from domestic and EU origins, as Bogaert and Gersie, Van der Zouwen, Boonstra and Padt all show. Another example is the interlinkage between water policy and spatial planning, as Wiering and Crabbé illustrate. However, these linkages might not only imply change, but also *stagnation*. Dutch regional policy, for example, is more constrained by traditional agricultural policy making than enabled as is Flemish nature policy by spatial planning.

INSTITUTIONALISATION AND GOVERNANCE CAPACITY

Compared to earlier publications on the PAA, this book has introduced new concepts to assess the extent of institutionalisation of emerging policy arrangements on the one hand and their governance capacity on the other. These are the concepts of *congruency* and *JEP-triangle* respectively. Congruence means 'sufficient coherence' among: (1) the policy views and interests of the different stakeholders in a policy arrangement (*strategic* congruence); (2) the four dimensions of a policy arrangement (*internal-structural* congruence); and (3) a policy arrangement and its wider institutional context (*external-structural* congruence). The assumption is that a certain level of congruence – strategically and structurally, internally as well as externally – is needed for any policy arrangement to institutionalise in the first place *and* to deploy a certain capacity to perform in the second. This assessment concerns the *institutional* side of policy analysis and evaluation: under what conditions can new arrangements become stable in a 'policy-crowded' environment and under what conditions will institutional capacity emerge to produce outcomes? Another question is whether these outcomes are *desirable*, e.g. from a 'good governance' perspective. For an assessment of the latter, which reflects the *strategic* side of policy evaluation, the JEP-triangle is introduced. Here different logics of and criteria for policy evaluation – juridical, economic, political – are integrated in order to enable the evaluator to judge the (performative) governance capacity of a certain policy field. With the introduction of these notions, the PAA also adds a normative framework to its original model.

It should be admitted that this normative model has not been widely applied in this book. We consider it a theoretical and methodological innovation for the PAA now that should be validated by empirical research at a later stage. Yet, in three chapters, congruence and (aspects of) the JEP-triangle play a role. As far as the case of Dutch organic farming is concerned, it turned out that the governance capacity of the policy arrangement cannot be considered very high, neither in institutional nor in performative terms. Reasons for this conclusion are the low level of strategic and structural congruence – given the internal fragmentation of the arrangement and the external, rather hierarchical embeddedness in the mainstream agricultural policy arrangement – and the rather low scores on 'good governance', i.e. on the JEP-triangle criteria. Subsequently, ideas for a 'reflexive design' of an alternative route for Dutch organic farming were presented.

Two other chapters in this book, however, use the concept of congruence. Boonstra analyses the extent of institutionalisation of newly emerging policy arrangements in integrated region-oriented environmental policy, whereas Verbeeck and Leroy do so with regard to Flemish target group policy. The former is rather optimistic about the (relative) stability of the majority of her cases, whereas the latter are very pessimistic about the institutional chances of target group policy in Flanders. With these kinds of analyses, the concept of congruence becomes a sort of indicator to predict the probability that policy arrangements will become successful in the near future, both in terms of institutional stability and in terms of institutional prerequisites for performance.

CONCLUSION

Given all the arguments and findings so far, the conclusion of this book on environmental politics can best be summarised as: 'lots of dynamics, not much change'. Dynamics are mainly the consequences of discursive innovations and the entrance of new actors in policy arrangements, stability of 'given' power relations and (domestic) institutional structures. As a result of this interplay between dynamics and stability, we do not find much policy change, which can be considered 'fundamental', 'deep' or 'third order'. With that, *government* has remained to be as important – or even more important – than *governance*. The shift from the former to the latter, which is so prominent in current public administration and political science literature, cannot be validated in the environmental domain, at least not as a *general* trend or as a *grand story*. At best, we find *small* stories of shifts from government to governance. At the same time, we cannot hold that 'everything remains the same'. Political modernisation, for example, is traceable, yet as a renewal of modernity that results in hybrid structures of 'the old' and 'the new'; environmental policy problem structures have become more complex and, with that, uncertainty rises; policy networks stretch over time and space beyond nation state borders; adjacent policy sectors can no longer be considered in isolation today; shock events raise new policy awareness; science reveals new insights, etc. All this puts pressure on policy arrangements to change or adapt. And so they do. But again, this does not result in real governance arrangements, sub-politics, or rule-altering politics to the extent as some have predicted.

A FINAL REFLECTION

With this book, we had two main ambitions in mind: (1) to renew our theoretical framework, in accordance with the agendas we formulated in earlier publications; and (2) to report on recent empirical research, which was conducted from the perspective of our framework. With regard to the latter ambition, we have brought together several authors, who have done environmental policy case studies from the PAA perspective. Overall, we believe, these cases offer a nice overview of developments in current environmental politics. The first, more theoretical ambition, urged us to do a number of analyses in this book: an elaboration upon the (contested) political modernisation thesis, an emphasis on methodology and operationalisation, an introduction of a policy evaluation model and more attention paid to *innovative* policy making and policy arrangements-in-development, to EU policy and *multi-level* governance and to the *explanation* of policy change (e.g. the role of shock events and adjacent policy fields). However, what we did *not* achieve with regard to our theoretical ambitions so far, is to make our model more dynamic, amongst others. We have debated the question whether the PAA is still a too static model, given the emphasis on stabilisation of policy making and given the language used (power instead of dis/empowerment, agency instead of action, discourse instead of deliberation and rules instead of governing, being pairs of words of which the first notions are those used by us, whereas the second ones are the more dynamic concepts). Also, not all relevant debates and approaches in current policy sciences are seriously addressed or accounted for by us, such as those on democracy or policy learning. Here and now, we see the challenges for future theorising emerging.

The two ambitions of this book have produced a dilemma too. Reporting on empirical research done so far is an *ex post* activity, while offering new theoretical and methodological insights is an *ex nunc* one. This leads to the situation that not all theoretical and methodological insights are covered in the case studies. For example, hardly any case study author refers to the 'tetrahedron' methodology (Chapter 3) or to 'reflexive' policy evaluation (Chapter 4). It is our ambition and intention that future case studies will nonetheless do so. Another difference between the two book parts is that the theoretical chapters urge for a balanced analysis of organisation and contents in policy arrangements, whereas most empirical chapters tend to focus on *discursive* change/continuity in the first place. However, a truly discursive-institutional approach, something we strive for, needs to do more justice to a balanced view on both, on organisation *and* substance. This also needs a more thorough theorising about institutions and discourses as well as on their distinctions and overlap. We are on the other hand convinced that the different empirical chapters do much more justice to the other dialectics the PAA stands for, namely the one of actor and structure. This duality is well embedded in the way the different cases are analysed.

A final point of reflection is our main conclusion ('lots of dynamics, not much change'). We are fully aware that this conclusion is biased by our framework, which focuses on long(er) term institutionalisation processes. With that, we might easily lose sight of, for example, day-to-day policy processes of change, temporary experiments with new modes of governance or subtle shifts in power. Hence, our theoretical lenses determine what we empirically observe. However, this is a common feature of science and, even more so, accepted as normal scientific practice since Popper. Consequently, we will *not* rewrite or nuance our conclusion here, under the heading of reflection, but make ourselves and the readers (again) aware of the perspective from which these were drawn.

Index

F

ENVIRONMENT & POLICY

1. Dutch Committee for Long-Term Environmental Policy: *The Environment: Towards a Sustainable Future.* 1994 ISBN 0-7923-2655-5; Pb 0-7923-2656-3
2. O. Kuik, P. Peters and N. Schrijver (eds.): *Joint Implementation to Curb Climate Change.* Legal and Economic Aspects. 1994 ISBN 0-7923-2825-6
3. C.J. Jepma (ed.): *The Feasibility of Joint Implementation.* 1995 ISBN 0-7923-3426-4
4. F.J. Dietz, H.R.J. Vollebergh and J.L. de Vries (eds.): *Environment, Incentives and the Common Market.* 1995 ISBN 0-7923-3602-X
5. J.F.Th. Schoute, P.A. Finke, F.R. Veeneklaas and H.P. Wolfert (eds.): *Scenario Studies for the Rural Environment.* 1995 ISBN 0-7923-3748-4
6. R.E. Munn, J.W.M. la Rivière and N. van Lookeren Campagne: *Policy Making in an Era of Global Environmental Change.* 1996 ISBN 0-7923-3872-3
7. F. Oosterhuis, F. Rubik and G. Scholl: *Product Policy in Europe: New Environmental Perspectives.* 1996 ISBN 0-7923-4078-7
8. J. Gupta: *The Climate Change Convention and Developing Countries: From Conflict to Consensus?* 1997 ISBN 0-7923-4577-0
9. M. Rolén, H. Sjöberg and U. Svedin (eds.): *International Governance on Environmental Issues.* 1997 ISBN 0-7923-4701-3
10. M.A. Ridley: *Lowering the Cost of Emission Reduction: Joint Implementation in the Framework Convention on Climate Change.* 1998 ISBN 0-7923-4914-8
11. G.J.I. Schrama (ed.): *Drinking Water Supply and Agricultural Pollution.* Preventive Action by the Water Supply Sector in the European Union and the United States. 1998 ISBN 0-7923-5104-5
12. P. Glasbergen: *Co-operative Environmental Governance:* Public-Private Agreements as a Policy Strategy. 1998 ISBN 0-7923-5148-7; Pb 0-7923-5149-5
13. P. Vellinga, F. Berkhout and J. Gupta (eds.): *Managing a Material World.* Perspectives in Industrial Ecology. 1998 ISBN 0-7923-5153-3; Pb 0-7923-5206-8
14. F.H.J.M. Coenen, D. Huitema and L.J. O'Toole, Jr. (eds.): *Participation and the Quality of Environmental Decision Making.* 1998 ISBN 0-7923-5264-5
15. D.M. Pugh and J.V. Tarazona (eds.): *Regulation for Chemical Safety in Europe: Analysis, Comment and Criticism.* 1998 ISBN 0-7923-5269-6
16. W. Østreng (ed.): *National Security and International Environmental Cooperation in the Arctic – the Case of the Northern Sea Route.* 1999 ISBN 0-7923-5528-8
17. S.V. Meijerink: *Conflict and Cooperation on the Scheldt River Basin.* A Case Study of Decision Making on International Scheldt Issues between 1967 and 1997. 1999 ISBN 0-7923-5650-0
18. M.A. Mohamed Salih: *Environmental Politics and Liberation in Contemporary Africa.* 1999 ISBN 0-7923-5652-7
19. C.J. Jepma and W. van der Gaast (eds.): *On the Compatibility of Flexible Instruments.* 1999 ISBN 0-7923-5728-0
20. M. Andersson: *Change and Continuity in Poland's Environmental Policy.* 1999 ISBN 0-7923-6051-6

ENVIRONMENT & POLICY

21. W. Kägi: *Economics of Climate Change: The Contribution of Forestry Projects.* 2000 ISBN 0-7923-6103-2
22. E. van der Voet, J.B. Guinée and H.A.U. de Haes (eds.): *Heavy Metals: A Problem Solved?* Methods and Models to Evaluate Policy Strategies for Heavy Metals. 2000 ISBN 0-7923-6192-X
23. G. Hønneland: *Coercive and Discursive Compliance Mechanisms in the Management of Natural Resourses.* A Case Study from the Barents Sea Fisheries. 2000 ISBN 0-7923-6243-8
24. J. van Tatenhove, B. Arts and P. Leroy (eds.): *Political Modernisation and the Environment.* The Renewal of Environmental Policy Arrangements. 2000 ISBN 0-7923-6312-4
25. G.K. Rosendal: *The Convention on Biological Diversity and Developing Countries.* 2000 ISBN 0-7923-6375-2
26. G.H. Vonkeman (ed.): *Sustainable Development of European Cities and Regions.* 2000 ISBN 0-7923-6423-6
27. J. Gupta and M. Grubb (eds.): *Climate Change and European Leadership.* A Sustainable Role for Europe? 2000 ISBN 0-7923-6466-X
28. D. Vidas (ed.): *Implementing the Environmental Protection Regime for the Antarctic.* 2000 ISBN 0-7923-6609-3; Pb 0-7923-6610-7
29. K. Eder and M. Kousis (eds.): *Environmental Politics in Southern Europe:* Actors, Institutions and Discourses in a Europeanizing Society. 2000 ISBN 0-7923-6753-7
30. R. Schwarze: *Law and Economics of International Climate Change Policy.* 2001 ISBN 0-7923-6800-2
31. M.J. Scoullos, G.H. Vonkeman, I. Thornton, and Z. Makuch: *Mercury - Cadmium-Lead:* Handbook for Sustainable Heavy Metals Policy and Regulation. 2001 ISBN 1-4020-0224-6
32. G. Sundqvist: *The Bedrock of Opinion.* Science, Technology and Society in the Siting of High-Level Nuclear Waste. 2002 ISBN 1-4020-0477-X
33. P.P.J. Driessen and P. Glasbergen (eds.): *Greening Society.* The Paradigm Shift in Dutch Environmental Politics. 2002 ISBN 1-4020-0652-7
34. D. Huitema: *Hazardous Decisions.* Hazardous Waste Siting in the UK, The Netherlands and Canada. Institutions and Discourses. 2002 ISBN 1-4020-0969-0
35. D.A. Fuchs: *An Institutional Basis for Environmental Stewardship:* The Structure and Quality of Property Rights. 2003 ISBN 1-4020-1002-8
36. B. Chaytor and K.R. Gray (eds.): *International Environmental Law and Policy in Africa.* 2003 ISBN 1-4020-1287-X
37. F.M. Brouwer, I. Heinz and T. Zabel (eds.): *Governance of Water-Related Conflicts in Agriculture.* New Directions in Agri-Environmental and Water Policies in the EU. 2003 ISBN 1-4020-1553-4

ENVIRONMENT & POLICY

38. G.J.I. Schrama and S. Sedlacek (eds.): *Environmental and Technology Policy in Europe.* Technological Innovation and Policy Integration. 2003 ISBN 1-4020-1583-6
39. A.J. Dietz, R. Ruben and A. Verhagen (eds.): *The Impact of Climate Change on Drylands.* With a focus on West Africa. 2004 ISBN 1-4020-1952-1
40. I. Kissling-Näf and S. Kuks (eds.): *The Evolution of National Water Regimes in Europe.* Transitions in Water Rights and Water Policies. 2004 ISBN 1-4020-2483-5
41. H. Bressers and S.Kuks (eds.): *Integrated Governance and Water Basin Management.* Conditions for Regime Change and Sustainability. 2004 ISBN 1-4020-2481-9
42. T. Flüeler: *Decision Making for Complex Socio-Technical Systems.* Robustness from Lessons Learned in Long-term Radioactive Waste Governance. 2005 ISBN 1-4020-3480-6
43. E. Croci (ed.): *The Handbook of Environmental Voluntary Agreements.* Design, Implementation and Evaluation Issues. 2005 ISBN 1-4020-3355-9
44. X. Olsthoorn and A.J. Wieczorek (eds.): *Understanding Industrial Transformation.* Views from Different Disciplines. 2006 ISBN 1-4020-3755-4
45. H. Aiking, J. de Boer and J. Vereijken (eds.): *Sustainable Protein Production and Consumption: Pigs or Peas?* 2006 ISBN 1-4020-4062-8
46. F. Brouwer and B.A. McCarl (eds.): *Agriculture and Climate Beyond 2015.* A New Perspective on Future Land Use Patterns. 2006 ISBN 1-4020-4063-6
47. B. Arts and P. Leroy (eds.): *Institutional Dynamics in Environmental Governance.* 2006 ISBN 1-4020-5078-X

GPSR Compliance

The European Union's (EU) General Product Safety Regulation (GPSR) is a set of rules that requires consumer products to be safe and our obligations to ensure this.

If you have any concerns about our products, you can contact us on ProductSafety@springernature.com

In case Publisher is established outside the EU, the EU authorized representative is:

Springer Nature Customer Service Center GmbH
Europaplatz 3
69115 Heidelberg, Germany

Batch number: 10762627

Printed by Printforce, the Netherlands